Mire Lee
Open Wound

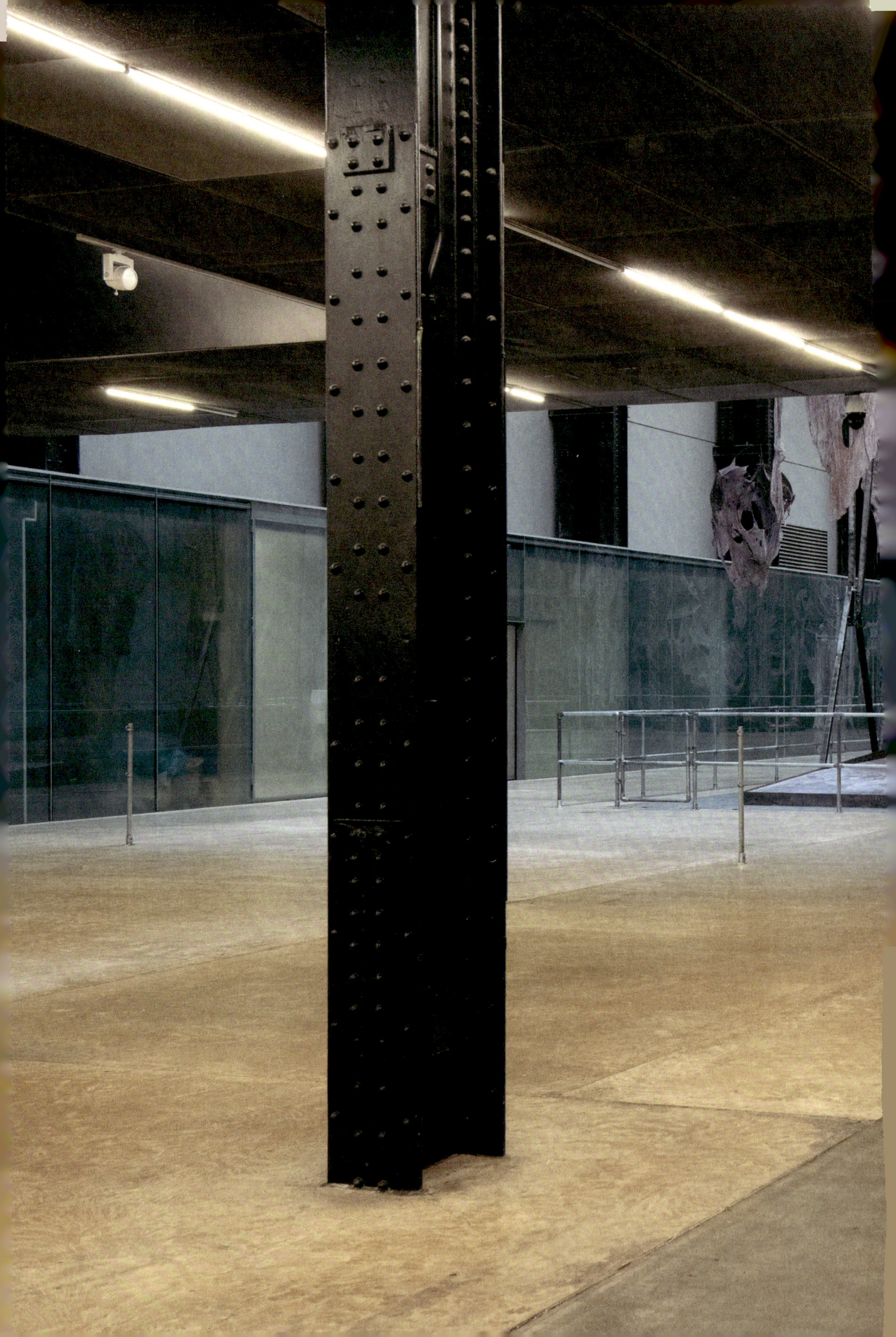

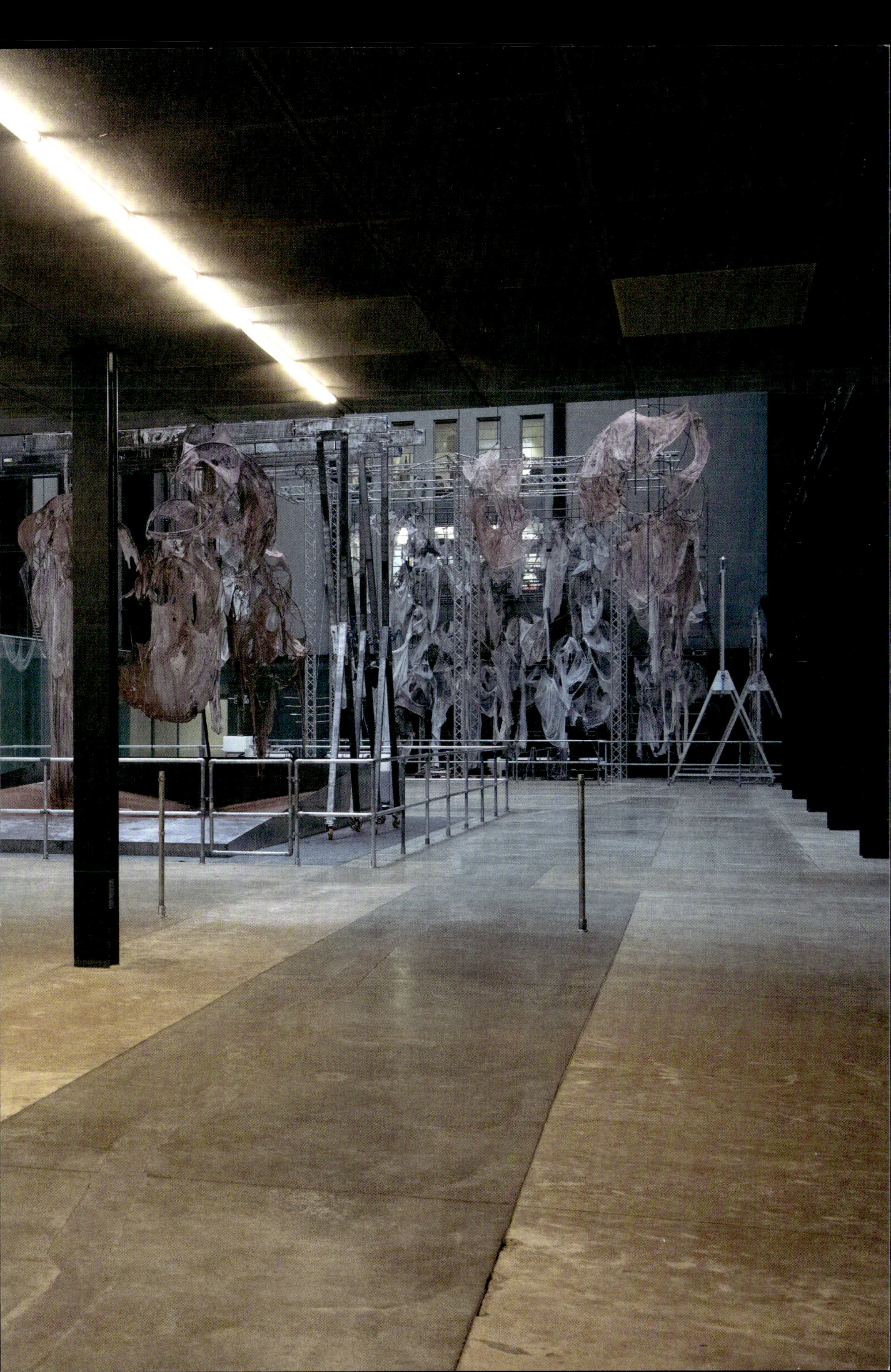

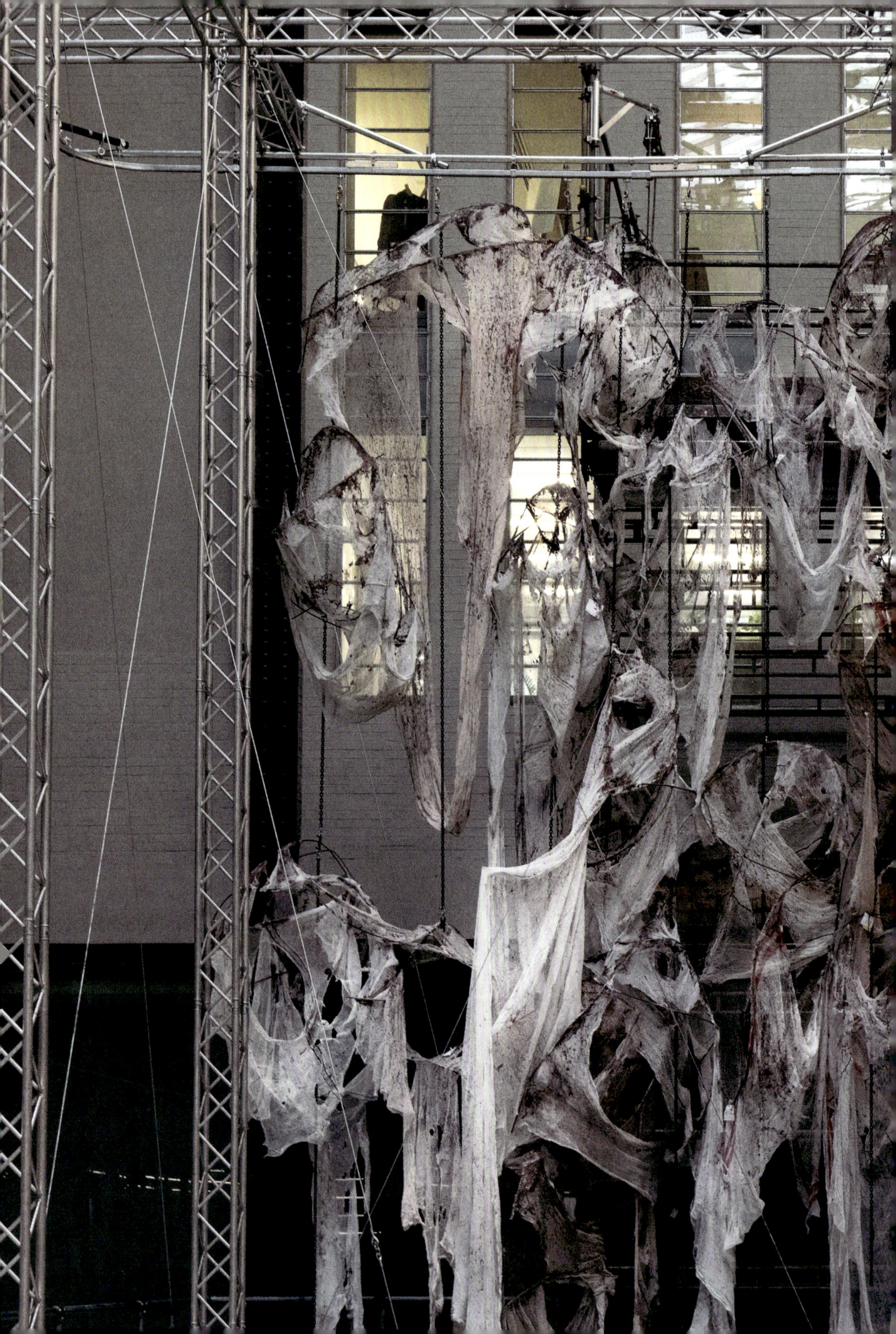

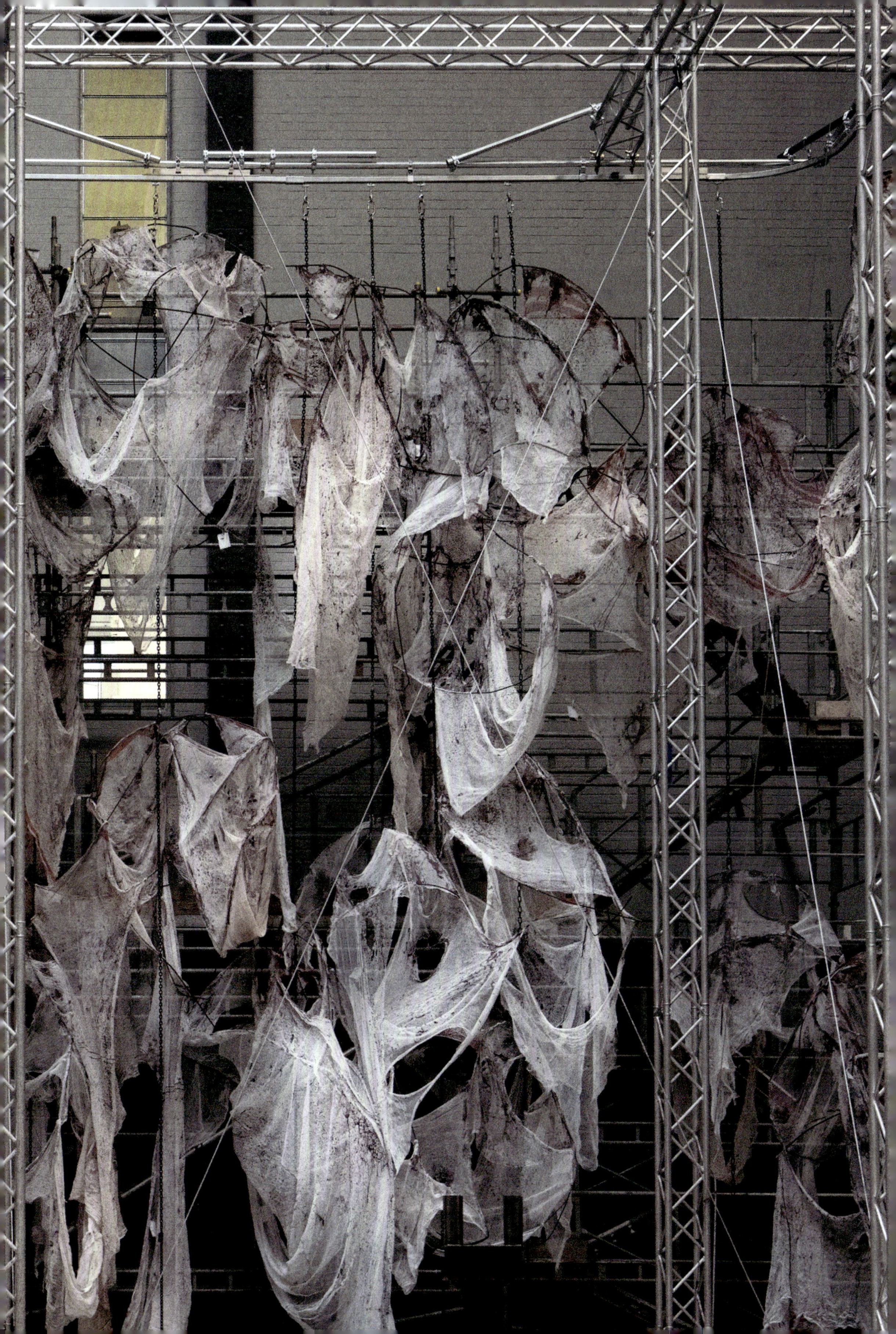

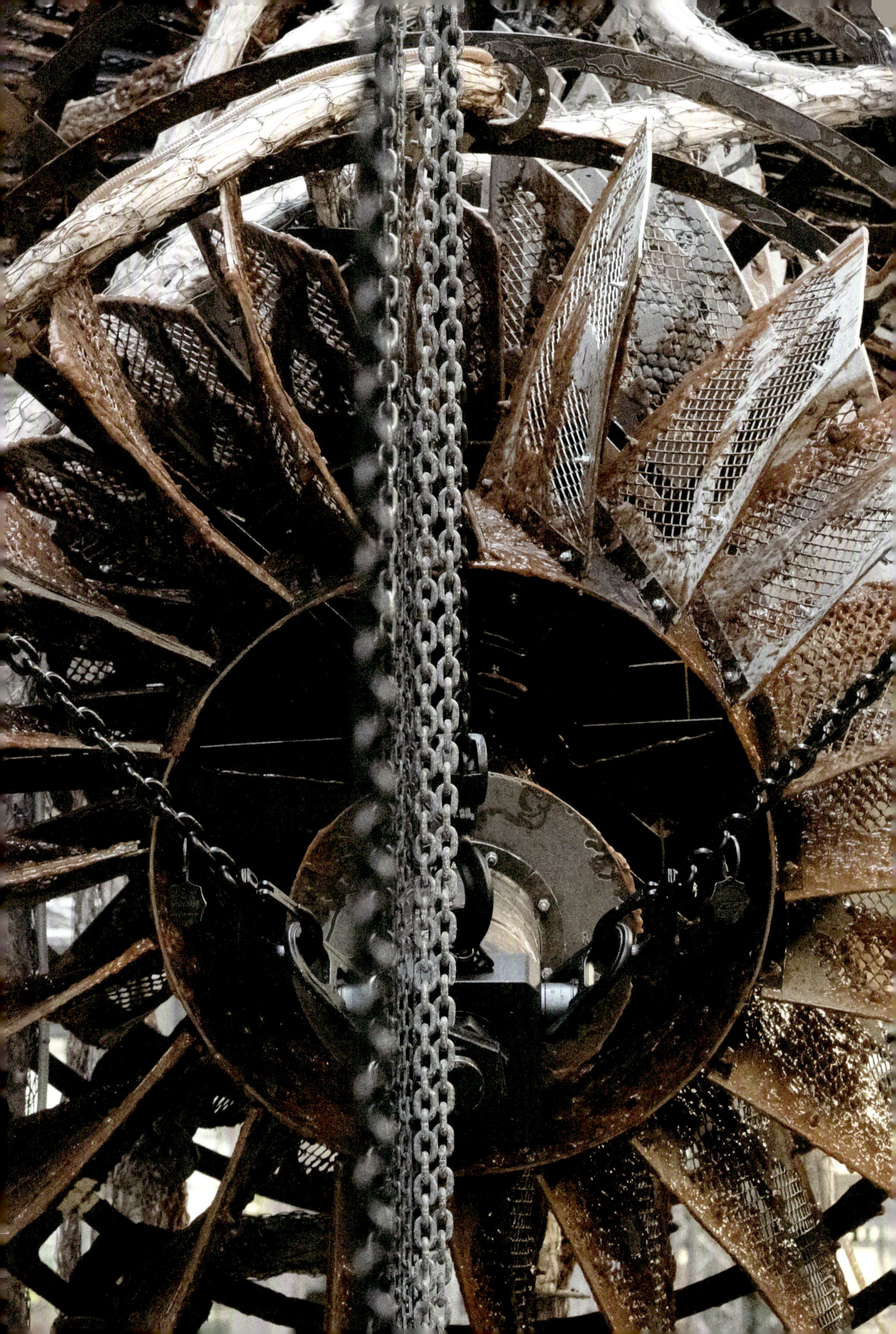

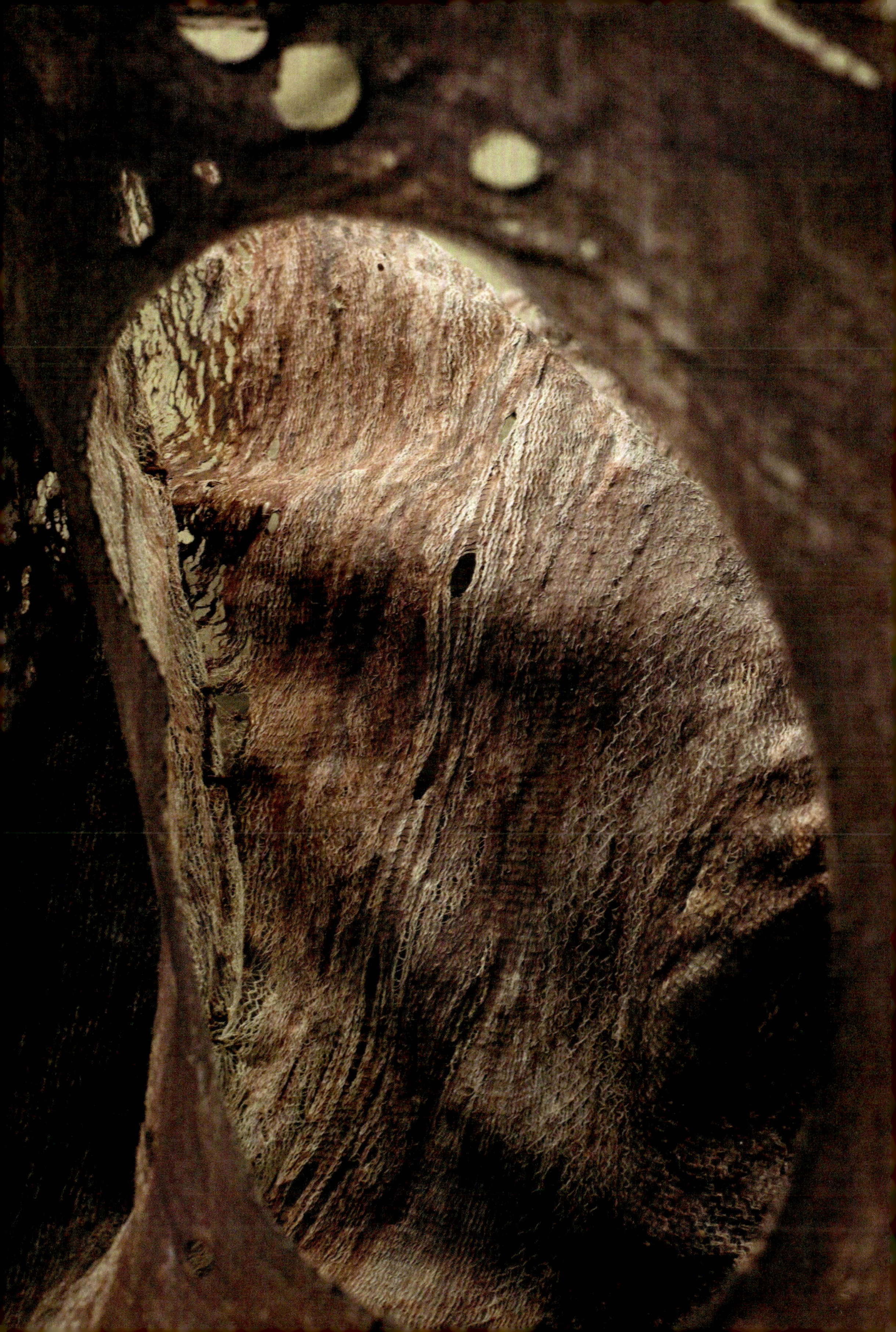

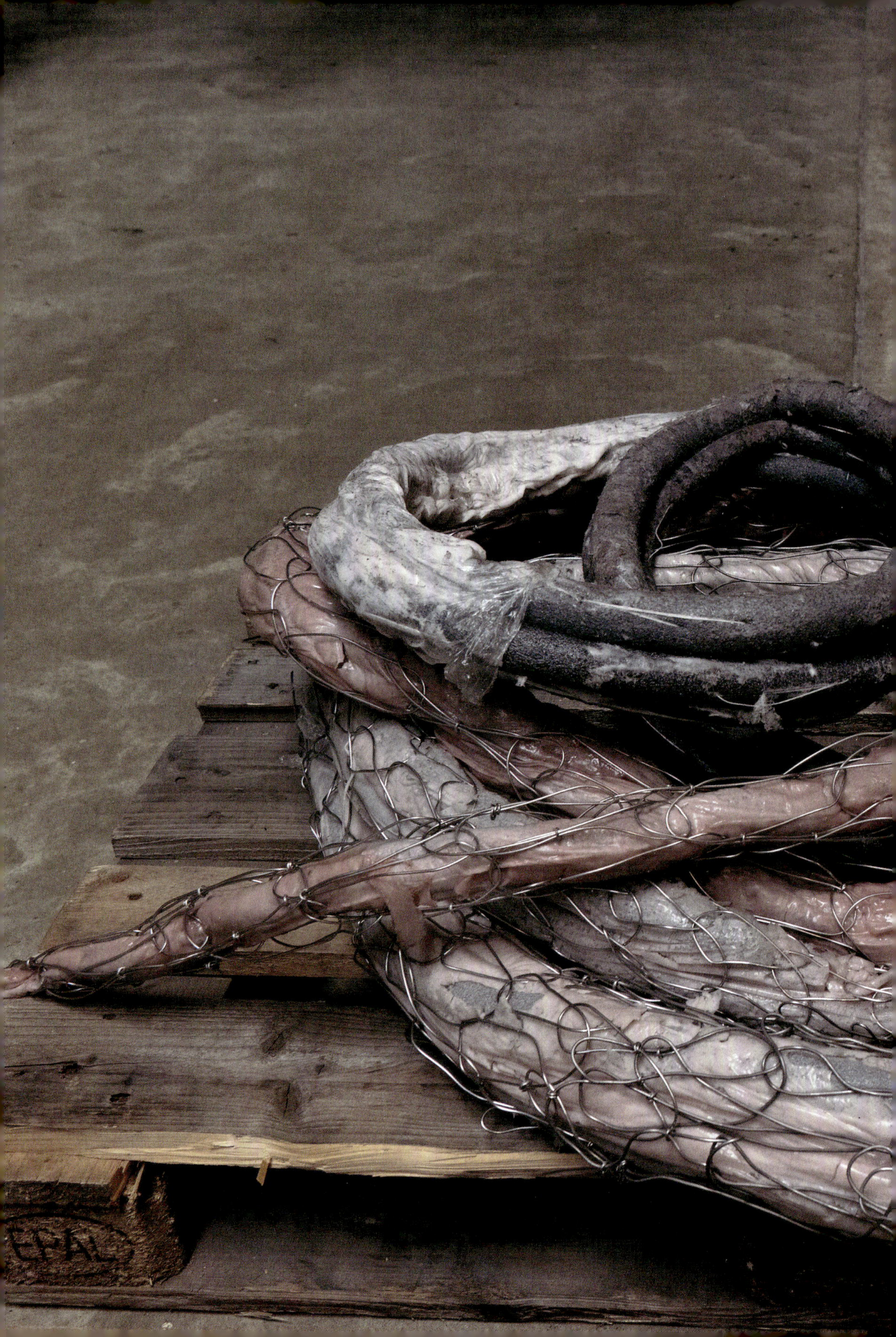

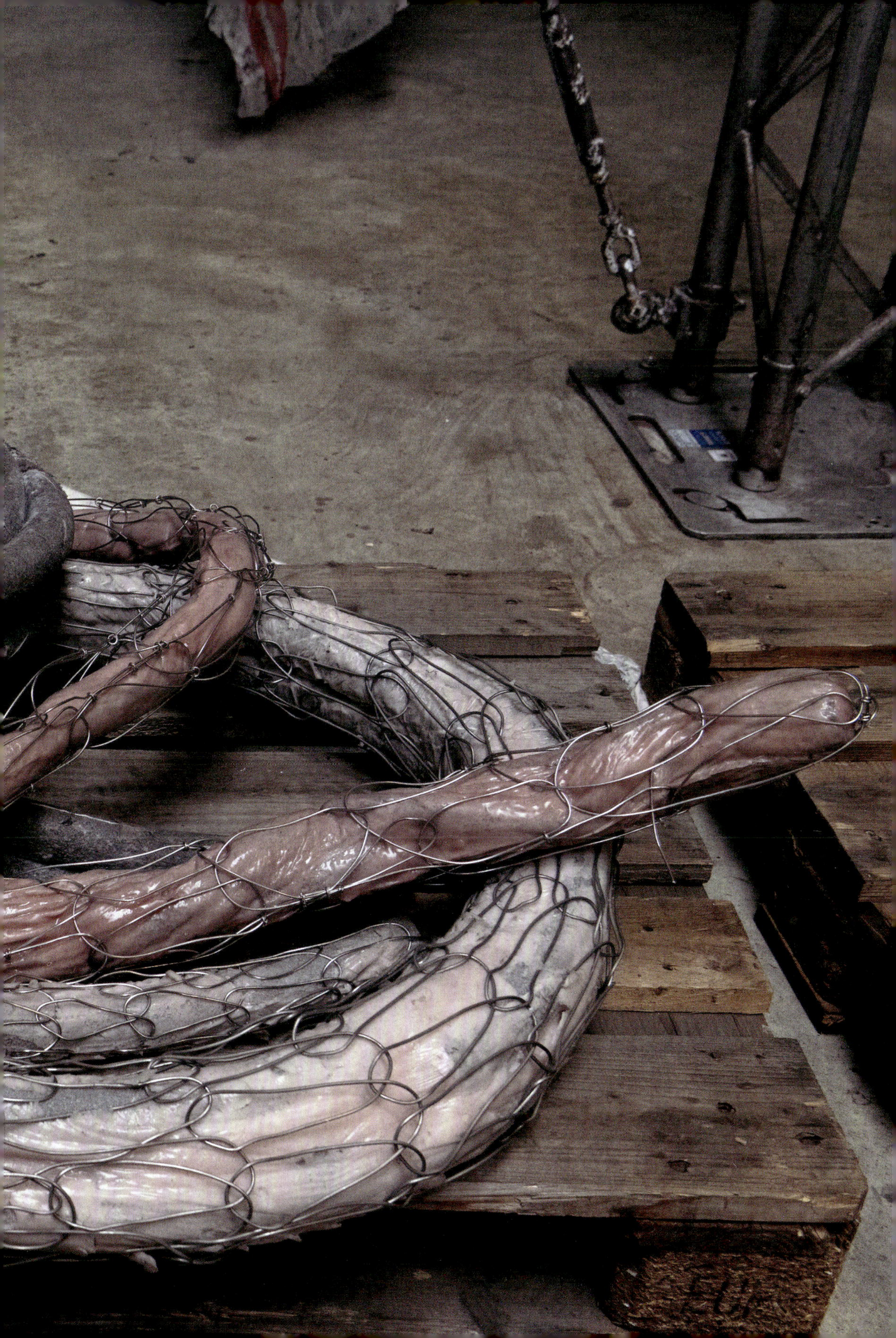

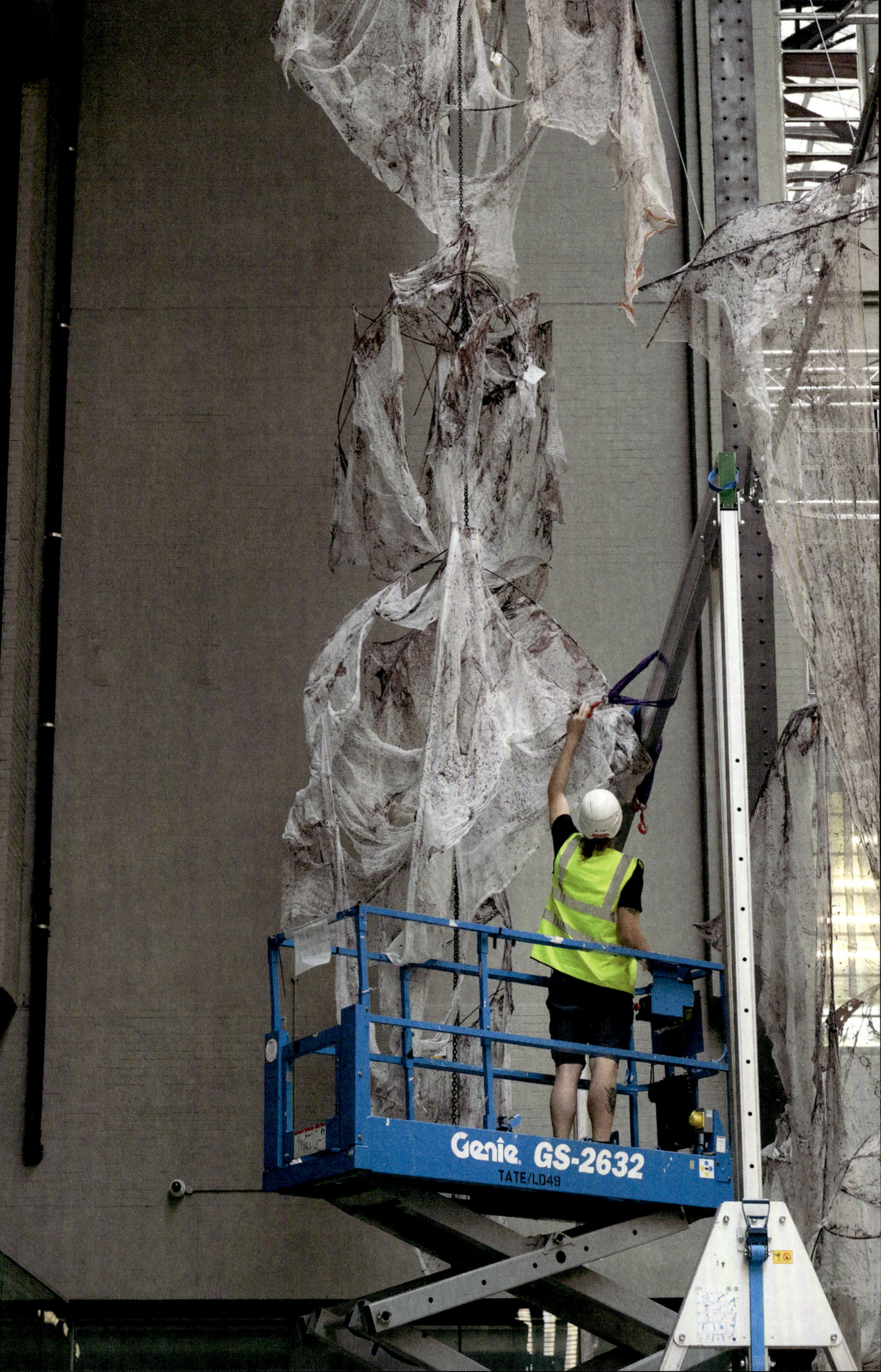
Genie GS-2632
TATE/LD49

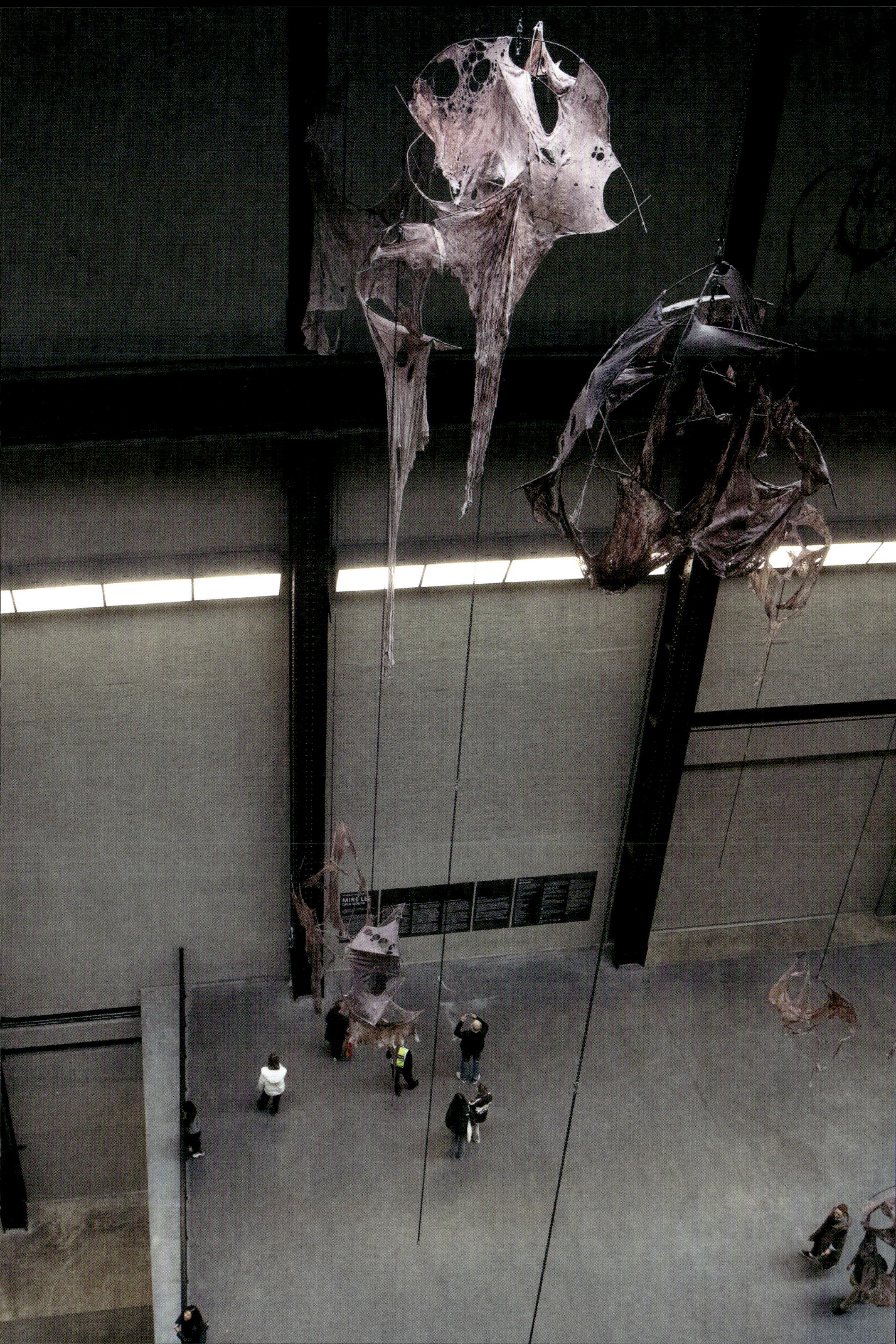

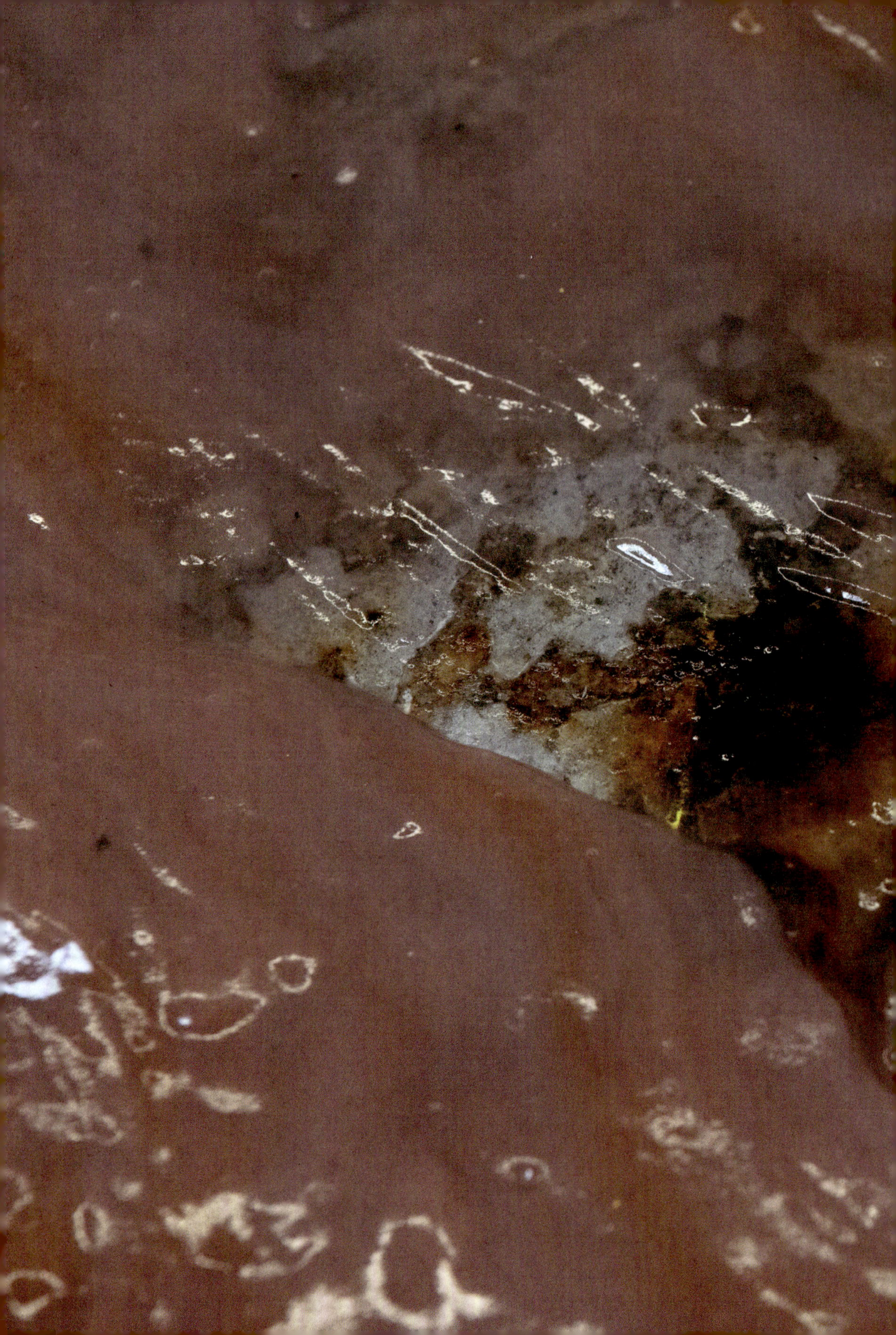

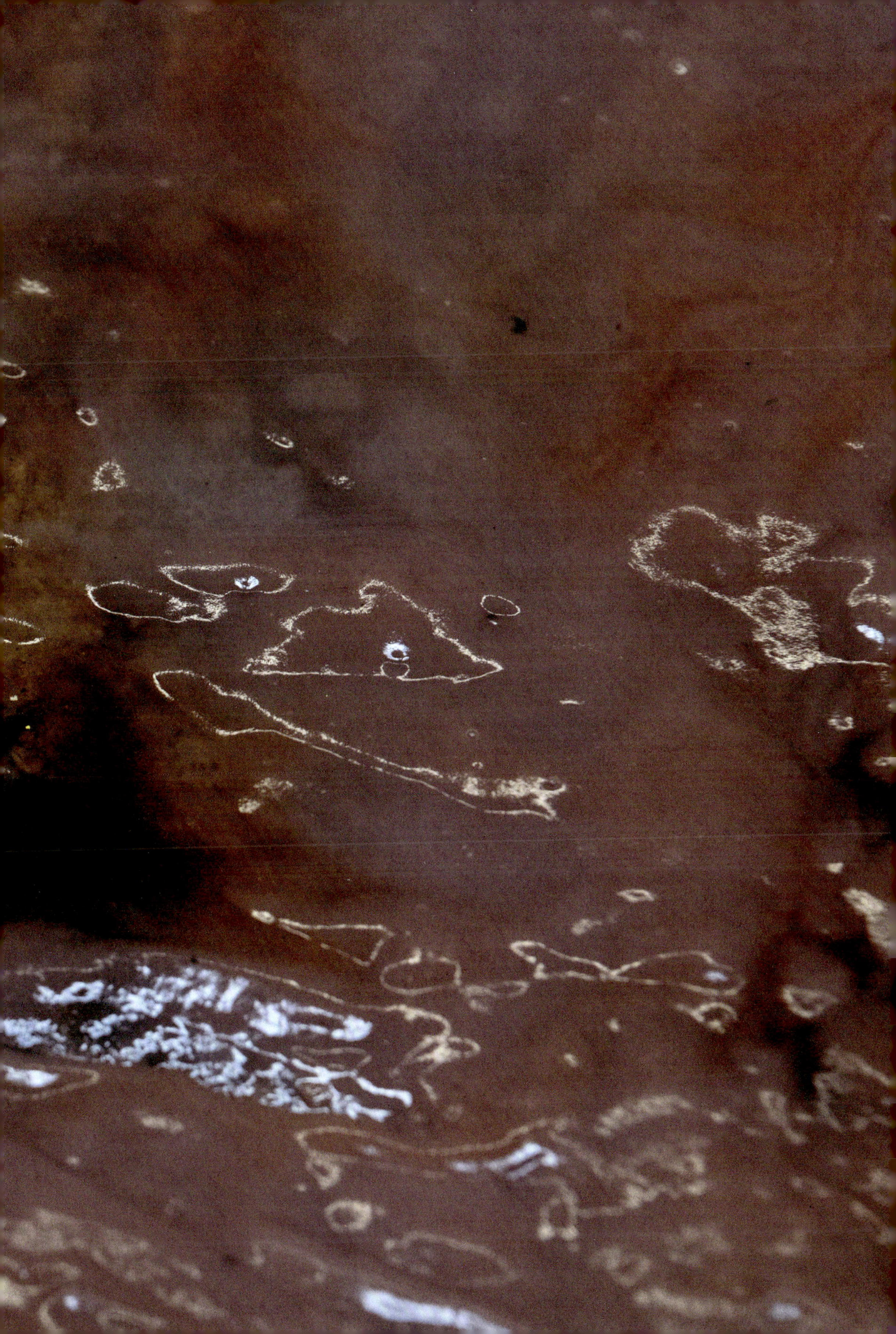

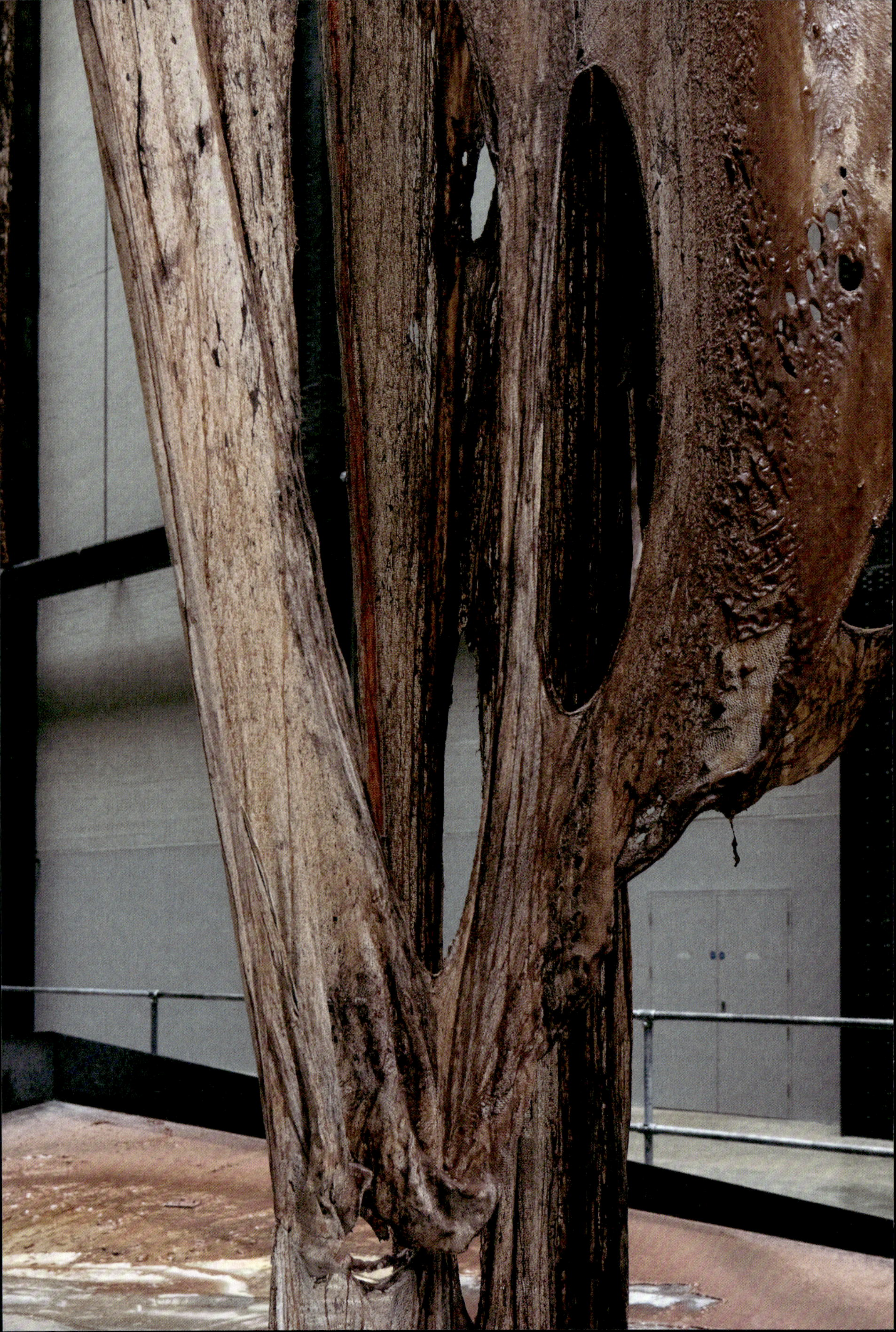

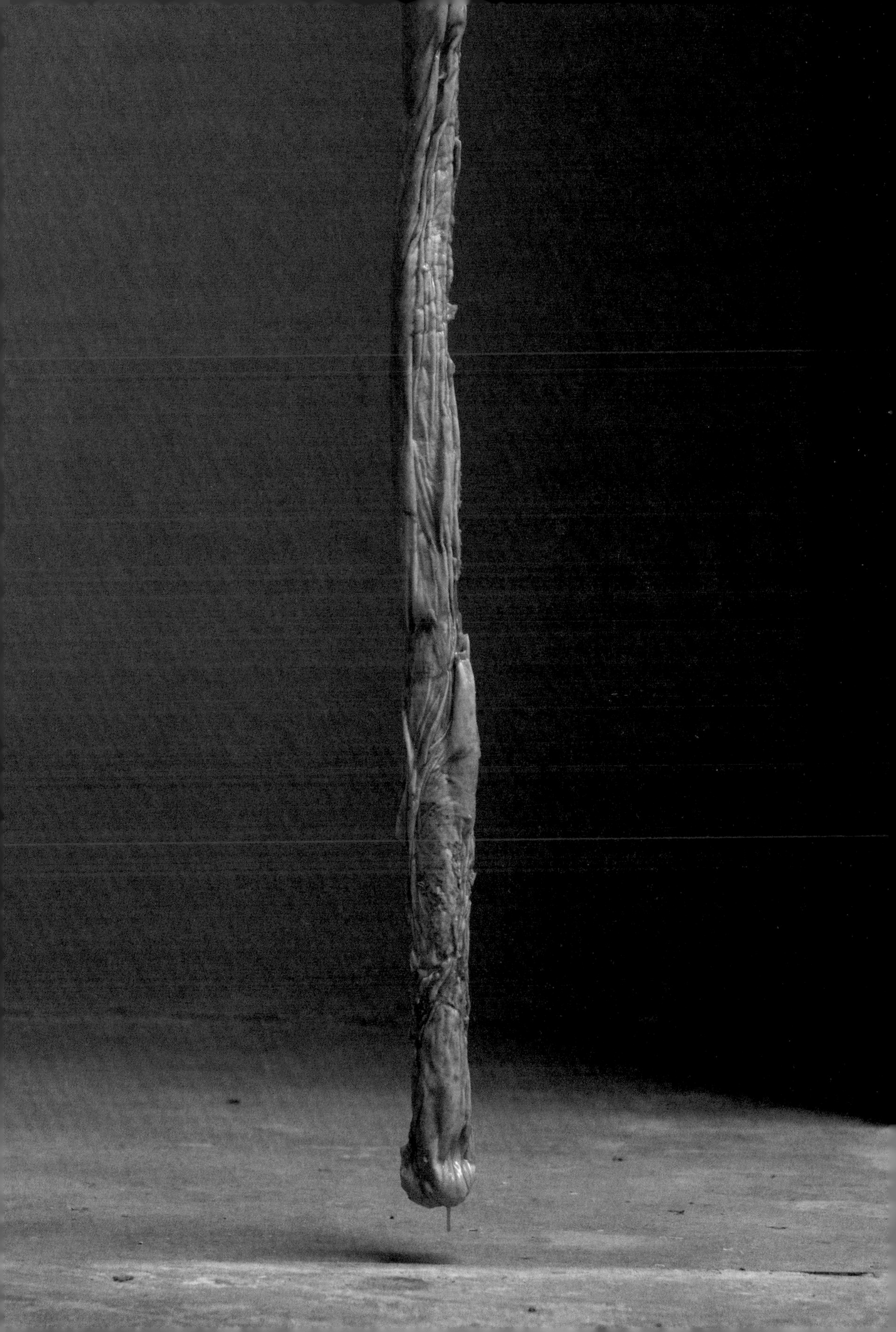

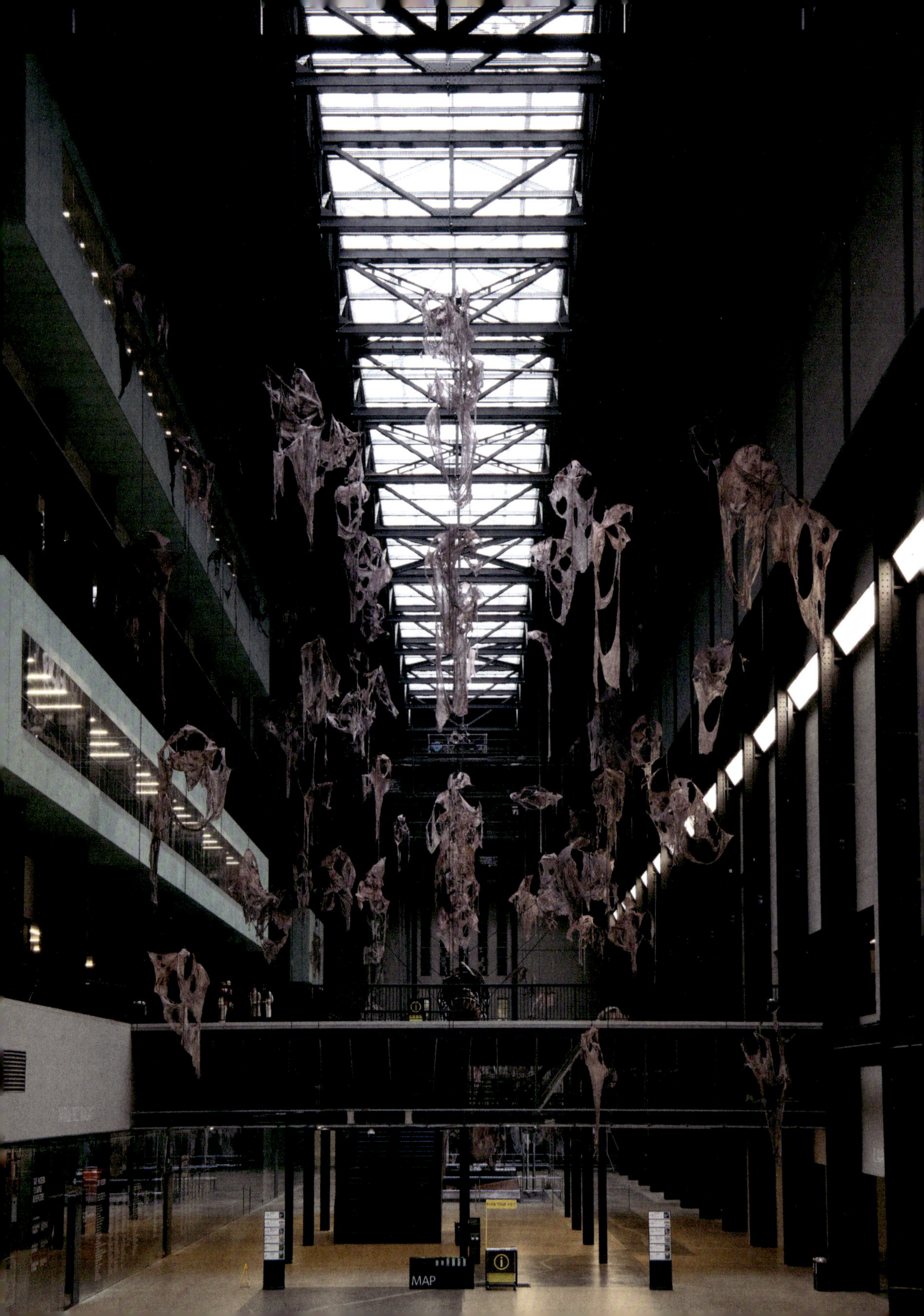

Hyundai Commission

Mire Lee
Open Wound

Edited by Alvin Li
With Bilal Akkouche

Contributions by Dina Akhmadeeva, Bilal Akkouche,
Mire Lee, Alvin Li

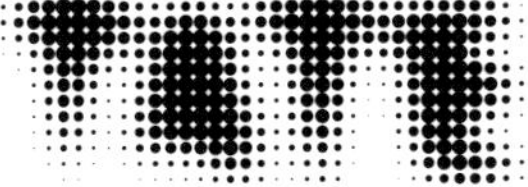

First published 2025 by order of the Tate Trustees
by Tate Publishing, a division of Tate Enterprises Ltd,
Millbank, London SW1P 4RG
www.tate.org.uk/publishing

on the occasion of the exhibition
Hyundai Commission: Mire Lee
Open Wound
Tate Modern, London
9 October 2024 – 16 March 2025

In partnership with Hyundai Motor

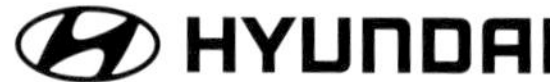

With additional support from

The Mire Lee Supporters:
    Ministry of Culture, Sports and Tourism of Korea,
    Korea Arts Management Service, and the grant
    program Fund for Korean Art Abroad
    Richard Chang
    Yan Du
    Lonti Ebers

The Mire Lee Supporters Circle:
    Tina Kim Gallery
    Antenna Space
    Sprüth Magers
    The Peter Magnone Foundation
    Mondriaan Fund
    Miyoung Lee and Neil Simpkins
    Eleanor and Francis Shen
    Victoria Bruhn
    Wendy Lee
    Dina Liu
    Allison Berg
    Kahng Foundation
    Lisa Kim and Eunu Chun
    Dana and Gregory Lee
    Kyungsoon Lee and Jungwoo Shon
    Teresa Tsai
    Yoonjung and Edouard Ullmo
    Margaret Wang
    Yang Won Sun Foundation
    Hee Yoon
    Salle Yoo and Jeff Gray

Tate Americas Foundation

This book is published with the support of
Ministry of Culture, Sports and Tourism of Korea
and Korea Arts Management Service

A catalogue record for this book is available from
the British Library

ISBN 978 1 84976 959 4

Distributed in the US and Canada by ABRAMS,
New York
Library of Congress Control Number applied for

Project Editor: Nicola Bion
Production: Bill Jones
Picture Research: Sarah Tucker
Designed by Mark Thomson
Set in Custodia (Fred Smeijers)

Colour reproduction by DL Imaging, London
Printed and bound in Italy by SIZ

Cover; pp.2–16, 20, 22, 26–7, 31, 32–3, 130–55:
Hyundai Commission: Mire Lee: Open Wound 2024
(details)

Measurements of artworks are given in
centimetres, height before width and depth

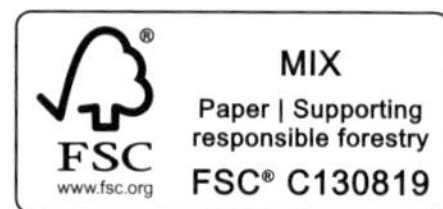

Contents

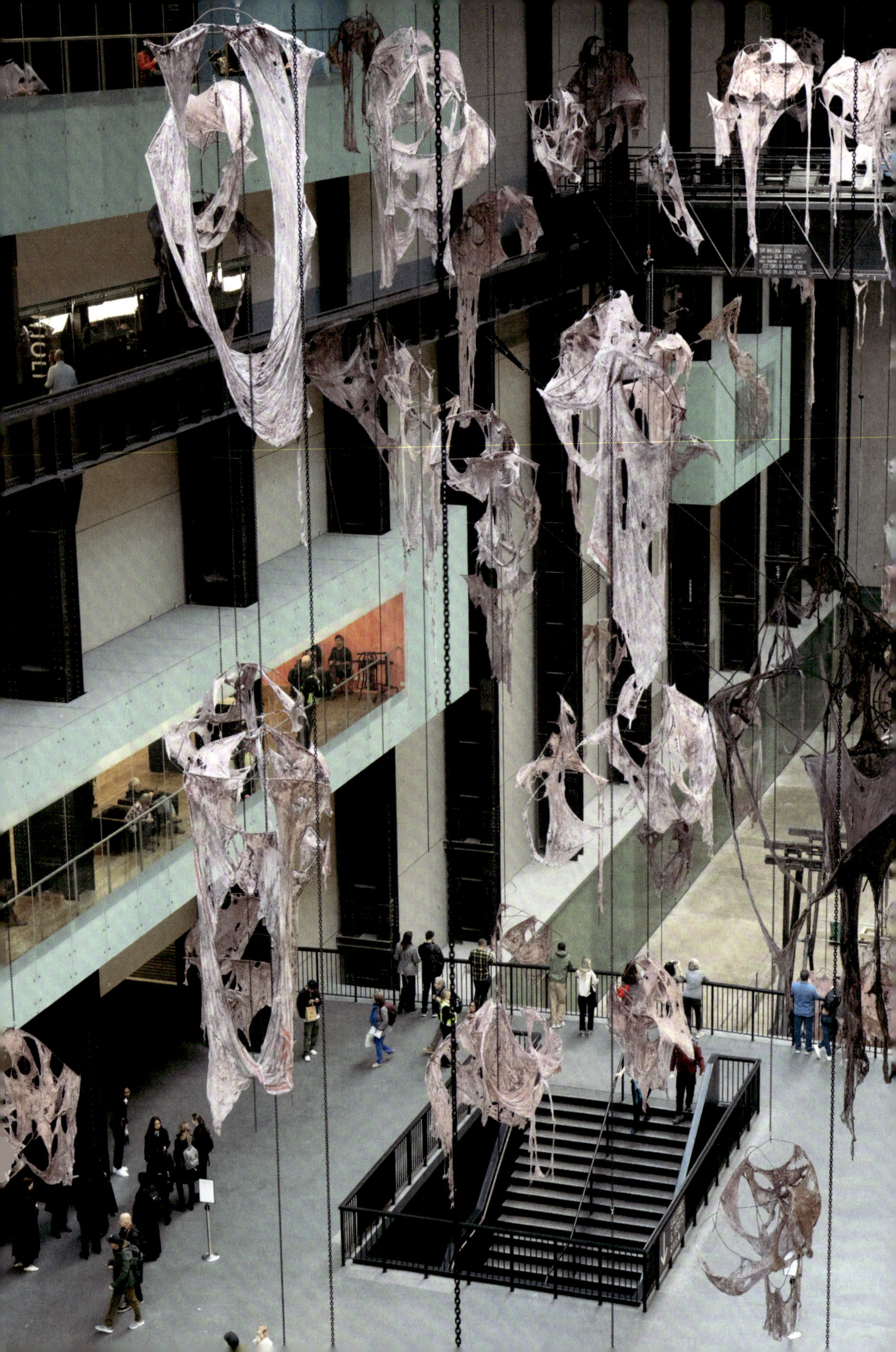

Supporter's Foreword

Hyundai Commission: Mire Lee: Open Wound blurs the boundaries of materiality as well as temporal and spatial territories, evoking a range of senses, emotions and memories. Mire Lee's daring explorations are renowned for juxtaposing contrasting elements in ever-changing spaces that intensify as they move in seemingly boundless loops. Occupying a delicate balance between resilience and vulnerability, Lee invites us to consider the nature of our interconnected existence in times of uncertainty.

This year's Hyundai Commission brings a motorised turbine back to Tate Modern's Turbine Hall. By recalibrating Tate Modern to recall the building's former purpose as a power station, Lee traces the evolution of this vast space through historical and societal transformations. Skin-like sculptures are produced by the action of the artwork to gradually fill the space. Immersed among the bodily forms, we are reminded of the necessity of human care in the process of production, and a sense of openness towards shared belonging emerges. The appealing yet uncanny sculptures recall cycles of gain, loss and renewal and become an invitation for us to move beyond our individual existence, to delve collectively into broader complexities that continue to shape our world. Lee's work, an open studio for production and reflection, serves as a compelling reminder that art can speak to the past, present and the untapped potential of the future.

Hyundai Commission: Mire Lee: Open Wound is the result of the collective vision of Tate and Hyundai Motor to embrace diverse perspectives and foster dialogue that forefronts voices from communities around the world. I would like to express my deepest gratitude to Mire Lee, as well as everyone at Tate and beyond for their tremendous efforts in making this meaningful project possible.

Euisun Chung
Executive Chair, Hyundai Motor Group

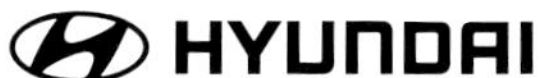

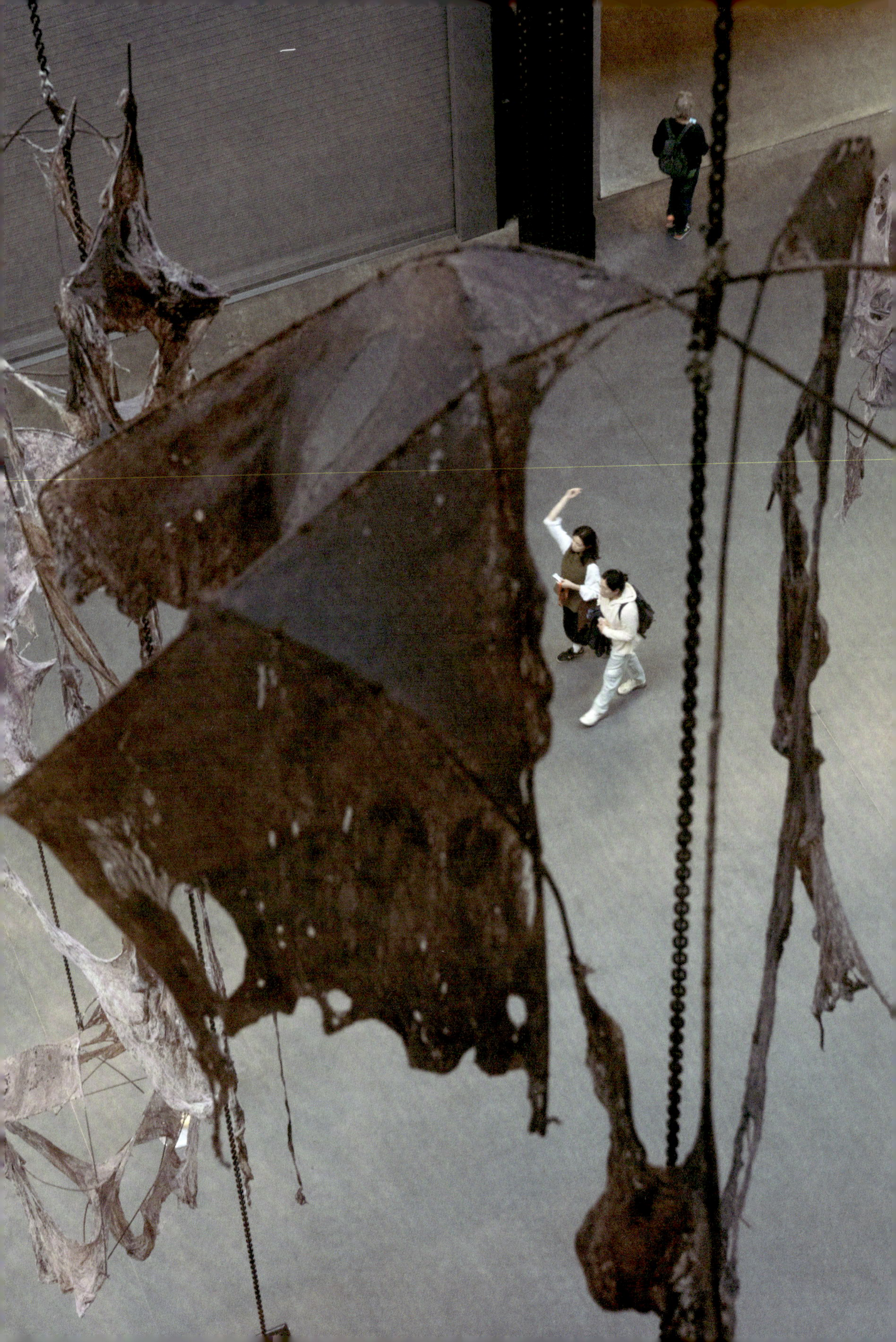

Foreword

Mire Lee's sculptural installations are visceral, emotional and existential.
By combining industrial materials such as steel, cement and silicone with
machineries to create fantastical environments with kinetic elements, her
work explores the tension between soft bodies and rigid systems. Unafraid
of pushing the boundaries between beauty and the grotesque, the familiar
and the uncanny, her experiments in materiality and form challenge norms
of acceptance to unsettling effect. As motors and pumps channel liquid clay
and silicone through sculptural fragments suggestive of living organisms, her
installations remain in a state of perpetual regeneration, in need of constant
care, and transforming over time. In the long aftermath of the Covid-19
pandemic, as we strive to recover amid the widespread collapse of healthcare
systems, economic stability and social security, Lee's work assumes a powerful,
prophetic urgency. It offers the public an intimate space where the physical and
emotional experience of living in a turbulent world is laid bare.

As the largest work by the artist to date, Mire Lee's Hyundai Commission,
Open Wound, continues the artist's commitment to creating site-specific,
monumental sculptural installations in response to the moods and histories
of buildings and public spaces. For her Hyundai Commission, she has
transformed the Turbine Hall into a living, breathing entity, where fabric
sculptures (termed 'skins' by Lee) will be produced throughout the exhibition
period, gradually populating the hall. Reimagining the Turbine Hall as at once
a factory and an industrial womb, Lee intends for the space to appear to 'shed'
increasingly over time, in a dual process of gestation and deterioration.

Lee's installation revives the history of the Turbine Hall, breathing new life
into dormant elements of the space. At the heart of this installation is a newly
built motorised turbine, suspended from a recommissioned ceiling crane,
slowly turning and discharging a viscous liquid within the hall's east end. The
crane, a relic of the Turbine Hall's power station days, is once again central
to the operation of the space, while the removal of cladding along the bridge
exposes the internal wirings of the building.

The strength of Lee's work lies in its ability to evoke an eclectic range
of emotions – from awe and discomfort to empathy and tenderness. Her
installation prompts us to reflect on the complex relationship between
technology and humanity, where progress is often accompanied by decay and

efficiency competes with an enduring need for connection. As these pulsating forms evolve within the Turbine Hall, they remind us of our shared human experience, as well as the collective vulnerabilities and aspirations that drive us forward, towards each other. Lee's work dissolves the boundaries of individual identity, highlighting the fluidity between the self and the collective and offering a profound meditation on existence itself.

This ninth annual Hyundai Commission is supported through the commitment and generosity of our long-term partner Hyundai Motor Company. On behalf of Tate Modern, I would particularly like to extend our gratitude to Executive Chair Euisun Chung, Hyundai Motor Group for his significant support of the Hyundai Commission and the Hyundai Tate Research Centre: Transnational. Tate, alongside artists, strives to address pressing contemporary issues through their work. The ongoing support of Hyundai Motor Company plays a crucial role in allowing innovative art projects to deepen our collective insight into future possibilities.

This year's Hyundai Commission benefited from a tremendous input of philanthropic support from individuals, foundations and public funds from across the globe, enabling the artist's vision to become a reality. We would like to offer thanks to the Mire Lee Supporters including the Ministry of Culture, Sports and Tourism of Korea, Korea Arts Management Service, and the grant program Fund for Korean Art Abroad, Richard Chang, Yan Du and Lonti Ebers for the leading commitment to the project. We are also further grateful to the Mire Lee Supporters Circle, including Tina Kim Gallery, Antenna Space, Sprüth Magers, The Peter Magnone Foundation, Mondriaan Fund, Miyoung Lee and Neil Simpkins, Eleanor and Francis Shen, Victoria Bruhn, Wendy Lee, Dina Liu, Allison Berg, Kahng Foundation, Lisa Kim and Eunu Chun, Dana and Gregory Lee, Kyungsoon Lee and Jungwoo Shon, Teresa Tsai, Yoonjung and Edouard Ullmo, Margaret Wang, Yang Won Sun Foundation, Hee Yoon, Salle Yoo and Jeff Gray for their support.

The successful realisation of this project stands as testament to the remarkable collaboration and dedication of many individuals. The project has been curated by Alvin Li, Curator, International Art, supported by Asymmetry Art Foundation, who has worked with Lee on many occasions and whose longstanding commitment to the artist has enabled this exceptional and ambitious commission to come to fruition. Alvin has been supported by Bilal Akkouche, Assistant Curator, International Art, whose insightful contributions have been essential in the presentation of this impactful commission. They were further assisted by Alexandra Dolgosheina. Ann Coxon, former Curator, International Art, provided additional support in the early stage of the commission. The commission was expertly managed by Nancy Cooper, Production Manager, Commissions, whose tireless commitment was crucial in bringing this complex and ambitious installation to life. Nancy was assisted closely by Isabella Pilcher who provided essential support. Catherine Wood, Director of Programme, Tate Modern and Neil Casey, Associate Director, Business and Operations, offered vital advice and direction.

This book, edited by Alvin and Bilal, is part of a series of publications ensuring the legacy of the Hyundai Commissions. We thank the authors for their insightful contributions: Dina Akhmadeeva, Alvin and Bilal. We are grateful to the Tate Publishing team: Tom Avery, Nicola Bion, Bill Jones and Sarah Tucker. Thanks are due to Mark Thomson for the design of the Hyundai Commission catalogue series and to the Tate Photography Department for the images of the installation.

Finally, my deepest gratitude goes to Mire Lee for her extraordinary vision and the generosity she has shown throughout this project. With *Hyundai Commission: Mire Lee: Open Wound*, she has created a space where the complexities of our emotional lives are explored in depth, offering us a powerful reflection on the fragility and beauty of existence in our ever-evolving world.

Karin Hindsbo
Director, Tate Modern

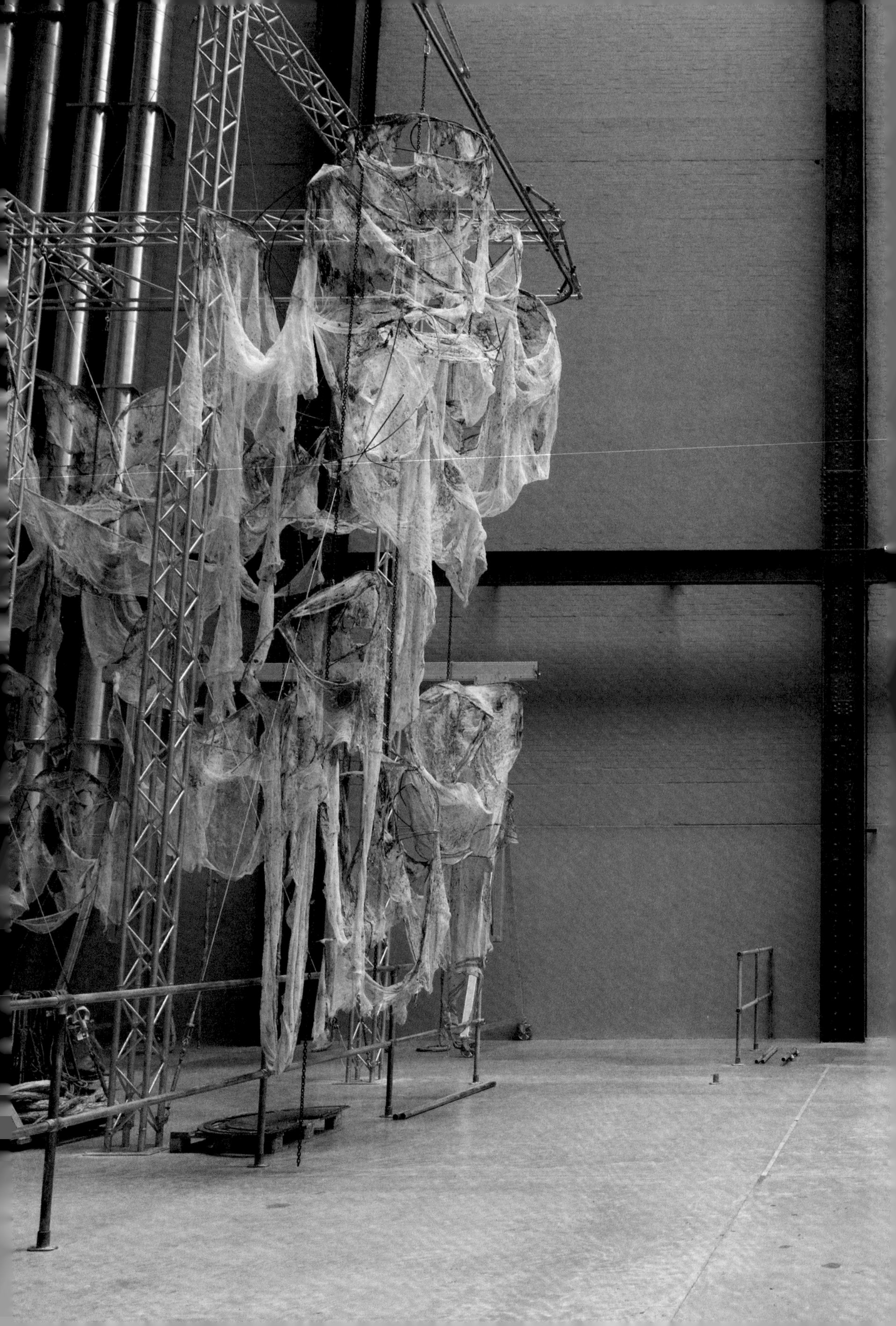

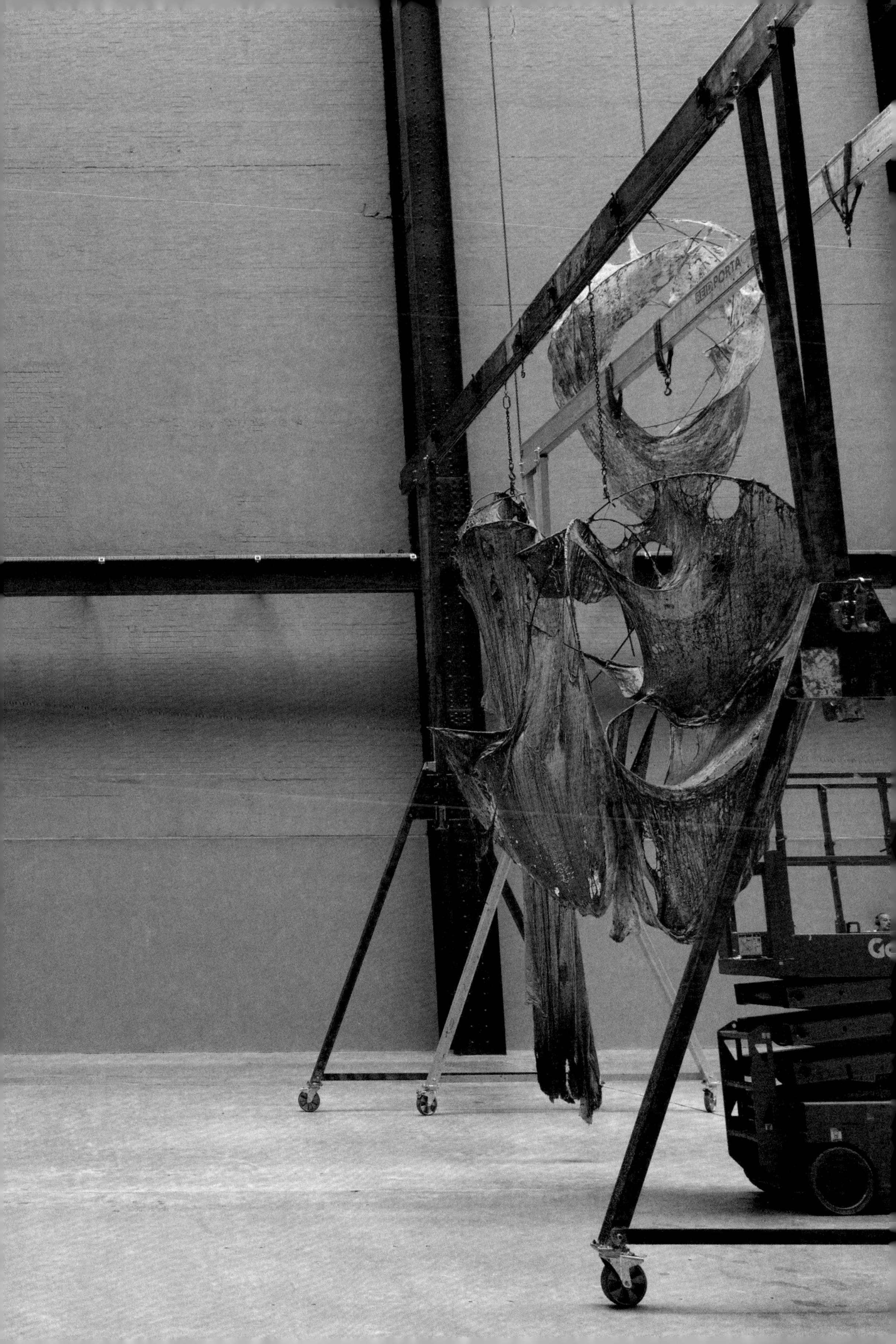

Acknowledgements

The realisation of a project as ambitious as Mire Lee's Hyundai Commission, *Open Wound*, inevitably involves an extended team of colleagues and supporters. In addition to the many individuals who have supported the commission, there is a community of dedicated collaborators who have championed the artist over many years. Many thanks are due to Tina Kim and the team at Tina Kim Gallery, as well as former gallery director Junni Chen, current Deputy Director of Para Site, Hong Kong; Simon Wang and the team at Antenna Space; and Monika Sprüth and Philomene Magers, Shine Oh, Andreas Gegner and the team at Sprüth Magers. We are grateful to Stephan Kuderna, who, having worked with the artist during her early years at the Rijksakademie, agreed to join us on this project as Lee's technical advisor. A special note of thanks must be extended to Mire Lee's studio teams in Seoul and Amsterdam, including Mingrui Jiang, Christian Otto, Joe Highton and Xenia Bond, whose tireless efforts have been fundamental to the realisation of this commission.

The intricate and evocative nature of Mire Lee's work has been brilliantly supported by the Brighton-based production studio millimetre. Their ingenuity and commitment to excellence have been vital in the realisation of this commission, ensuring that the complex and delicate elements of Lee's vision were brought to life with precision and care. We are deeply appreciative of their diligent research, meticulous planning and collaborative spirit, which have made this project a true success.

We would like to express our deepest appreciation to Karin Hindsbo, Deputy Director, Tate and Director, Tate Modern; Catherine Wood, Director of Programme, Tate Modern; and Neil Casey, Associate Director, Business and Operations, Tate Modern, for their unwavering support and guidance throughout the project. At every juncture of *Hyundai Commission: Mire Lee: Open Wound*, my colleague Bilal Akkouche has contributed with great efficiency. His clarity of organisation has been matched by production manager Nancy Cooper, whose dedication to the project and attention to detail is unparalleled, and I should like to thank them both for this concentrated energy. We are grateful to Ann Coxon for her curatorial input in the early stage of the commission. I would also like to acknowledge former and present Tate colleagues who joined me early on in advocating for Mire's work: Clara Kim, Chief Curator & Director of Curatorial Affairs, The Museum of Contemporary Art, Los Angeles; Katy Wan, Managing Curator, D.Daskalopoulos Collection Gift, Tate Modern; and Hera Chan, Adjunct Curator, Asia-Pacific, Tate.

In addition to the abovementioned individuals at Tate, the project has been supported by a wide array of departments across Tate Modern, and we are very grateful for the contributions of many. Special thanks go to Emma Garrett, Head of Visitor Experience; Sandra McLean, Senior Visitor Experience Manager; Kathleen Patterson, Diary Coordinator; Roger Miller, Risk, Health and Safety Manager; Joanna Sandler, Press and Communications Officer; Kirsteen McSwein and Elliott Higgs in Interpretation; Charlotte Reeves and Sophie Busby in Corporate Partnerships; Nancy Hitzig, Sarah Monteath and Grace England in Major Gifts; Sandra Sykorova and Fikayo Adebajo in Public Programmes; Megan Pottle and Georgina Ramkoleea in Marketing; Jessye Bloomfield at Tate Lates; Scott Morris and Ben Wells in Digital; Tylar Napolitano in Advocacy and Events; and Lavinia de Nazelle in Legal. I also appreciate the dedicated work of our colleagues in the Security and Audiences Division, as well as the Learning and Design teams.

Additionally, I would like to thank the artist James Richards, who has remained an interlocutor throughout the project, and has agreed to lend his vision to the commission's closing event, taking place in March 2025, as my co-curator. Further thanks to artist Ami Lien, whose feedback, shared over many late-night conversations, provided Mire and me with great inspiration – a snippet of the conversation between Ami and Mire is published in the September issue of *Tate Etc.*

As Senior Editor at Tate Publishing, Nicola Bion has masterminded this volume with remarkable sang-froid, and I should like to thank her colleagues, Tom Avery, Bill Jones and Sarah Tucker. Thanks to Mark Thomson for the wonderful design. I would also like to thank Dina Akhmadeeva, Assistant Curator, International Art, Tate Modern, for the beautiful introduction essay she penned for this book.

Finally, I would like to thank Mire for her unconditional trust and friend-ship. In the many years we have worked together she has never ceased to inspire me with her vision and earnestness. Back in 2022, in a conversation published in the September 2022 issue of *Frieze* magazine, I asked Mire about her interest in the work of poet Eon Hee Kim. Mire said: 'What I love about Eon Hee's work – and I know this from talking to her – is that she wanted to write poems so brutal that the paper itself would tear. And her poems truly feel that way to me. Poetry as a form cannot contain Eon Hee's words: they flow right out.' It is with the same intensity, fearlessness and devout allegiance to alterity that Mire Lee builds her sculptural worlds. The inexhaustible impact and depth of *Open Wound* remains for the visitors and readers of this current volume to explore in the many years to come.

Alvin Li
Curator, International Art, supported by Asymmetry Art Foundation

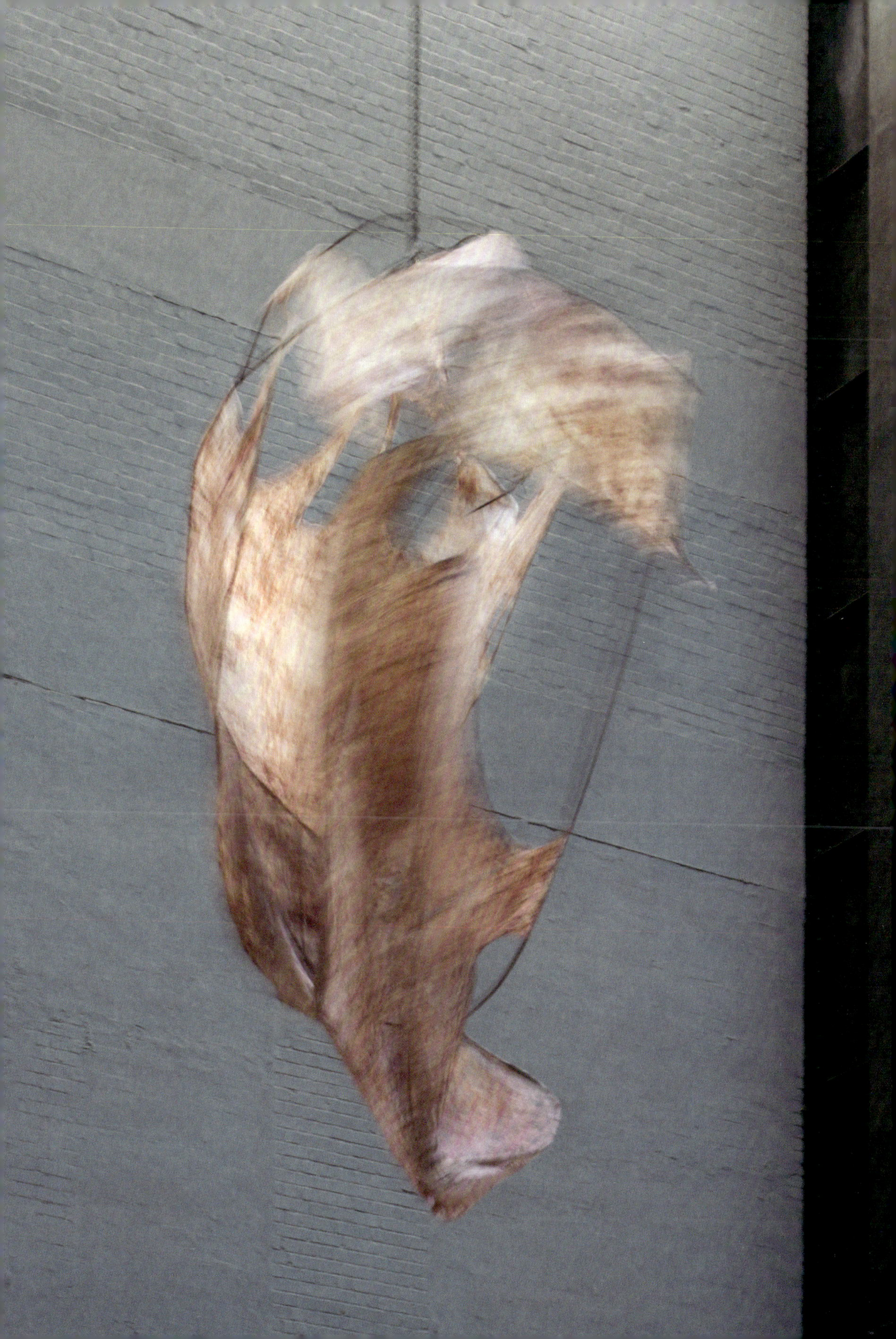

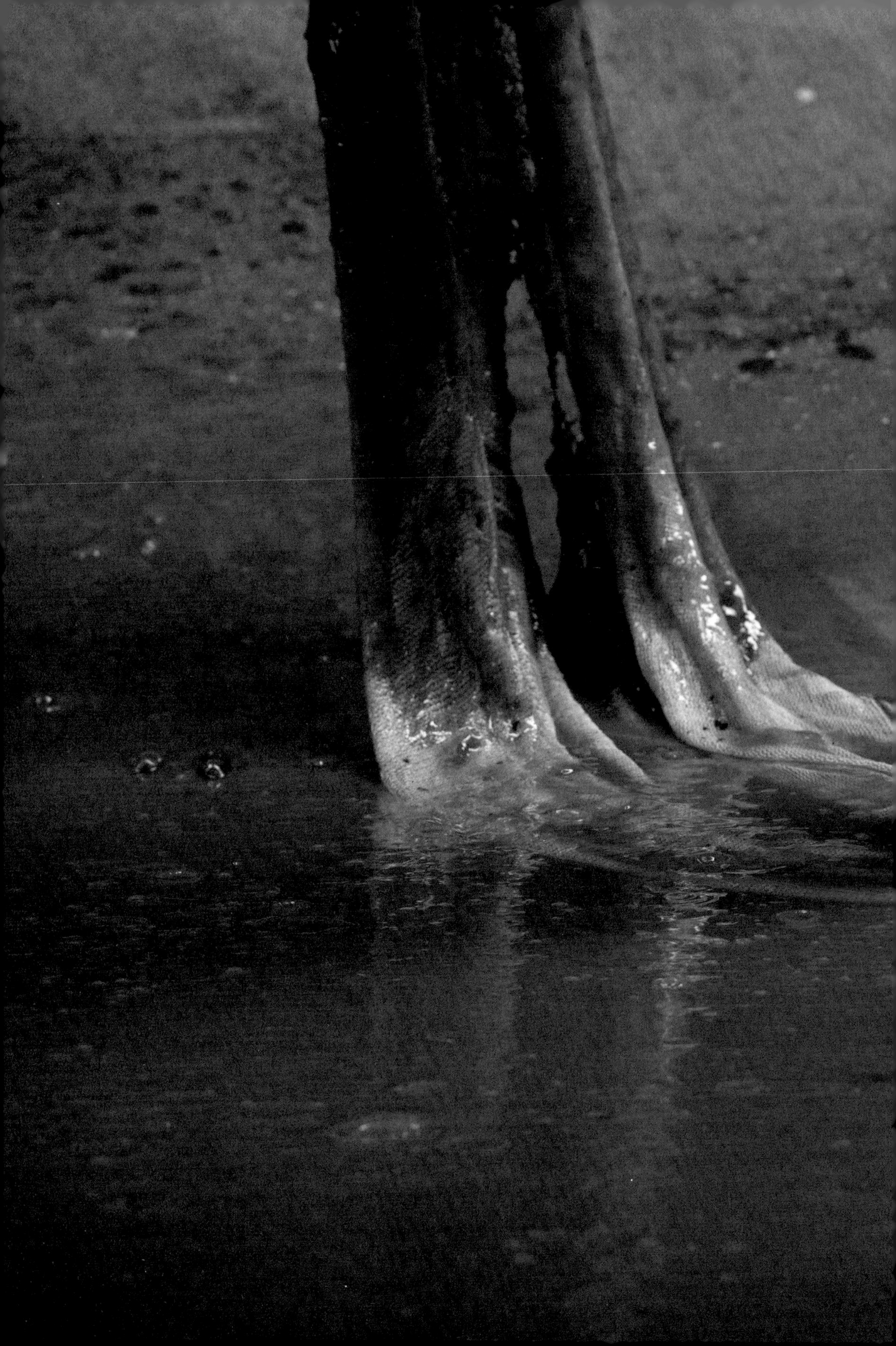

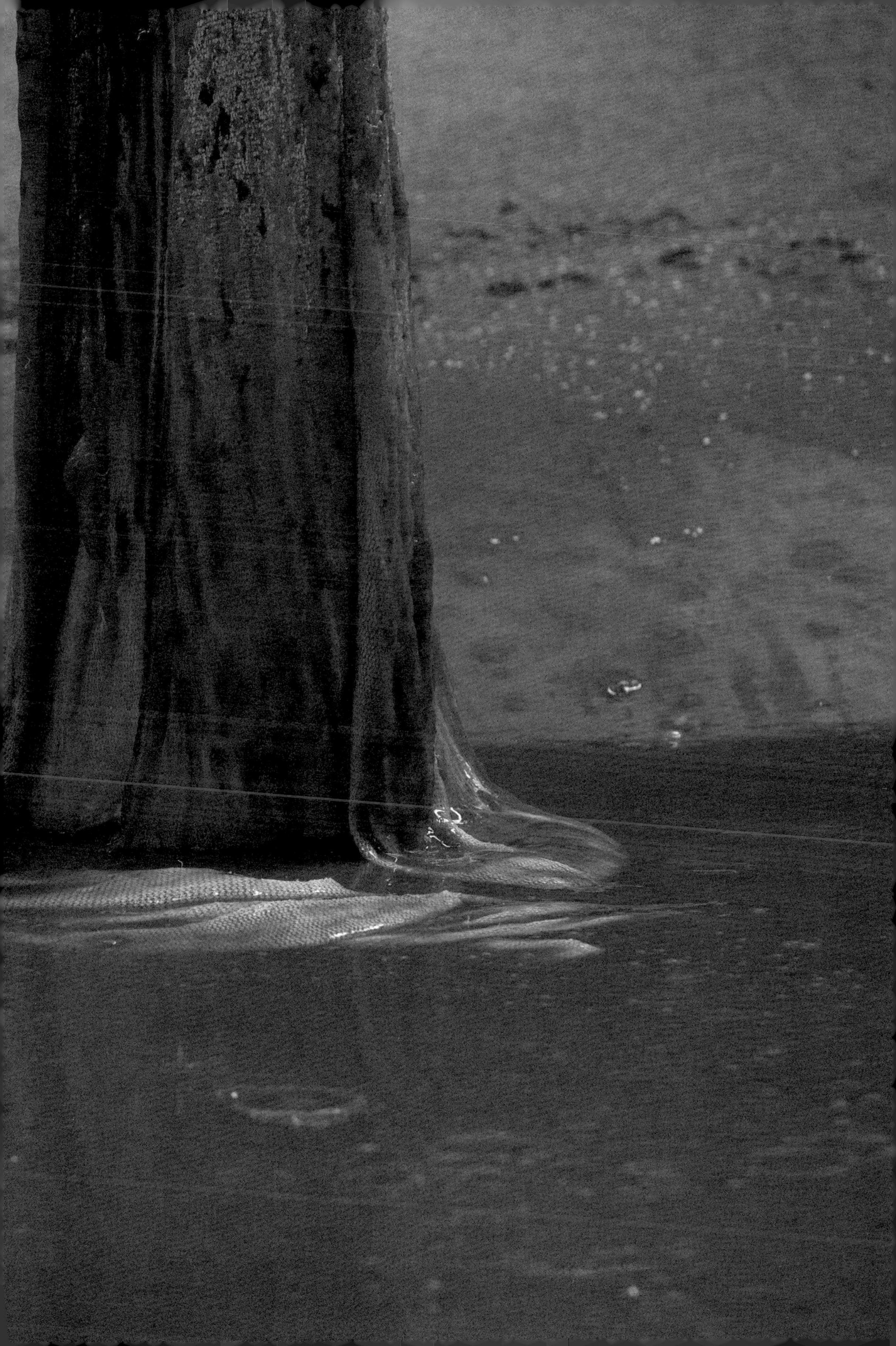

Convulsing, Devouring, Rotating, Feeling

Dina Akhmadeeva

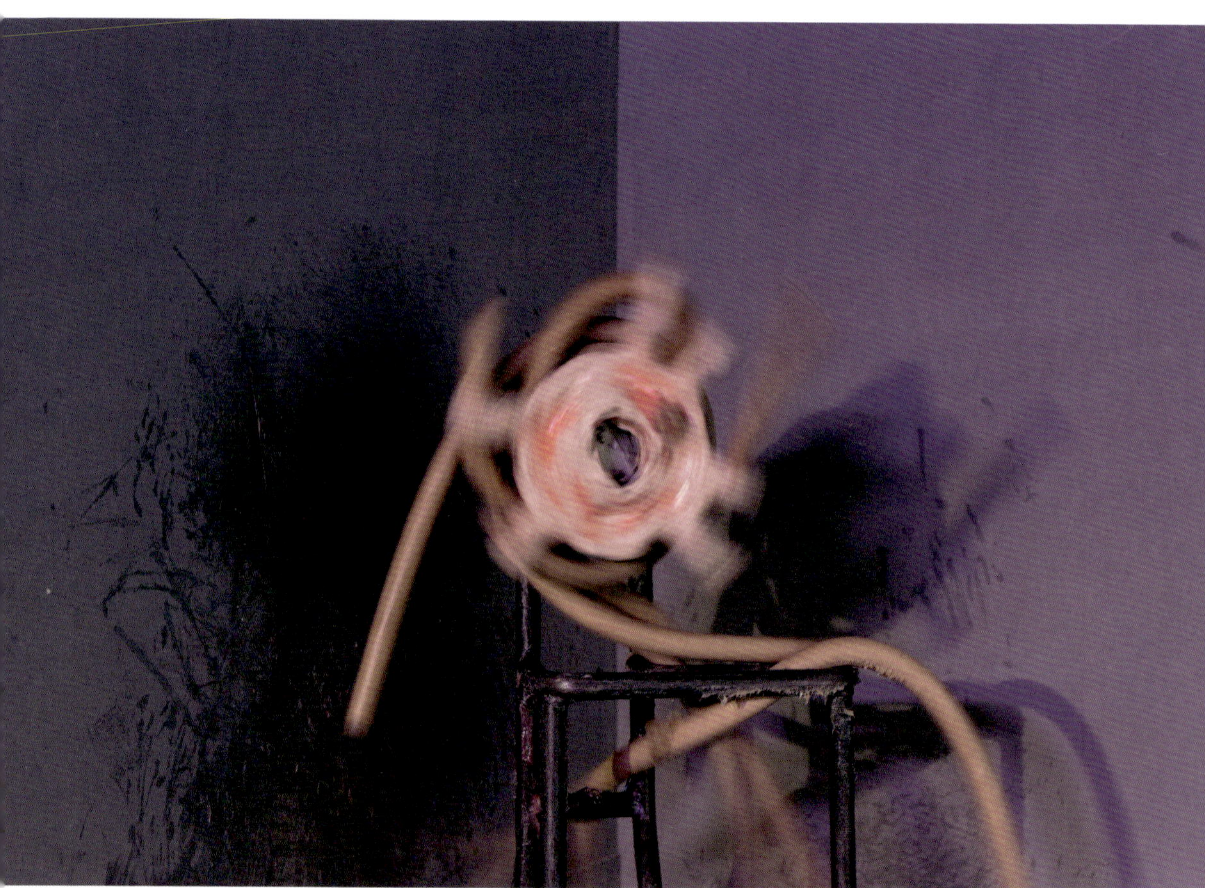

Hysteria, Elegance, Catharsis; the islands 2017 (detail); series of different sculptures in mixed media, dimensions variable

I'm watching a video documenting the movement of a sculpture by Mire Lee. It comes in at barely over a minute, but I play it on a loop, near-obsessively, my attention trapped in the rotation of the sculpture, pulled along with it. A plasticine starfish-wheel-cog with a hole for an eye that's not an eye turns on a makeshift low-fi mechanism that sits on an armature of three welded metal rod-legs. I follow its motion as it pulls along solid, floppy tubular lengths of rubber with no compromise or respite. These thin, pathetic tendrils, the colour of ultra-processed meat (flesh that is not flesh), twist and tighten around the cog. For a moment, they form a blockage of sorts. Responding to this accumulation of concentrated energy, my body stiffens, anticipating the inevitable release of built up mechanical-material tension. I imagine it will be a relief. Instead, twitching a little, the tentacles unfurl not dramatically but languidly, caught between the downward pull of gravity and their rubbery stretch in a comically sluggish bounce that marks the walls with a greasy substance: motor lubricant.

Anticlimactic, comical, a bit repulsive, *Hysteria, Elegance, Catharsis; the islands* 2017 contains in its concentric tightening action the motions of Mire Lee's all-consuming fixations, which exist prior to the moment of this work and recur in shifted, expanded states beyond it: the uncertain formation and messy undoing of both body and psyche; the transgression of orchestrated social limits through non-normative sexuality and the embrace of desire; the errant motion and movement of low-fi kinetic technologies; the comedic theatrics of failure; an attunement to contradictory, ambivalent emotional conditions. Its rotation pulls in Lee's own no less restless motion, from Seoul to Paris to Amsterdam to Berlin, its gestures giving unruly form to the emotional states of Lee's work. As each springy tentacle languidly drops, leaving behind successive splashes of lubricant, so too, one by one, do Lee's motions and preoccupations unfurl.

CONVULSING, TWITCHING: LEE'S LIVING CADAVERS

Always indirect, through relation to a body, a part of a body, not a person, a whole thing, unless a spirit, a being, a strange character, a beautiful creature, a child, a vision, a parasitic body, a cadaver, a living cadaver, a phantom, an other, a beloved body, a body, an inanimate body, a sphinx. That one did not speak or hardly spoke, a silent life of scent, hair, thighs, a curved neck, skin, an arm, a shoulder, dancing divinely, drunkenly.
Sharon Kivland[1]

Where does a body begin and end? Lee's kinetic sculptures, marked by
decay and violence, have simultaneously become interlinked with a sense
of bodily formation, being repeatedly recognised as forms marked by decay
and violence, 'reminiscent of mutilated bodies or organs', during the course
of her career.[2] Lee's sculptures evoke bodily functions, function like bodies,
malfunction like bodies, disintegrate like bodies. Their abject horror speaks
directly into bodies, while their distinct forms and part-forms force their way
out of and beyond a somatic relation to the human body. Yet increasingly, in
the growth and expansion of her practice from sculpture to installation, Lee's
works draw attention to themselves as sites, environments and choreographies
of ambiguous, unsettled, restless bodies in a tension between breakdown
and a morbid liveness. Her sculptures and structures – particularly since her
introduction of industrial lubricants, glycerine, ceramic glaze and other liquids
into their forms – are at the mercy of an errant, unpredictable vitality that
courses its way through them. Propelled by rudimentary motors, these liquids
force their way through translucent hoses and tubes, forcing their carriers to
come to life – pulling some upwards off the floor, making others thrash side to
side, hissing. With the violence that is characteristic of Lee's sculptures, the
liquids find their way out eventually, spitting themselves out under pressure,
or oozing lazily from orifices and cracks either introduced deliberately into
her materials by Lee or produced by slip-ups she embraces. Lee's commission
for the main exhibition of the 2022 Venice Biennale, which she titled *Endless
House: Holes and Drips* 2022, existed as a dramaturgy of the pumping, oozing
and splattering of a red-coloured liquid clay that coursed its way through hoses
and tubes, throwing these vessels into frantic, unpredictable convulsions.
Presented in the manner of a spectacle on a vertical scaffolding structure
above metal grates that both drained the liquid and became stained with their
remnants, Lee set up a scene of implied deathly violence heightened by a
desperate, gushing final moment of life.

The technologies that Lee embraces – peristaltic and dosing pumps
that move liquid, spinning motors belonging to engine machinery, clamps,
PVC hoses – are decidedly and deliberately low-tech and, in contrast to
the comparatively dematerialised digital technologies of her own time,
infrastructurally emphatically physical. In their design, these elements have
a proximity to the body and biological mechanisms: peristaltic pumps, which
originate technologically in blood transfusions, imitate the swallowing and
movement of food through the digestive system and the production of waste,

while hoses and tubing 'act out' a circulatory system, their leakages and spurts mimicking physical damage with the theatrical flair of comedic horror. While Lee's works have previously been framed in the context of futuristic and sci-fi hybrids that speak to the ongoing enmeshment of body and technology, these aging, distinctly analogue systems benefit from being understood as more akin to the historical tradition of the mechanical automaton.[3] These devices had a 'parasitic' relationship to the body: they were mechanisms modelled on and made in imitation of the human form. Among them, for example, was the Euphonia, a talking machine exhibited for the first time in Philadelphia in 1845, that replicated human speech: comprising a mechanical throat and vocal organs, jaws, mouth and tongue behind a female mask, this unnerving figure stood as part of a tradition that stretches back to antiquity via cuckoo clocks, singing birds, floating orchestras and moving knights.

This is the context in which Mire Lee stages her dramaturgy. Dead, her sculptures play alive. When they simulate living, they stage dramatic deaths. States of production (the accumulation of glaze, the solidification of pooling cement) are simultaneously states of – often – the self-sabotaging material collapse of analogue, already aging systems and infrastructures. 'When I first began to work with deformity of material and figures, I was putting soft and hard materials next to each other in kinetic operations, and was fascinated to see how they destroy each other', Lee has said.[4] The choreography of these sculptures' movements exists in the notation of the convulsion, the twitch, the cramp. It is a desperate, volatile liveness that emerges together with their theatrical disintegration.

Roger Caillois, the surrealist philosopher and historian of science, wrote at length on a figure in nature capable of standing in as a counterpart to Lee's sculptures for its capacity to *act* dead while also *being* dead: the praying mantis.[5] Specifically, it is the mantis's decapitated body – Caillois's object of reflection as a cadaverous figurehead of the living dead – that points the way toward imagining the specificity of Lee's liveness as centred on the knotted, unresolved tussle of these two states. 'There are very few reactions the mantis cannot perform in a decapitated state – that is, without any center of representation or of voluntary activity', Caillois wrote in his 1934 text:

> In this condition, it can walk; regain its balance; sever a threatened limb; assume the spectral stance; engage in mating; lay eggs; build an ootheca; and (this is truly frightening) lapse into feigned rigor mortis in the face of danger or

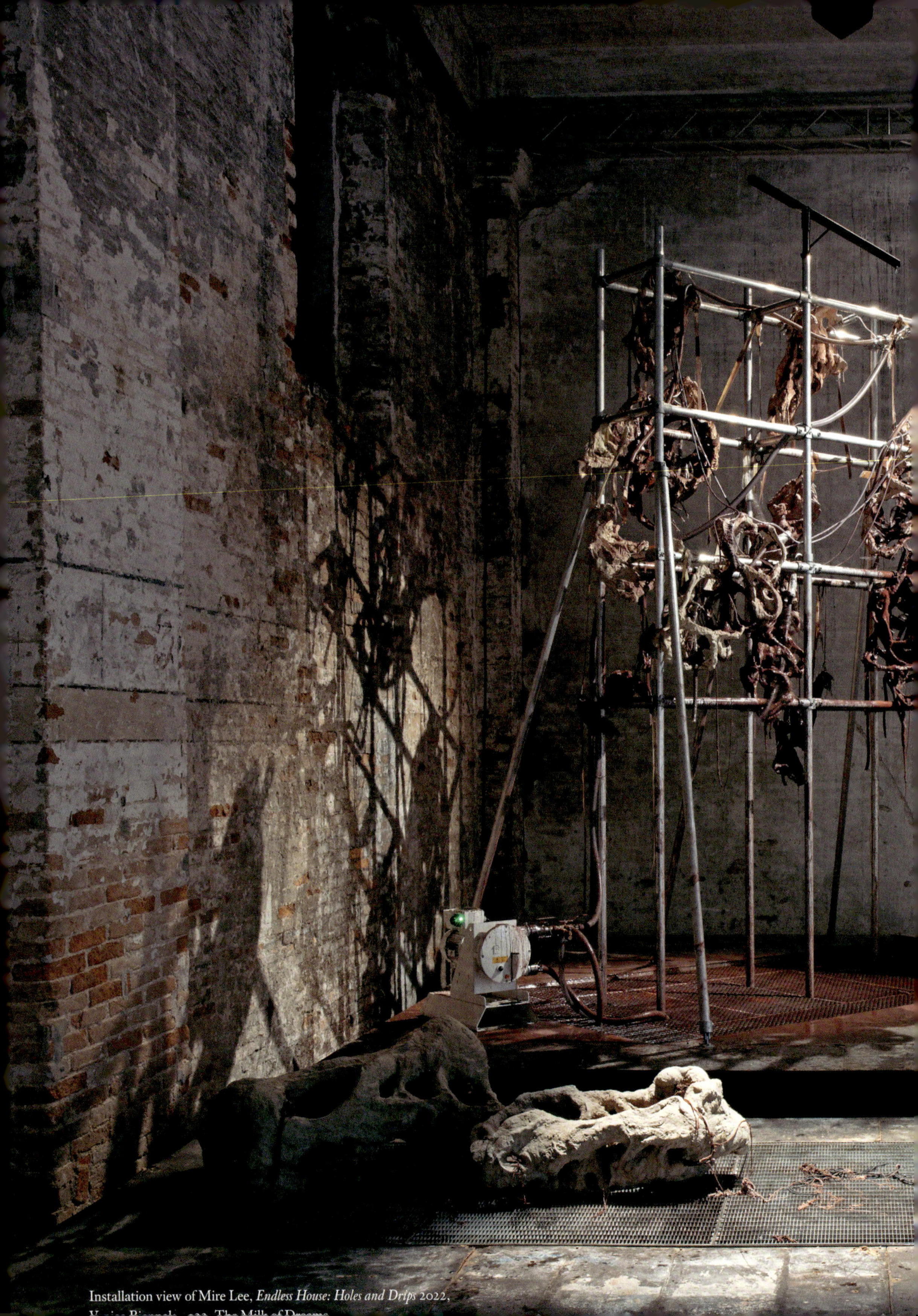

Installation view of Mire Lee, *Endless House: Holes and Drips* 2022,
Venice Biennale 2022 The Milk of Dreams

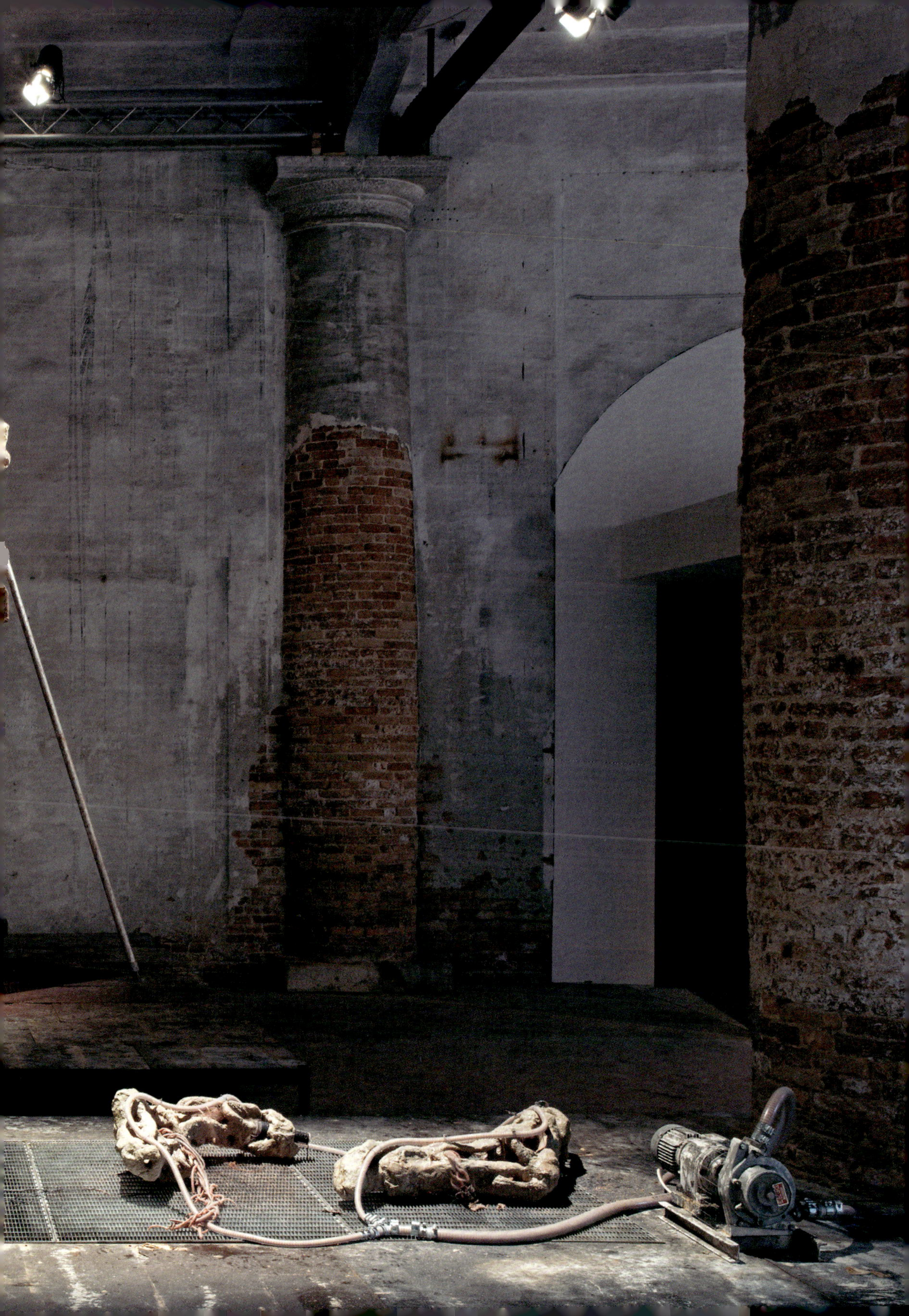

when the peripheral nervous system is stimulated. I am deliberately expressing
myself in a roundabout way as it is so difficult, I think, both for language
to express and for the mind to grasp that the mantis, when dead, should be
capable of simulating death.[6]

What must precede any actions of the headless insect, however, is the
moment of primordial violence enacted by its cannibalistic counterpart. The
moment of decapitation, which captured the surrealists' imagination, is part
of the female mantis's sexual practice of beheading and devouring the male
after, or even in the moment of, copulation.[7] She is the anxiety-tinged animal
personification of the castrating, devouring mouth. Within it, glimpses of
primordial violence and voracious sexuality point onwards to the importance of
non-normative sexuality and forms of desire for Lee's own explorations. Or, in
the words of Kim Eon Hee, the Korean poet whose words continue to animate
and permeate Lee's practice – most directly in her 2022 exhibition at the
Museum für Moderne Kunst (MMK) in Frankfurt (we will return to it later) –
and for whom Lee expressed her admiration for 'writ[ing] poems so brutal that
the paper itself would tear':[8]

> It was
> The mantis, crunch crunch
> The lustful lower jaw chews
> The back of my head, it was
> The old mother, with morning sickness for twenty-four hours
> A mouth that's not the mouth
> With the jet-black smile
> The mantis'
> Day has five nights[9]

Together with the mantis's prey, we enter the mouth of Lee's work through
the moment of ingestion.

DEVOURING: THE HOLE, THE VOID

In and through the mouth, voracious sexuality and negation coalesce across
Lee's practice as ways toward being in the world, toward opening to the world.

For nearly a decade, she has looked to the sexual fetish of vorarephilia to feed her exploration. Vorarephilia, or vore, is the desire to consume or be consumed by another ('soft vore' prefers that the victim be swallowed alive and whole, resting in the stomach; less commonly, 'hard vore' imagines the chewing apart and digestion of the victim). In the paraphilic imagination of vorarephilia, the mouth as an orifice into the body of another is interconnected with the anus, the breast, the penis as points of entry for the ingested being. The vagina becomes a site of a particular strand of vore fantasy, that of going back into the womb: a body full of holes. Lee has described the lure of the phenomenon for her in terms of a form of openness to another. 'You want to be inside the other, to become one with them', she has said. 'No porn caters to people who engage in the fetish because it would be impossible to enact it. I find this very romantic.'[10]

The work *i wanna be together* 2019 (p.43), exhibited at the Seoul Museum of Art (and subsequently the title of shows in Amsterdam and Rotterdam) enacted the dynamics of the fetish in its workings. Lee invited ten artists in her circle – many of whom she had met during her residency at the Rijksakademie in Amsterdam in 2018–19 – to offer up their artworks to be 'fed' into her sculptural process. These works, presented in fragments on a rotating spherical steel armature, at once depicted the destructive act of material ingestion and exemplified Lee's vision of reconfigured, dissipated boundaries between one and another. It is a logic that permeates Lee's works more latently, too: in titling her spindly, spurting and twitching mechanisms *Carriers* 2020 at Art Sonje Center in Seoul and *Carriers: Offsprings* 2021 – exhibited at her joint exhibition with H.R. Giger at the Schinkel Pavillon in Berlin – Lee gestured toward imagining her mechanisms as bodily systems filled with substances or other bodies: 'carrying a child, carrying a disease, carrying fluids'.[11] Curator Alvin Li has traced the transition of Lee's preoccupation with vore 'from its paraphilic origin into a creative attitude and an ontological metaphor', as a relational way of being.[12] The intense sexual desire to be engulfed by or engulf another being is also the desire to lose the bounds and thresholds of the self, to drop the image of self-contained coherence, to negate the singular identity, to open out. Or, in Mire Lee's words, 'it is about wanting to be absorbed – a total obliteration of distance.[13] Each one of us, filled with others.

The holes that permeate Lee's works are markers of these thinning boundaries between selves, ripped open to the possibility of relation, transgression, spillage. 'I have been interested in the idea of a being with lots of holes that make it permeable so that something could come in and out of it', she has said. 'I like this image of bodies so open that they can no longer contain.[14] Through these openings, we enter into Lee's investigation of infrastructures, emotional landscapes, systems. The body is never solely a body. Holes appear as marks of Lee's exploration of industrial disintegration in *Landscape with Many Holes: Skins of Young-do Sea* 2022 (pp.44–5), an expansive site-specific work installed in a former shipyard building on Yeongdo Island, South Korea for the 2022 Busan Biennale. Made up of a criss-crossing scaffolding structure of architectural proportions, holding shreds of construction mesh marked by used oil, cuts and perforations, the work was the first of Lee's site-specific explorations of aging systems of manufacture, a strand she continues in Tate Modern's Hyundai Commission by reactivating the museum building's former role as an industrial facility. Lee imagined the Busan commission as a building-body-infrastructure relation, 'an organism swallowed by the abandoned factory, like a battered whale', an image to which she has returned multiple times.[15] Soon after *Skins of Young-do Sea* was installed, a typhoon ripped through the already storm-damaged building, perforating the walls and roof with fresh holes.

Holes as tunnel-like bodily cavities appear also in *Endless House*, an interconnected body of works made for Lee's 2021 exhibition at the Schinkel Pavillon and the 2022 Venice Biennale which made reference to Lee's ongoing interest in the imagined architectural concept of the Endless House by Frederick Kiesler. Kiesler developed this unrealised project of a house-as-organism from the 1920s through to the 1960s, imagining a series of rounded, symbiotic spaces interconnected by openings and 'endless like the human body'.[16] Digested by Lee as 'the warmth of the womb and the darkness of a torture chamber at the same time', *Endless House* is a site of the conflicting emotional atmospheres that underpin Lee's practice.[17] Its endlessness, meanwhile, registers a development in Lee's understanding of how the space of her own installations and exhibitions can function in a charged way. With it, we see the spaces of Lee's exhibitions *become* voids, holes of their own in their spatial expansion outwards from singular objects to environments. Writer and curator Wong Binghao described Lee's 2022 exhibition *Look, I'm a fountain of filth raving mad with love* at the Museum für Moderne Kunst in Frankfurt as permeated with an 'utter, complete emptiness … a mélange of zero … It smelled a lot like nothing … A big, vacant hole growing inside of and

i wanna be together 2019, work-in-process fragments from 10 different artists, motor, and other mixed media, 3 x 3 x 6 metres

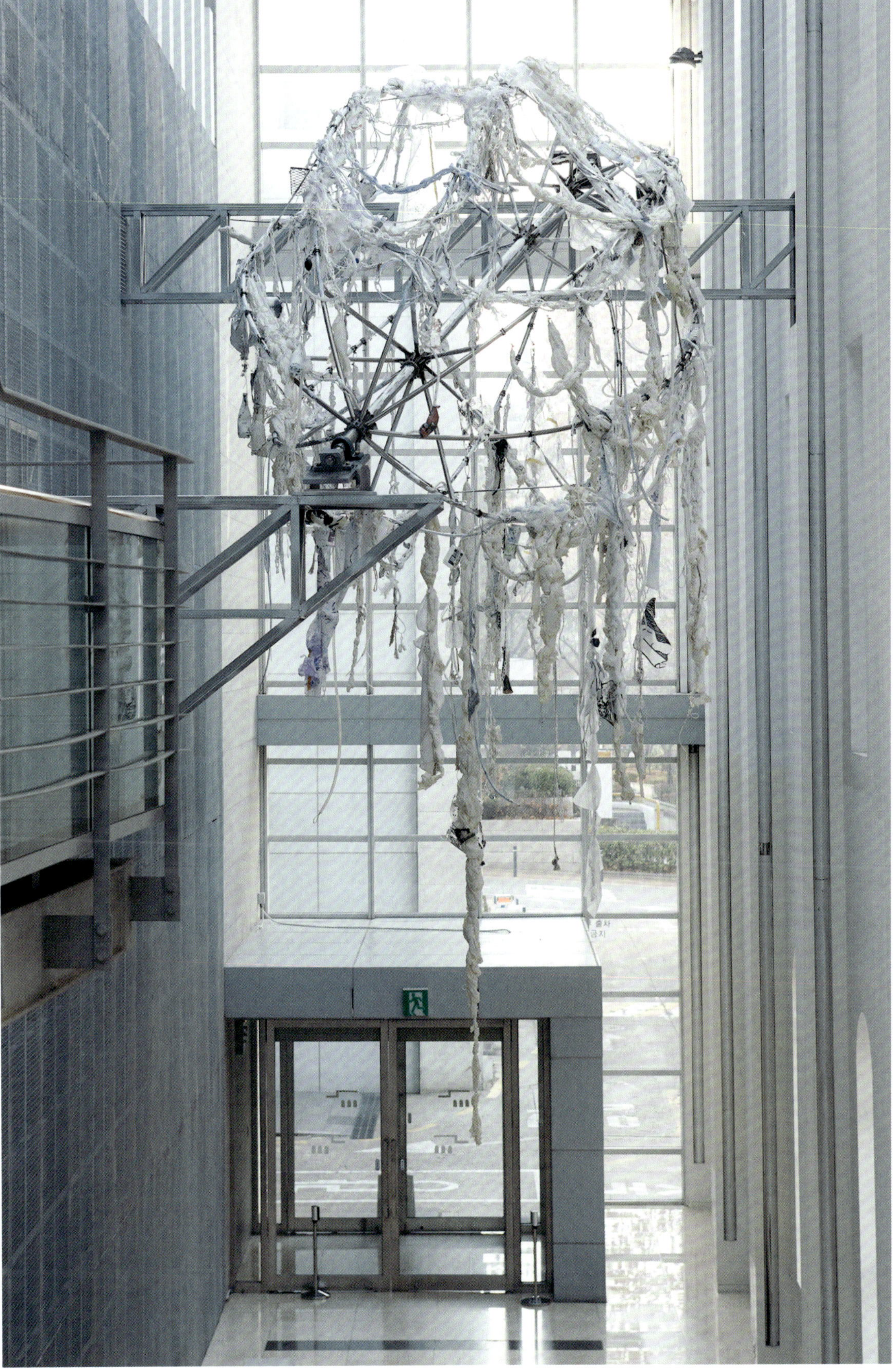

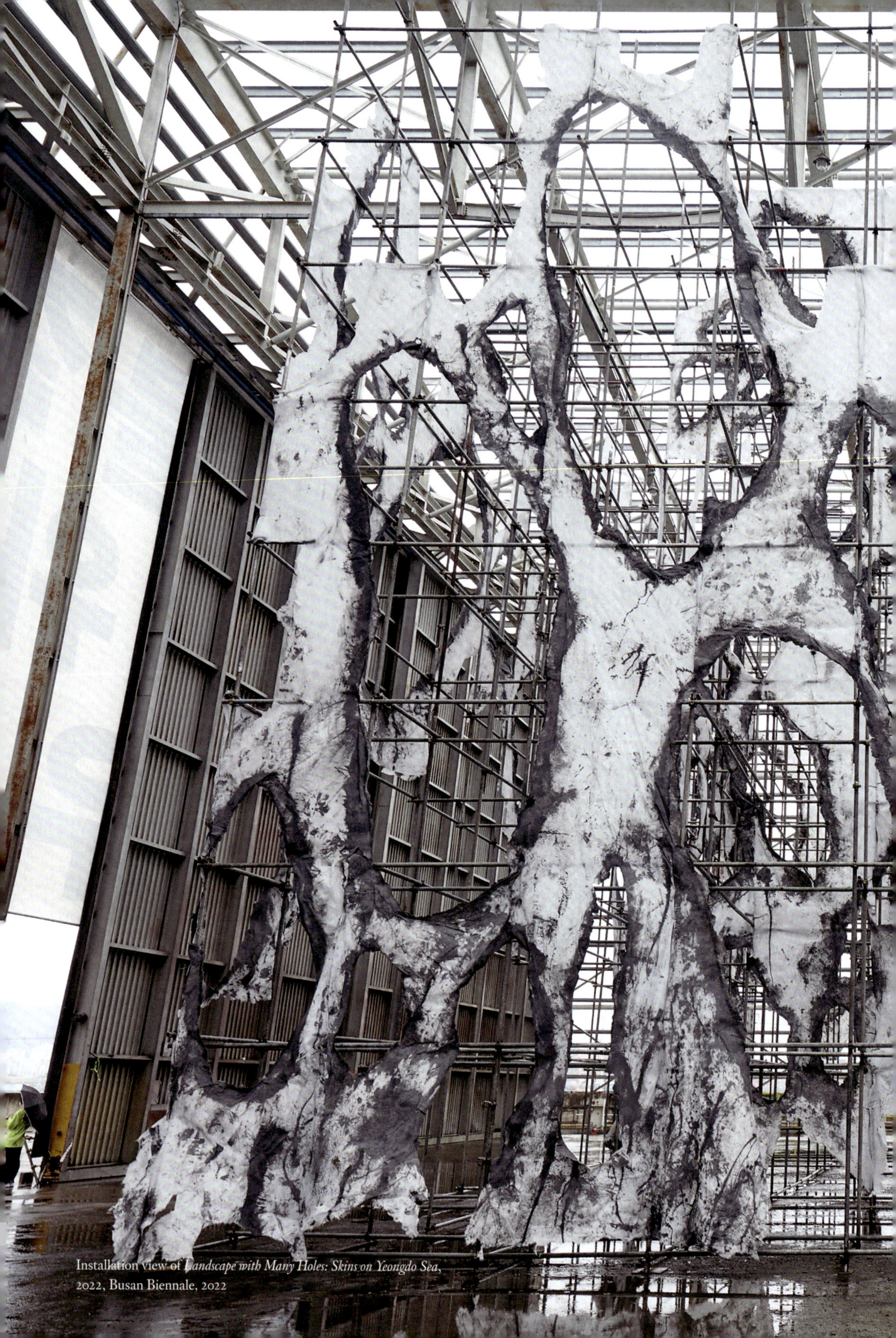

Installation view of *Landscape with Many Holes: Skins on Yeongdo Sea*, 2022, Busan Biennale, 2022

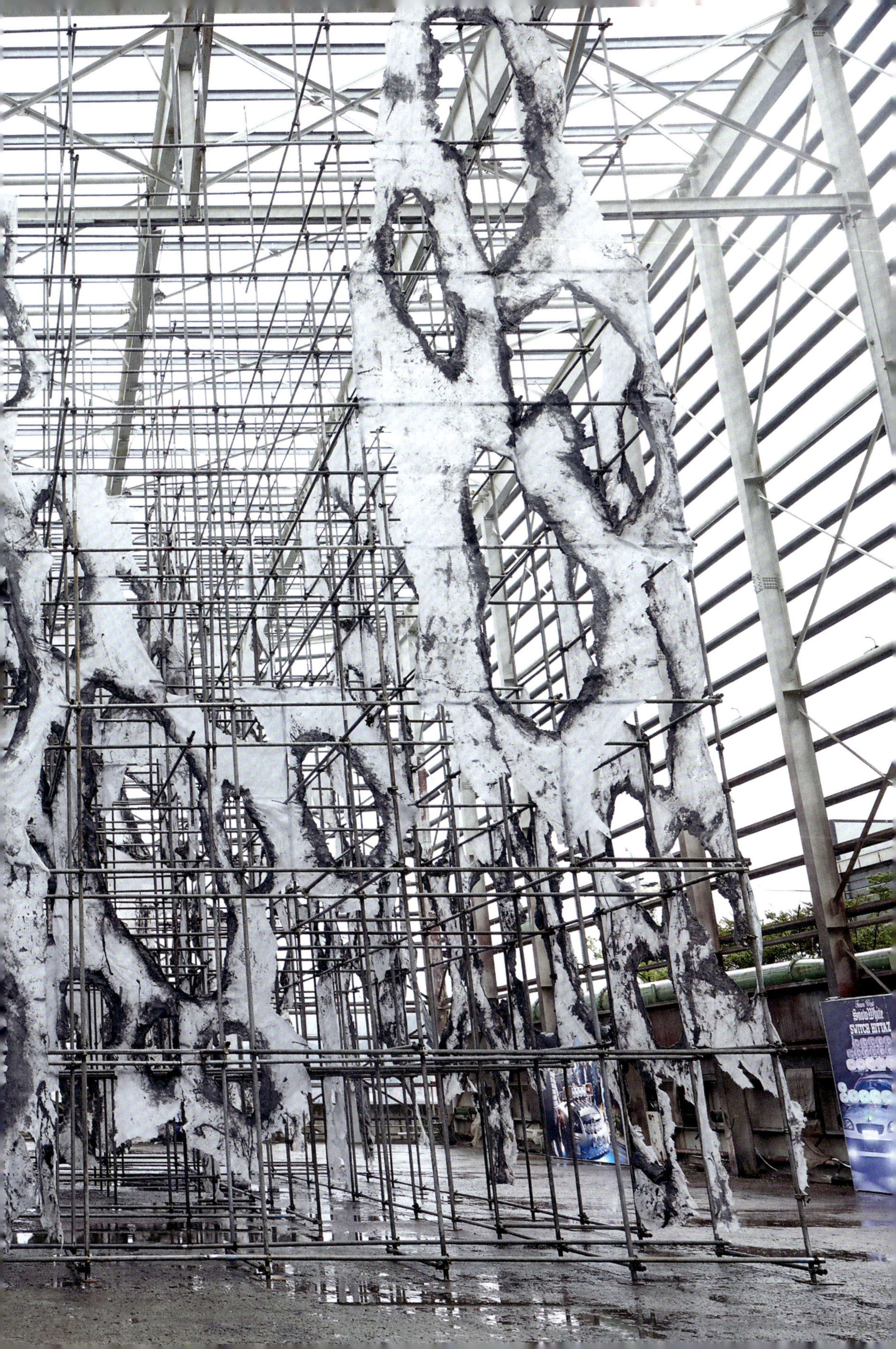

around you'.[18] There, a body as a hole encountered the spatial arrangement of the void.

ROTATING: A MOUTH THAT'S NOT THE MOUTH

Wong's sensitivity to emptiness and nothingness within Lee's exhibition in Frankfurt is one that has grown attuned to Lee's commitment to creating stoppages in language, reason and concept. '[I] like the quality of cancelling all the intellectual or communicative capacities we have as cultural beings. I'm interested in the obliteration of all these areas', Lee has stated.[19] This outlook animates her studio working process, which operates on the level of what Lee has described as 'infantile form[s] of association' sparked by material experimentation: collisions between the qualities of soft and hard and the destruction that ensues; tangles that form; the sound of something falling into a tub of liquid.[20] It likewise moves through each of her projects, sites through which others might come undone. To achieve this, Lee operates a kind of speculative structural reorganisation of the body, starting with its openings. In her own bodily imaginary, there is a direct channel between the mouth and anus, with the latter signifying the capacity for stoppage: 'I like evoking the anus or genitals in general because they cannot speak', she has explained.[21]

In the second issue of *Documents*, published in 1929, Georges Bataille, the writer and philosopher whose work on eroticism Lee has cited as an influence on her practice,[22] wrote an entry under the title 'Mouth' as part of his ongoing section 'Critical Dictionary', which for Bataille and his collaborators functioned as a site of free association that undid the meaning of words and opened up the contingent state of language. It is worth quoting at length:

> The mouth is the beginning or, if one prefers, the prow of animals … But man does not have a simple architecture like beasts, and it is not even possible to say where he begins. He possibly starts at the top of the skull … However, the violent meaning of the mouth is conserved in a latent state: it suddenly regains the upper hand with a literally cannibalistic expression such as *mouth of fire*, applied to the cannons men employ to kill each other. And on important occasions human life is still bestially concentrated in the mouth: fury makes men grind their teeth, terror and atrocious suffering transform the mouth into the organ of rending screams. On this subject it is easy to observe that the

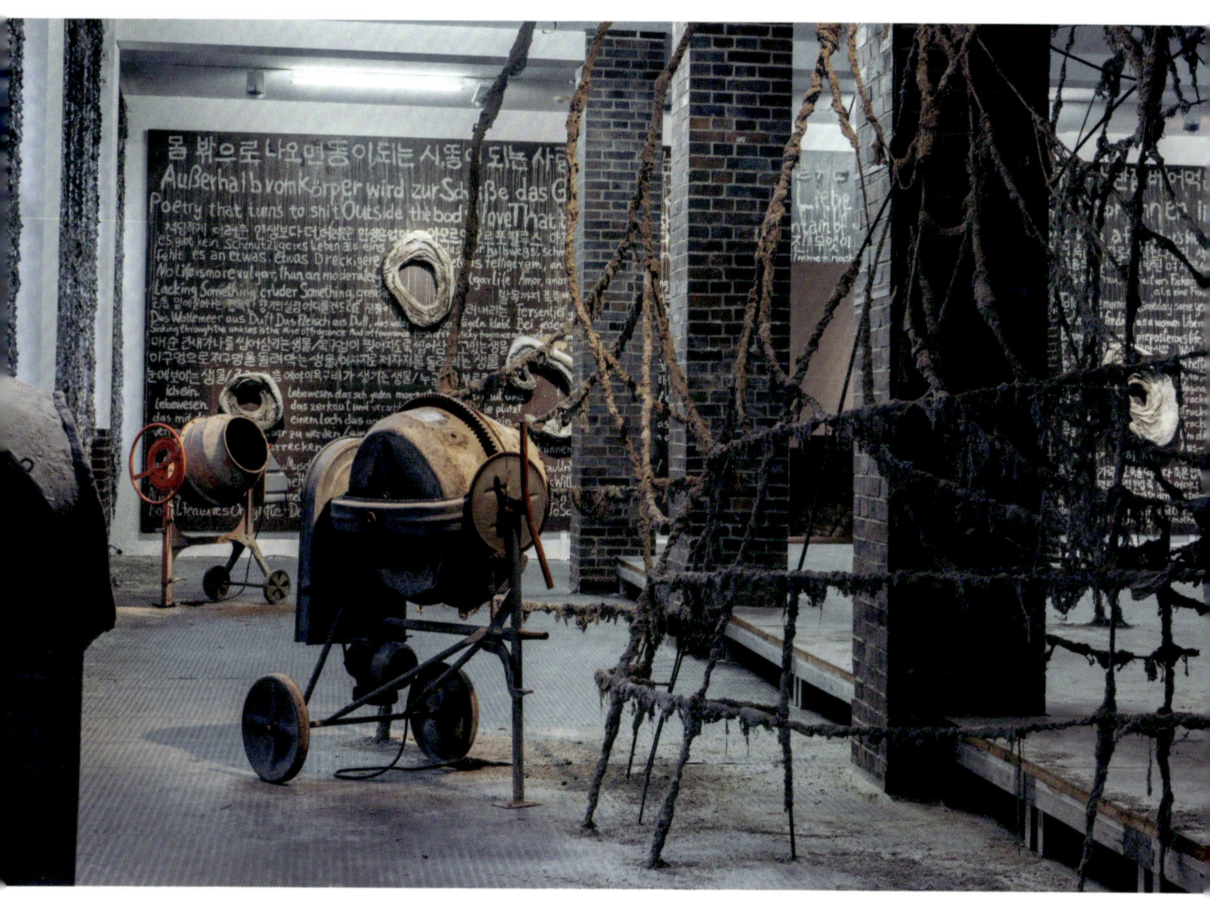

Installation view of *Look, I'm a fountain of filth raving mad with love*
2022, Museum fur Moderne Kunst (MMK), Frankfurt, 2022

overwhelmed individual throws back his head while frenetically stretching his neck so that the mouth becomes, as far as possible, a prolongation of the spinal column, *in other words, it assumes the position it normally occupies in the constitution of animals.*[23]

As developed in a commentary by the art historian Rosalind Krauss, Bataille's chains of association work toward the undoing of the mouth as a site of verbal expression, reclaiming its (and its human possessors') bestial signification. Making explicit Bataille's shift between the vertical human axis and the horizontal animal axis, Krauss speaks of the human mouth as linked to the 'possession of speech'; the animal's mouth is, by contrast, 'the leading element of the system of catching, killing, and ingesting prey, for which the anus is the terminal point'.[24] Noting Bataille's focus on overwhelmingly heightened emotional states (fury, terror, suffering) as activating the rotation from the vertical to the horizontal, Krauss makes explicit his impulse to 'reorganise the orientation of the human structure and conceptually to rotate the axis of loftiness onto the axis of material existence'.[25]

Bataille's words form a prescient foundation for Lee's own deep-rooted instinct for her works, environments and atmospheres to perform their own rotation, rotating the axis of loftiness onto the horizontal axis of material existence. Her exhibition *Look, I'm a fountain of filth raving mad with love* invoked three figures: her own mother, who appeared in a video by Lee as a sleeping figure, a choice which Lee described as rooted in her observation that 'people immediately become like meat when they fall asleep';[26] the late porn actress Veronica Moser, who specialised in scatology, interviewed in a video in which she described her enjoyment of consuming excrement; and Kim Eon Hee, through giving the poet's words a sculptural form. Even in this first instance of directly using language in her work, Lee's sculptural forms worked towards its undoing by invoking the excretive function of the anus. Surrounding the void-space of the exhibition – at the centre of which was a spindly structure made of metal rebars swaddled in hemp fibre and cement that resembled the form of an enormous spider, flanked by the rotating vessel-mouth-forms of working cement mixers – Lee built walls covered in Kim's words written out in cement to form a cramped, staccato visual rhythm. The visceral lines of Kim's poem 'Mightily, Mightily' begin with 'Poetry that turns to shit';[27] within Lee's chains of association, both cement and clay are forms of shit, and in her act of writing in cement, Lee both dutifully and irreverently turned Kim's words into shit, describing this disintegration of language through writing as 'the action of picking up shit and smearing it'.[28]

At the limits of language, at the limits of thought, Lee wants us to sink ourselves from our heads and downwards into our own bodies, to sit with the shit. Like Bataille's prompt – which suggests that the reorientation to material existence happens among intense emotional states – Lee makes room for (and makes rooms *of*) a spate of emotions, which have developed through her projects into an affective scale. She wants us to sink ourselves into feeling.

FEELING: AS INFRASTRUCTURAL IN ITS EFFECTS AS A FACTORY[29]

We enter through the heavy plastic curtains that mark the threshold of Lee's exhibition-installation *Black Sun*, which opened at the New Museum, New York in 2023 (pp.50–1). These curtains turn the gallery into a contained, womb-like chamber. At Tate Modern, Lee will continue to engage with the idea of a built environment interior as an industrial womb. Though physically sparse, the space is atmospherically full with the heaviness of air, the smell of liquid clay and the haze of humidity. These atmospheres permeate the crevices and holes that have been ripped through sheets of fabric weighed down by solidifying washes of clay, and ooze from the two slurry pits receiving drips from the bulbous, gristly, hanging twists of rope, chain, clay, ceramic, cement, fabric and machinery suspended above. The viscous liquids that are propelled, rotated, dropped and otherwise drudgingly moved through Lee's tired and sputtering machinery are weighed down by both gravity and an accumulation of anxiety, melancholy, fear. Disgust and paranoia leak out, mixed in the substance of Lee's liquids, splattering comically to the floor and seeping through metal grates.

An affective vocabulary has emerged around Lee's works, built out of the discursive repetitions that circle around them. It encompasses a kaleidoscopic range of both sludgy and agitated states – from anger to emptiness, frustration to inadequacy, overwhelmedness to failure, sadness to unease. These sensations are a manifestation of what Alvin Li has described as Lee 'giv[ing] room to the kinds of thorny affects that are irrational at best, extreme, ambivalent, or taboo, even destructively antisocial – feelings, however incoherent or ignoble, as real as any other building blocks of today's social worlds.'[30] In a disorientating affective slippage, this vocabulary is made up of

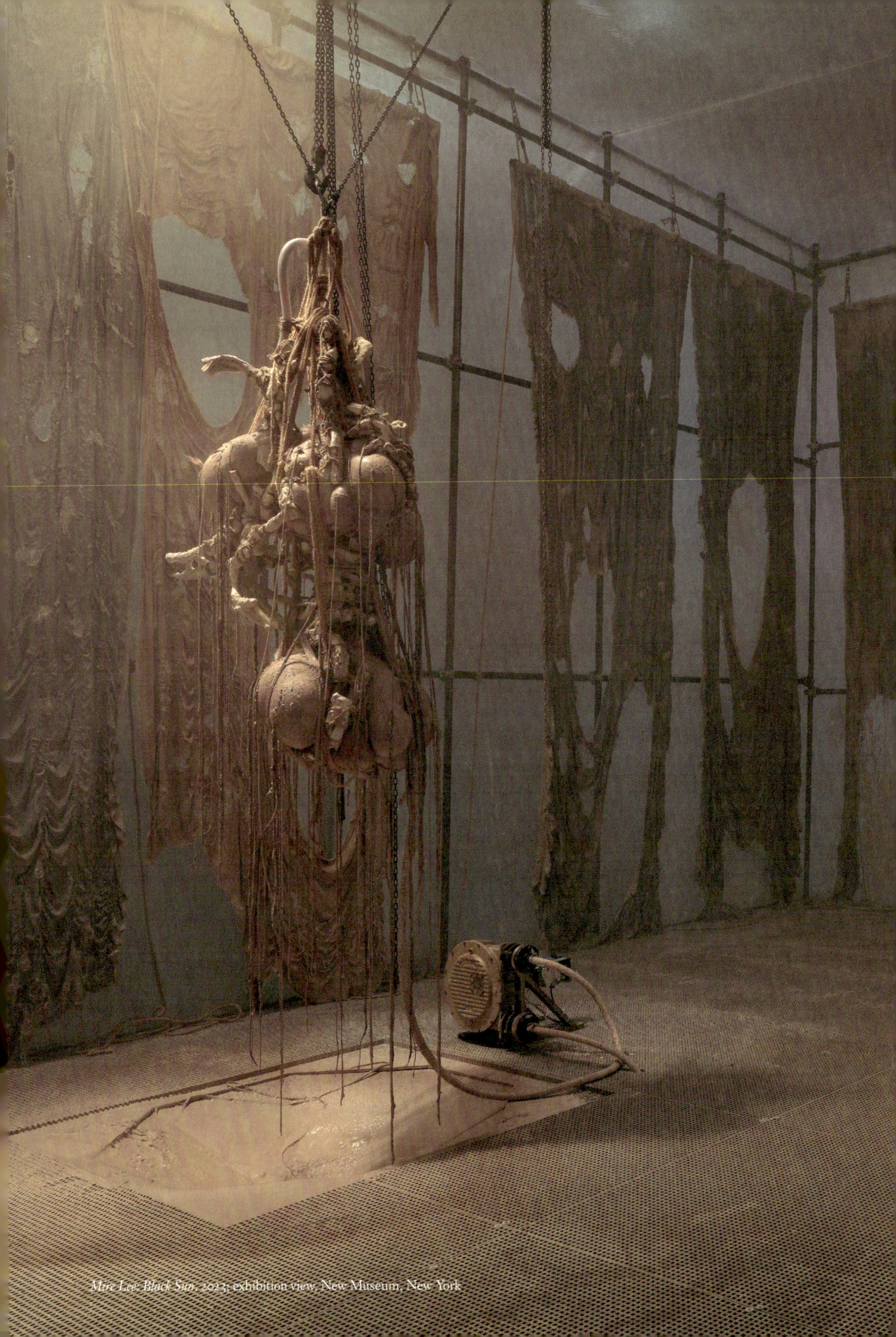

Mire Lee: Black Sun, 2013; exhibition view, New Museum, New York

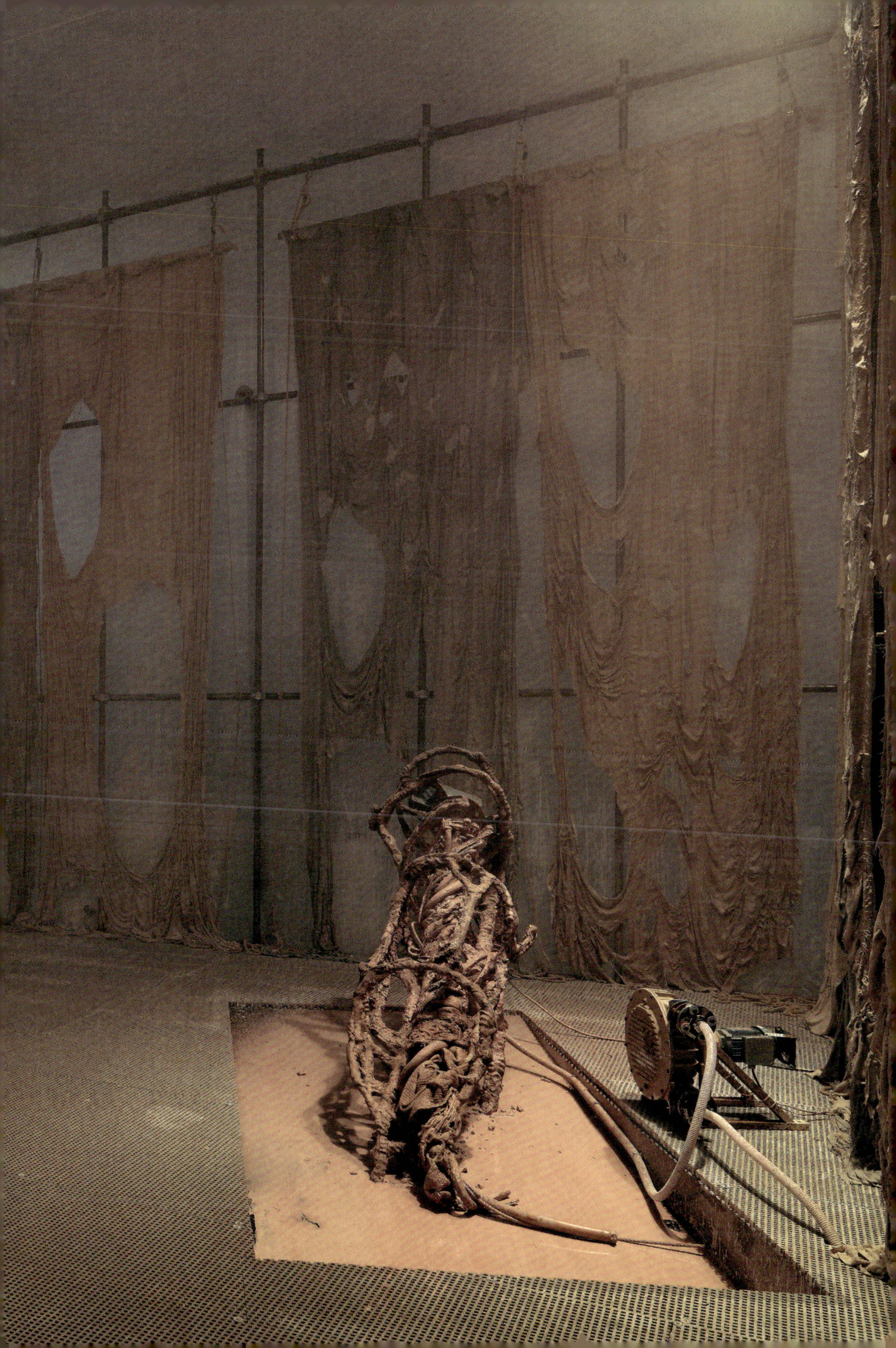

emotive states that arise from an encounter with Lee's works, ascribed to the works themselves as a 'registry of potential emotions, moods and reactions'[31] and 'realisations of senses and emotions'.[32] These slippages and confusions between inside and outside, psyche and world, recall the thinning, unstable boundaries of Lee's worlds as they spill into the body and become surfaces onto which to pour out the stickiest of sentiments.

Lee has embraced this dizzying transposition of emotion-into-material-into-emotion, drawing a comparison with her 'lik[ing] to create sensations that enter the inside of the spectators' bodies: the estrangement, the tension between contrasting affects such as love/hate, motherly/violent, birth/decay'.[33] While this intention pervades the entirety of her practice, it is *Black Sun* that has been most explicit in its embrace of negative affects, taking them as its subject matter as well as material. The starting point for the exhibition was Lee's relationship with the 1987 book *Black Sun: Depression and Melancholia* by philosopher and psychoanalyst Julia Kristeva. Kristeva's study located and theorised depression and melancholia in linguistic terms, identifying a loss of speech and loss of meaning as its symptoms, and suggesting that the focus of the symptoms was an unrepresentable 'Thing', the loss of which continues to radiate its effects 'without presence, a light without representation: the Thing is an imagined sun, bright and black at the same time'.[34] Impossible to name or show, Kristeva articulated the Thing as being felt 'in the tension of ... affects, muscles, mucous membranes, and skin'.[35] Lee was drawn to imagining the space of the New Museum as a manifestation of this state, free-associating between images of an eclipse, a hole and an anus, as 'a kind of non-space that you collapse or fall into'.[36]

Black Sun is part of a wider exploration by Lee that, in its manufactory of a specific emotional register of the thorny, the ambivalent, the negative, the ignoble, aligns itself with generations of theorists – including Lauren Berlant, Sara Ahmed, Eve Kosofsky Sedgwick and Sianne Ngai – whose work has committed to attuning to 'negative affects' as part of a larger effort in examining how emotion might be reclaimed as part of a critical project. In this, Lee is grounded in a commitment to attending to emotion not as solely personal, introspective or navel-gazing, but instead capable of registering the state of the world-at-large. As Sianne Ngai wrote in her 2005 book *Ugly Feelings*, 'sociohistorical and ideological dilemmas, in particular, produce formal or representational ones': it is through paying attention to one that the other can be reached.[37] Lee's sculptural environments possess the quality of film sets between action – somewhere in the genre of horror – in which such dilemmas can be located, rehearsed and played out in their full ambivalence. Spatially, they are full of voids in which to face them; temporally, they are sites of sluggishly repetitive mechanised gestures that themselves recur in the manner of emotional patterns that demand to be confronted. Offering no promise of emotional release, nor of valorising feelings as ways toward action, Lee's spatial experiments instead offer up states of languid suspension in which we are left to sit with the state of things, inside and out.

To suspend is to interrupt, to bring action to a halt temporarily or permanently; to suspend is to hang something. The two motions intersect in Lee's Hyundai Commission. Making the most of the spatial voids afforded by Tate Modern's Turbine Hall's 3,600m² space, Lee invokes the building's industrial past as a power station, reanimating it as a site of manufacture coming undone. Starting its journey at the discharge points of a turbine inserted by Lee into the space, a viscous liquid seeps and drips down the vertical thirty-metre expanse of the Turbine Hall, landing and coagulating in thin layers onto forms that hang in the air, a skeletal or 'substrate' layer made up of construction mesh and rebar. Over time, this runoff clots together on its support structures to form bodily allusions that Mire Lee terms 'skins'. In that state of flesh-still-in-formation, Lee's manufactory suspends. Never gaining deeper tissue to surround, Lee's skins are manually moved and hoisted upwards on industrial chains, still as ambivalent membrane-thresholds. There, in their downward pull, they are subjected to a spectacle of curing – air-drying, a slower form of rotting, already moving toward their un-form. Once complete, they are moved one final time, to be suspended in their state of preserved deathliness. Turning the Turbine Hall into a manufactory of suspended action that is as much affective in its formation and undoing of the body as it is infrastructural in its reckoning with the legacy of industrial capitalism, Lee has formed a space that intersects the infrastructural and emotional, and that demands we pay due attention to stuckness and entropy on an individual level as symptoms of a collective social and political reality.

Borrowing some questions from another of Kim Eon Hee's poems offers a series of precise prompts as one way to begin that self-analysis. Have you been feeling blue these days? Do you want to suffer more from your sense of guilt? Even though you're alone are you really not alone?

Do your words come out like mushed rotten strawberries?
Are both your hands fool's gold, one holding amnesia and the other
delirium?
Are you boundless and trapped? Suffocating and
In pitch-black?
You'll likely go crazy soon
But like, only like
Are you like that?[38]

1 Sharon Kivland, *ABÉCÉDAIRE*, Nottingham 2022, p.135. This passage is, in turn, Kivland's own translation, reimagining and rewriting of lines from Anne Garréta, *Sphinx*, Paris 1986.

2 Agnes Gryczkowska, 'Mire Lee and H.R. Giger', in *HR Giger & Mire Lee*, exh. cat., Schinkel Pavillon, Berlin 2021, p.17.

3 See, for example, McKenzie Wark, 'Dysmorphia/Dysphoria', in Ibid, p.102. Wark writes: 'In Lee's work there is only flesh and tech, as if tech were the condition of possibility of all flesh'. Leaning into its sci-fi evocations, Lee's work was paired for this 2021 exhibition at the Schinkel Pavillon with that of H.R. Giger, who had been responsible for creating the titular xenomorph creature in the *Alien* film franchise.

4 Quoted in Gryczkowska 2021, p.109.

5 Roger Caillois, 'The Praying Mantis: From Biology to Psychoanalysis', in Claudine Frank (ed.), *The Edge of Surrealism: A Roger Caillois Reader*, London and Durham, NC 2003.

6 Ibid, p.79. Callois uses the term 'ootheca', meaning the substance that contains a mass of eggs.

7 On the praying mantis and surrealism, see William Pressly, 'The Praying Mantis in Surrealist Art', *Art Bulletin*, vol.55, no.4, Dec. 1973, pp.600–15.

8 Mire Lee and Alvin Li, 'Mire Lee's Deep-Rooted Romanticism', *Frieze*, no.229, Sept. 2022, https://www.frieze.com/article/mire-lees-deep-rooted-romanticism, accessed 9 June 2024.

9 Kim Eon Hee, *Have You Been Feeling Blue These Days?*, trans. Sung Gi Kim and Eunsong Kim, Blacksburg, VA 2019, p.94.

10 Stephanie Bailey, 'Mire Lee's Visceral Bodies: In Conversation with Stephanie Bailey', *Ocula*, 21 Sept. 2022, https://ocula.com/magazine/conversations/mire-lee-visceral-bodies, accessed 11 June 2024.

11 Quoted in Gryczkowska 2021, p.105.

12 Alvin Li, 'Vorarephilia: Mire Lee', *Mousse*, 12 Nov. 2019, https://www.moussemagazine.it/magazine/mire-lee-alvin-li-2019, accessed 11 June 2024.

13 Quoted in Gryczkowska 2021, p.107.

14 Gary Carrion-Murayari, 'Biotechniques: Mire Lee in Conversation with Gary Carrion-Murayari', in *Mire Lee: Black Sun*, exh. cat., New Museum, New York 2023, p.47.

15 'Mire Lee', *Busan Biennale 2022: We, On the Rising Wave*, http://www.busanbiennale2022.org/en/exhibition/artists/mire-lee, accessed 12 June 2024. Lee has spoken about the image of a whale in reference to being in the belly of Monstro from *Pinocchio*. See Gryczkowska 2021, p.107

16 Frederick Kiesler, *Model for the Endless House* 1959, Whitney Museum of American Art, https://whitney.org/collection/works/7371, accessed 13 July 2024.

17 Lee and Li 2022.

18 Wong Binghao, 'Blood Line', in *Mire Lee: Black Sun*, exh. cat., New Museum, New York 2023, p.26.

19 Mire Lee, 'Biotechniques', in ibid., p.43.

20 Ibid, p.44.

21 Ibid, p.43.

22 Ágrafa Society, 'Interview with Mire Lee: Deforming Sculpture as Emotional Portal', Seminar, no.8, 2021, http://www.zineseminar.com/wp/issue08/mirelee-eng/?ckattempt=1, accessed 13 June 2024.

23 Georges Bataille, 'Mouth', in Allan Stoekl (ed.), *Georges Bataille: Visions of Excess: Selected Writings 1927–1939*, Minneapolis, MN 1986, p.59.

24 Rosalind Krauss, 'Corpus Delicti', *October*, vol.33, Summer 1985, p.43.

25 Ibid.

26 Mire Lee, 'Conversation: Mire Lee/Susanne Pfeffer', in *MIRE LEE: Look, I'm a fountain of filth raving mad with love*, exh. booklet, Museum für Moderne Kunst (MMK), Frankfurt 2022, https://cms.mmk.art/site/assets/files/7673/mmk_booklet_mire_lee_en.pdf, accessed 30 June 2024.

27 For full translation, see Kim Eon Hee, 'Mightily, Mightily', trans. Soje, *Waxwing*, no.49, https://waxwingmag.org/items/issue30/49_Hee-Mightily-Mightily.php#top, accessed 14 June 2024.

28 Bailey 2022.

29 This is an adapted, truncated quotation from Brian Massumi, *Parables for the Virtual: Movement, Affect, Sensation*, Durham, NC 2002, p.45.

30 Alvin Li, 'Deterioration, lost futures, melancholy, endurance…: Mire Lee's Infrastructural Thoughts', forthcoming.

31 Madeline Weisburg, 'In the Shadow of the Black Sun', in *Mire Lee: Black Sun*, exh. cat., New Museum, New York 2023, p.12.

32 Kim Eon Hee, 'A Few Thoughts for Carriers', in *Mire Lee: Carriers*, exh. cat., Art Sonje Center, Seoul, 2020, p.75.

33 Mire Lee quoted in 'Hans Ulrich Obrist & Mire Lee, 2021', in *HR Giger & Mire Lee*, exh. cat., Schinkel Pavillon, Berlin 2021, p.105.

34 Julia Kristeva, *Black Sun: Depression and Melancholia*, New York 1989, p.13.

35 Ibid, p.14.

36 Mire Lee, 'Biotechniques', in Mire Lee: Black Sun, exh. cat., Schinkel Pavillon, Berlin 2021, p.43.

37 Sianne Ngai, *Ugly Feelings*, Cambridge, MA 2005, p.12.

38 Here I quote, and slightly reformat, the lines beginning and ending 'Have you been feeling blue…' from Kim Eon Hee's poem 'Have You Been Feeling Blue These Days?'. See Kim 2019, p.38.

Hell is Better with Other People

Alvin Li

A Fact'ry is a Gothic Hell.
    Thomas Man[1]

Hell is – other people!
    Jean-Paul Sartre[2]

Mostly, though, other people are not hell ... Mostly, people are inconvenient, which is to say that they have to be dealt with. 'They' includes you ... The sense of the inconvenience of other people is evidence that no one was ever sovereign.
    Lauren Berlant[3]

For a period of six months, Mire Lee undertook to transform Tate Modern's Turbine Hall into a living factory in a state of animated suspension – between production and decay, hope and disillusion. Two thirds of the Turbine Hall are populated with chains hanging from the ceiling. At the end of the hall, visitors encounter a motorised structure (a 'turbine') suspended from a crane. The turbine spins continuously throughout museum opening hours, as flesh-like 'tentacles' attached to it discharge a viscous liquid to be collected in a large, sloped tray underneath. Over the course of the exhibition, pieces of fabric ('skins', in Lee's term) are wetted with the liquid discharged from the turbine structure, then placed by technicians on nearby racks to dry and harden before being hauled into the air to hang overhead. Over the months, the Turbine Hall is gradually filled with these draped pieces, as if it were the interior of a body – an 'industrial womb', the artist calls it – shedding its lining inwardly.

What is this eerie play, this theatre of cruelty? As Lee's focus has moved in recent years from standalone kinetic sculpture to atmospheric sculptural installation, she has begun to express her artistic ingenuity in more than sculptural terms, as a director of moods and atmospheres. Beyond its initial assault on the senses, which aims to obliterate the audience's 'intellectual and communicative capacities', Lee's factory yields manifold allegories.[4] I propose to approach this new work through the lens of 'the gothic', as the installation's hybridity and liminality condense key moments in the historical transition from industrial modernity to the present, bringing our attention to the fearsome – and sublime – in the sprawling technological systems that shape our lives. Meanwhile, by making tangible our collective vulnerabilities amid the overwhelming austerity of contemporary life, Lee's factory also becomes a sphere of public intimacy, inviting us to indulge in the hopes and dreams that make our precarious lives together bearable.

'Gothic' is a convoluted term with a wide variety of uses in different fields. Originally a demonym referring quite literally to the Goths, northern European 'barbarians' blamed, among others, for the collapse of the Roman Empire, the word's semantic breadth had grown exponentially by the eighteenth century, when it became used loosely – and still pejoratively – to designate all things medieval (as opposed to 'classical'), such as the gothic architecture prominent from the twelve to the sixteenth century. As David Punter summarises: 'Where the classical was well-ordered, the Gothic was chaotic; where simple and pure, Gothic was ornate and convoluted; where the classics offered a set of cultural models to be followed, Gothic represented excess and exaggeration, the product of the wild and the uncivilized.'[5] However, a shift in cultural values during the second half of the eighteenth century prompted a positive revival of the medieval, the primitive and the wild. This sowed the seeds for the birth, in the Britain of the late 1700s, of the 'original gothic fiction' of writers such as Horace Walpole and Mary Shelley, as well as for the revival of gothic architecture.

While early gothic fiction was marked by such signature, oftentimes supernatural motifs as haunted castles, vampire bats and secret passageways, these standard trappings – as the late gothic scholar Linda Bayer-Berenbaum observes – are no longer the defining features of later gothic creations. Throughout the following two centuries, the style would continue to hybridise, germinating a rich spate of literary, cinematic and musical subgenres, as well as artistic productions. More recently, Bridget M. Marshall, in her study of transatlantic nineteenth-century literature, has coined the term 'industrial gothic' to describe a subgenre of nineteenth century gothic fiction informed by the gruesome realities of industrial labour and invested in the horrors, both physical and psychic, of industrialism. As Marshall points out, a number of major nineteenth-century writers, including Thomas Man, William Godwin and Friedrich Engels, employed standard gothic tropes and themes such as paranoia, manipulation and injustice, 'placing traditional Gothic victims into factories and mills instead of castles and monasteries [to] portray the terrible costs of industrialisation, framing the Industrial Revolution as a site of Gothic torture, excess and horror'.[6]

While an attempt to distil a list of quintessential gothic characteristics would be doomed to failure, it is generally agreed that gothicism is nourished by the typically romantic qualities of yearning, aspiration, mystery and

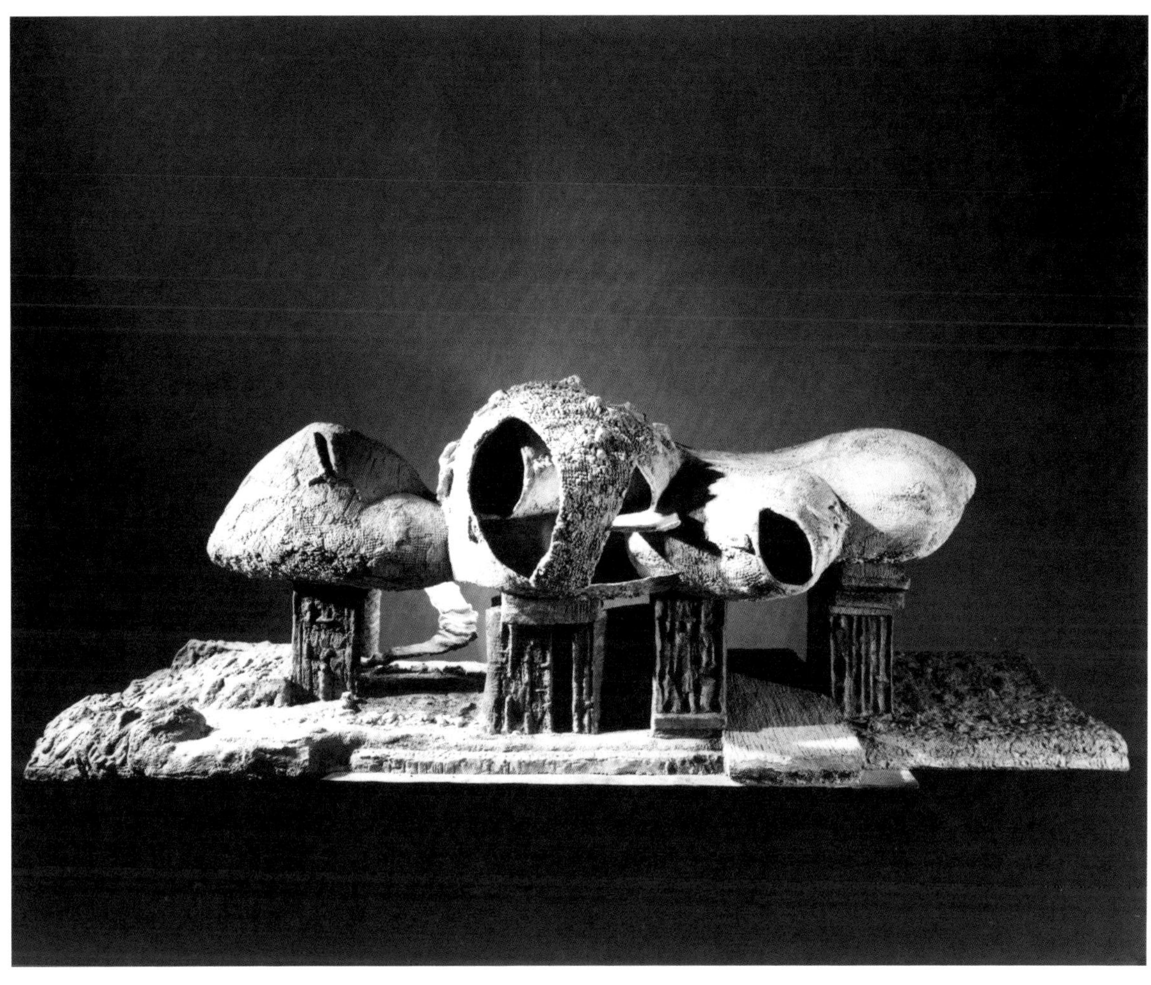

Frederick Kiesler, model for his Endless House (1958)

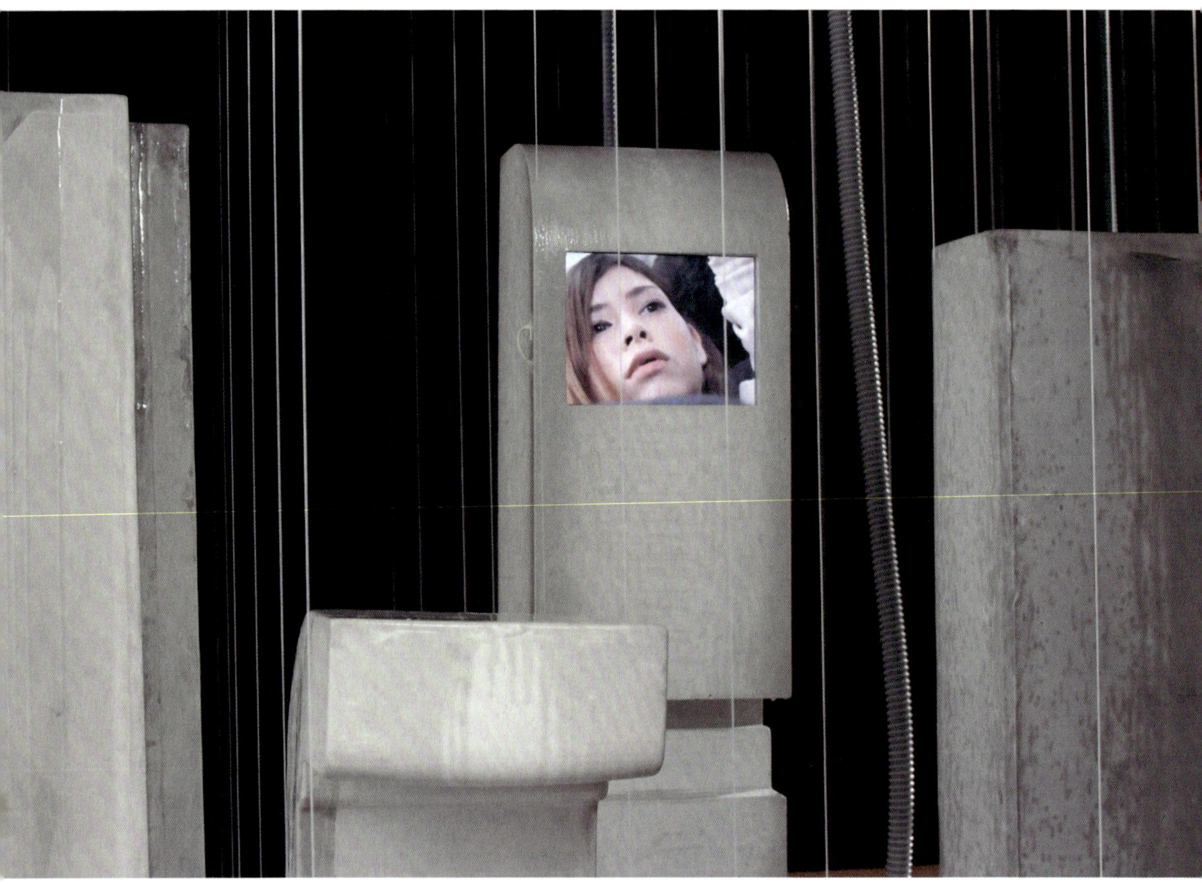

Installation view of *Andrea, in my mildest dreams* 2016; four plaster
sculptures, one sculpture with an i-pad screen mounted from inside,
single-channel looped video (4 min 23 sec), silicone oil, pump, and
other mixed media, sculpture size varies within roughly human size,
stage scale 4 x 6 metres

wonder, but takes them in a darker direction. What defines the gothic mode is a lingering atmosphere of dread, often combining terror, horror and mystery.[7] Formally, the gothic mode, as Bayer-Berenbaum observes, is marked by the use of persistent contrasts in setting, characterisation and theme: the gothic landscape plunges from extreme to extreme; idealised femininity serves as a backdrop for cruelty; gushing sentimentality is pitted against brutality. Such heightened and sustained contrasting 'discourages adjustment ... any dulling of the senses is averted'. Gothicism is an aesthetic that traces the boundaries of a greater reality – one that is not transcendental but immanent and integral to the world around us. It is this consciousness-raising character that has prompted its mutation into sociopolitically engaged forms such as industrial gothic.

In his theoretical work on gothic Marxism, which examines the vampiric spirit of contemporary capitalism, Jon Greenaway highlights 'spatial enclosure' as a leitmotif in the gothic imagination (in contrast to science-fiction's fascination with spatio-temporal expansion), and emphasises 'hybridity', 'instability' and 'liminality' as its foremost features.[8] Greenaway's diagnosis resonates vividly with Jack Halberstam's reading of the gothic form in *Skin Shows* (1995), a study of evolving mechanisms of othering in both gothic literature and cinema, wherein Halberstam argues that the gothic is marked by a breakdown of genre such that its texts verge on the unclassifiable. The gothic, he writes, 'marks a peculiarly modern preoccupation with boundaries and their collapse.'[9] A particular ingenuity of the form, according to Halberstam, is evidenced by its efficient condensation of various common fears (especially regarding racial, sexual and class-based threats to nation, capitalism and the bourgeoisie) in the singular body of the monster. While highlighting the gothic propensity for pathologisation, Halberstam identifies a peculiar affective structure that fuels the consumption of gothic horror: 'The Gothic ... inspires fear and desire at the same time – fear of and desire for the other, fear of and desire for the possibly latent perversity lurking within the reader herself.'[10] With his diagnosis of the instability of the gothic mode, Halberstam joins a wave of feminist and queer scholars in taking an recuperative approach to the gothic canon, long deemed conservative, by highlighting its potential to raise awareness regarding social issues like xenophobia.

With these fundamental qualities in mind, we may begin to appreciate the particular sensibility of Lee's maximalist commission. Lee's factory is a gothic phantasmagoria, collaging together several moments in the transition from

industrial modernity to the present. While the continued wetting and drying
of textile sculptures (construction mesh on rebar) discretely comments on the
prosaic processes of textile manufacture, the hanging system for the fabric
sculptures is inspired by a vernacular design widely utilised in pithead baths
around the world: its pulley mechanism, first adopted in Germany during the
late nineteenth century, which allowed miners to hang their street or work
clothes from the bathhouse's ceiling while labouring in the mines or resting
at home. Heating the ceiling area, architecture historian Gary A. Boyd notes,
served collieries as a hygienic and efficient method to dry miners' clothing.
Given the enormous numbers employed by the coal industry at its turn-of-
the-twentieth-century height, this practice resulted in 'voluminous, almost
cathedral-like changing areas ... articulated by a series of vertical suspending
chains holding bundles attached to pew-like structures beneath, where the
men could let down and access their change of clothes.'[11] In these transitory,
semi-public spaces, generations of miners washed away dirt, pain and fatigue,
reinforcing their developed camaraderie and collective identity as men, as
workers and – in the context of the United Kingdom – as what miner Thomas
Watson, a veteran of the 1914 Battle of Mons, called the 'backbone of the
nation'.[12] The space is a symbolically charged one, teeming with contrasts: rise
and fall, pride and precarity.

In addition to soaking in these histories, Lee's skin factory also alludes
to the new industrial formations that shape contemporary subjectivity.
As the shell of our individual forms, the skin is where signs of difference –
most commonly racial, and increasingly class-related (procedures deemed
emancipatory, such as gender confirmation or ability enhancement surgery,
often remaining out of financial reach of the less privileged) – are most
immediately registered. 'In my work I've thought a lot about the threshold
between what is considered normal and acceptable, and what is deemed
disabled, deformed or grotesque', Lee says. 'I've always been interested in
skin because it is something that registers otherness.'[13] Lee's observation
resonates with Halberstam's description of the gothic text as an 'elaborate skin
show'; if we 'measure one skin job against the other,' she writes, 'we can read
transitions between various signifying systems of identity.'[14] Manufactured
as a micro-prosthetic, skin also lies at the heart of the ever-expanding global
cosmetic surgery industry, which is heavily indebted to post-war technological
advancements. In his prophetic studies of the mutation of industrial capitalism
into a contemporary regime he terms 'pharmacopornographic capitalism',

Saboteurs 2019, installation view at the Lyon Biennale 2019;
peristaltic pump, motor, pigmented glycerine, and other mixed
media, dimensions variable

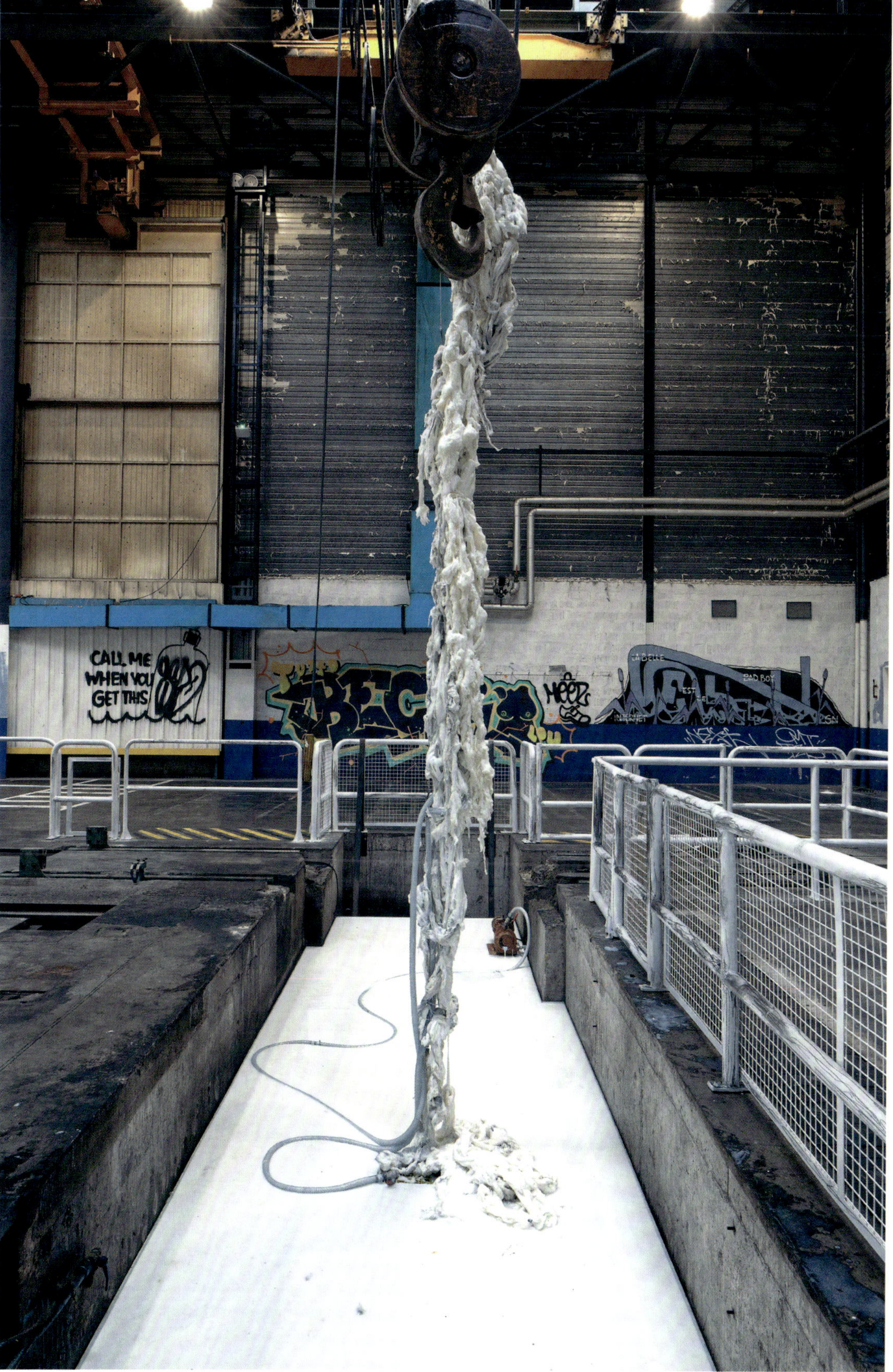

CALL ME
WHEN YOU
GET THIS

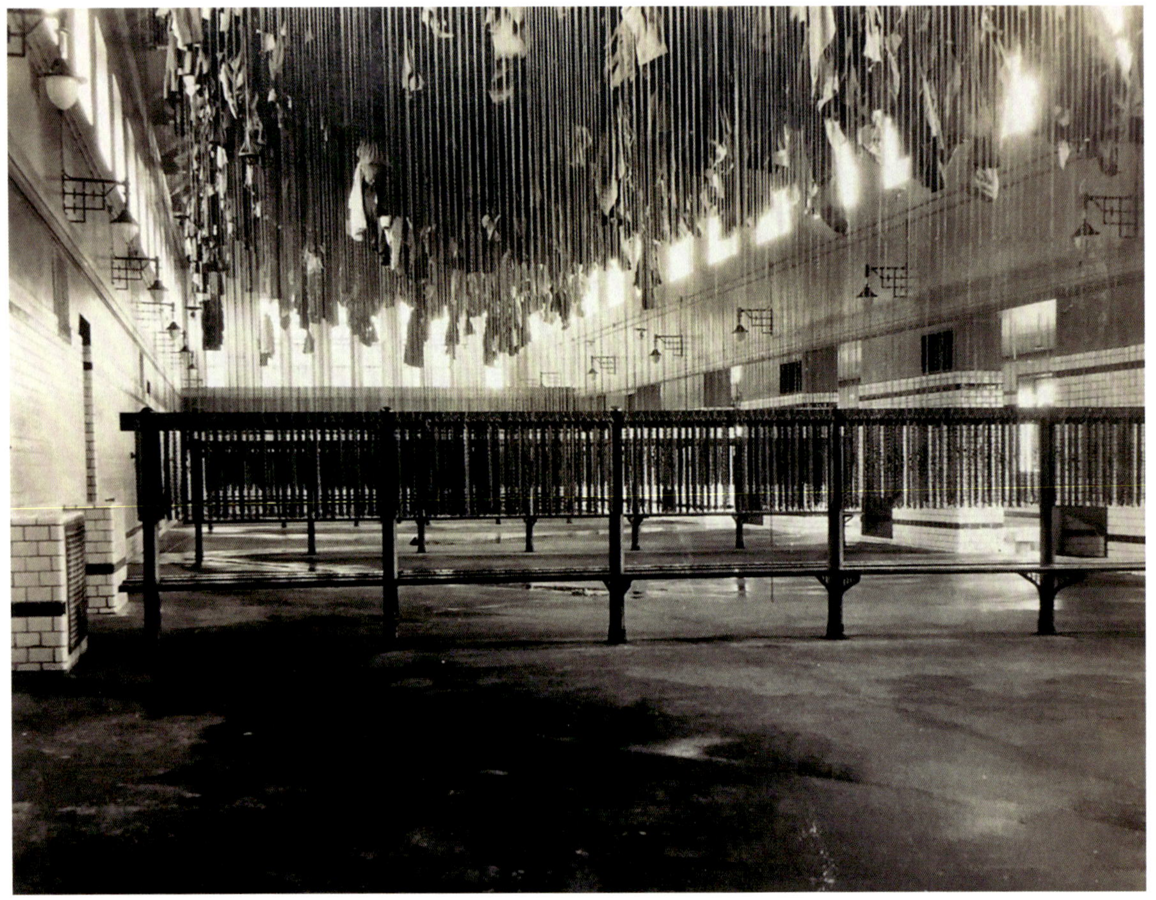

Interior of Gewerkschaft Gottessegen, Germany, photographed
in 1928

the philosopher Paul P. Preciado identifies the new dynamics of advanced biotechnologies in the second half of the twentieth century as the site at which gender, sex, sexuality and pleasure are transformed into objects that enable political management of the body.[15] Among other references, Preciado draws from American historian David Serlin's study of prostheses developed for Second World War veterans as tools for rehabilitating bodies and social identities. Prosthetics, as Serlin points out, were 'powerful anthropomorphic tools that refracted contemporary fantasies about ability and employment, heterosexual masculinity, and American citizenship'.[16] In Preciado's analysis, such technologies have in recent decades flourished into ever more nuanced forms, including gender confirmation surgeries such as phalloplasty. While acknowledging the promise of social acceptance, mobility and medical aid offered by prosthetic biotechnologies, Lee's skin factory begs us to consider the fraught tension between agency and control underlying advances in industrialised production under capitalism.

In alluding to these actually existing moments of industrialisation, Lee's commission refracts the cartography of a century-long transformation in industrial production. Yet in lieu of realistic portraiture, she opts for gothic theatricality; never resolving onto a specific source of evil, she locates a pervasive cruelty in the looming sense of an unfathomable reality beset with contradiction, a reality we cannot control. Underlying Lee's carefully orchestrated industrial environments, replete with signs of decay and expulsion, is an understanding of the world as increasingly governed by sprawling technological systems that depersonalise and dispossess in ever more abstract processes, making it increasingly difficult – indeed, impossible – to pinpoint a specific origin for one's own passivity. 'I'm naturally drawn to witnessing individual lives getting caught in a larger system', says Lee.[17] Slow, erratic, prone to malfunction unless constantly maintained, Lee's gothic factory, like all her precarious, breathless assemblages, is in sync with other systems slowly dying throughout our world.[18]

To come with terms with a truth as harsh as one's structural fixedness and fundamental powerlessness can be excruciating. This sense of 'the unbearable' courses throughout Lee's work. 'I am driven by emotion and affect, but when my feelings become too much and there's something I can't elaborate on, I just want to collapse.'[19] Indeed, Lee often stages such moments of breakdown in her sculptural environments. 'I like the quality of cancelling all the intellectual or communicative capacities we have as cultural beings', she says. 'I'm

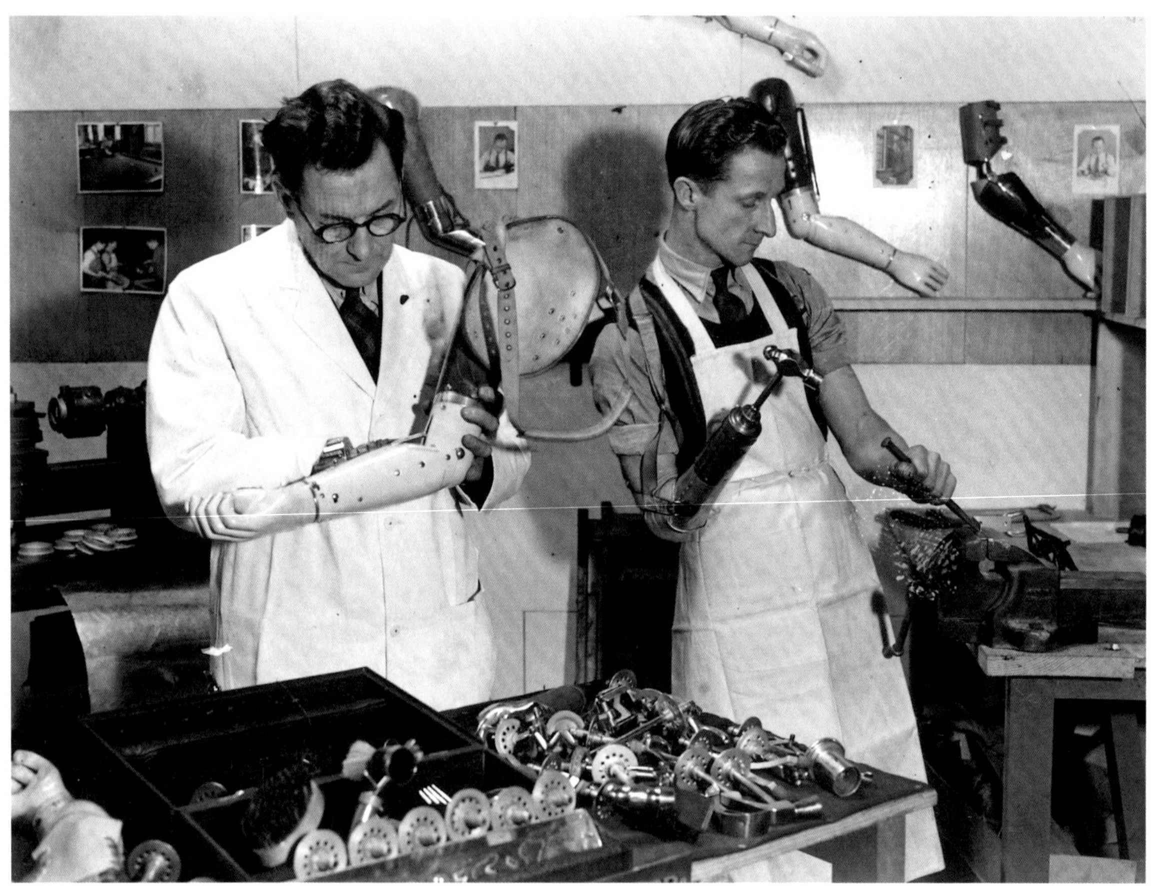

Two men making artificial limbs during an exhibition sponsored
by the Ministries of Health and Labour. They are each wearing an
artificial forearm.

interested in the obliteration of all these areas.'[20] But Lee's environments are not mirror images of the bleak world outside; nor do they suggest a romantic retreat from an insufferable present into a supposedly glorious moment in industrial modernity. What is exceptional, albeit all too easily overlooked, is her insistence on what comes after the obliteration. Consider the durational aspect of Lee's work: these kinetic sculptural environments plainly demand of us that we work through our initial disorientation and nausea and spend time with(in) them, that we commit to the perdurance of a damaged life. This explains the artist's decision that the factory must remain in operation during museum opening hours, throughout the run of the exhibition. To paraphrase Donna Haraway: Lee asks us to stay with the trouble, together.

In the French existentialist Jean-Paul Sartre's *No Exit,* a play with the eeriness of a gothic tale (and first performed in May 1944, just before the liberation of Paris), three morally corrupt petit-bourgeois find themselves locked in the same room in Hell. Following a slew of altercations without resolution, with the trio caught in eternal, mutual condemnation and denial, the male character Garcin declares: 'Hell is – other People!'[21] This line, one of Sartre's most-quoted lines, is frequently taken out of context as representing a heroic individuality vis-à-vis the burden of others. In fact, by assigning the declaration to a morally corrupt coward who by the play's end still cannot recognise his own shortcomings, *No Exit* implies something quite different: the world only becomes hell when we refuse to take responsibility for our own actions and their effect on others. In Sartre's classic apotheosis, individual freedom is tethered to interpersonal entanglements and social responsibility.

The work of the late American affect theorist Lauren Berlant, whose thinking Lee has cited as a major influence, further elaborates Sartre's emphatically social philosophy into the notion of a 'non-sovereign relationality'. As Berlant explains:

> Briefly, in the liberal tradition, sovereignty is a model of self- or jurisdictional governance that presumes rights of responsibility and control, or that presumes the legitimacy of one's relation to action (so some models of sovereignty locate sovereignty in the singularity of ungoverned desire and some in the legitimacy of the decision-space that distinguishes the citizen from all others, for example). 'Non-sovereign relationality' assumes that there is no sovereignty outside of relationships, and that we are always in a loosely woven state of becoming.[22]

This fundamental inseparability of I and other, replete with the accompanying frictions between individuality and collectivity, lies at the heart of Lee's commission. The multitude of near-identical skins slowly filling the Turbine Hall evokes the dream (or nightmare) of universal sameness – the ultimate form of collectivity – while their differences in scale remind us of the harsh reality that, in the artist's words, 'while dreaming itself is a universal thing ... everyone's dream is dressed and shaped by gender, race, class and where they belong. It's shaped, in other words, by their limitations.'[23] And yet, despite social hierarchies and structural determinants, we are all equally caught in the same, massive machine, equally subject to the weight of time and entropy.

When asked about the feeling she hoped to provoke in the audience with this commission, Lee, to the surprise of some, said: 'Warmth!'[24] This sense of *warmth* Lee hoped to bestow on visitors resembles, perhaps, a kind of eerie solidarity in the face of the unbearable, something that requires relinquishing our fantasies of individual sovereignty in favour of a more realistic projection of a social infrastructure to be collectively improvised. Echoing gothic writers who called for an immanence within the earthly realm, and existentialists who fearlessly affirmed the value of life in a historical period rife with moral debasement, Lee thrusts us into the abyss of reality, guided by the darkest truths. Such a confrontation does not invite nihilism. Quite the opposite: terror, in the gothic sense, gives rise to a liberated awareness, a sober agency. As Linda Bayer-Berenbaum writes, 'The chill of eternity incites a rush of activity; we run toward and away from our fear.'[25] In our moment of economic crisis, austerity, global uprisings and conflicts coupled with widespread emotional disillusionment, it is all the more necessary to be realistic about the objective constraints on life in our world. Lee's work for the Turbine Hall invites us to cherish our collective lives in our industrial ruins and carry on, not without a sense of melancholy or a touch of vengeance, but with utter lucidity. Utopia may not be possible, but this world can feel bearable when we face up to possibility as well as dread, embracing our shared passion and fragility.

1   Thomas Man, *Picture of a Factory Village: To Which are Annexed, Remarks on Lotteries*, Providence, RI 1833, p.11.

2   Jean-Paul Sartre, *No Exit and Three Other Plays*, trans. by Lionel Abel, New York 1955, p.47.

3   Lauren Berlant, *On the Inconvenience of Other People*, London and Durham, NC 2022, pp.1–2.

4   *Biotechniques*, exh. cat., New Museum, New York.

5   David Punter, *The Literature of Terror: A History of Gothic Fictions from 1765 to the Present Day*, vol.1, New York 1996, p.4.

6   Bridget M. Marshall, *Industrial Gothic: Workers, Exploitation and Urbanization in Transatlantic Nineteenth-Century Literature*, Cardiff 2021, p.3.

7   G.R. Thompson, 'Introduction: Romanticism and the Gothic Tradition', in G.R. Thompson (ed.), *The Gothic Imagination: Essays in Dark Romanticism*, Washington, DC 1974, p.3.

8   Adam Jones, Craig Laubach, William Conway, hosts, with Jon Greenaway, 'What is Gothic Marxism?: A Conversation with the LitCrit Guy', podcast, *Acid Horizon*, 12 Oct. 2021.

9   Jack Halberstam, *Skin Shows: Gothic Horror and the Technology of Monsters*, London and Durham, NC 1995, p.23.

10 Ibid., p.13.

11 Gary A. Boyd, *Architecture and the Face of Coal: Mining and Modern Britain*, London 2023, p.47.

12 Robert Gildea, *Backbone of the Nation: Mining Communities and the Great Strike of 1984–85*, London and New Haven, CT 2023, p.1. Gildea takes his title from a line in his interview of 16 June 2021 with miner Thomas Watson in the onetime mining village of Ballingry, Fife.

13 'Mire Lee in Conversation with Alvin Li and Bilal Akkouche' in this volume.

14 Halberstam 1995, p.6.

15 Paul B. Preciado, *Testo Junkie: Sex, Drugs, and Biopolitics in the Pharmacopornographic Era*, trans. by Bruce Benderson, New York 2013. See also Paul B. Preciado, *Pornotopia: An Essay on Playboy's Architecture & Biopolitics*, New York 2014.

16 David Serlin, 'Engineering Masculinity: Veterans and Prosthetics after World War Two', in Katherine Ott, David Serlin, and Stephen Mihm (eds.), *Artificial Parts, Practical Lives: Modern Histories of Prosthetics*, New York 2002, pp.45–74.

17 'Mire Lee in Conversation with Alvin Li and Bilal Akkouche' in this volume.

18 The sentence is a revised version of a previous statement from another text by the author. See Alvin Li, 'Deterioration, lost futures, melancholy, endurance … : Mire Lee's Infrastructural Thoughts' (forthcoming publication).

19 Mire Lee and Alvin Li, 'Mire Lee's Deep-Rooted Romanticism', *Frieze*, no.229, Sept. 2022, https://www.frieze.com/article/mire-lees-deep-rooted-romanticism, accessed 5 Aug. 2024.

20 *Biotechniques*, exh. cat. New Museum, New York.

21 Sartre 1955.

22 Charlie Markbreiter, 'Can't Take a Joke: An interview with Lauren Berlant', *The New Inquiry*, 22 March 2019, https://thenewinquiry.com/cant-take-a-joke, accessed 1 Aug 2024.

23 'Mire Lee in Conversation with Alvin Li and Bilal Akkouche' in this volume.

24 Mire Lee in conversation with the author, 2023.

25 Bayer-Berenbaum 1982, p.146.

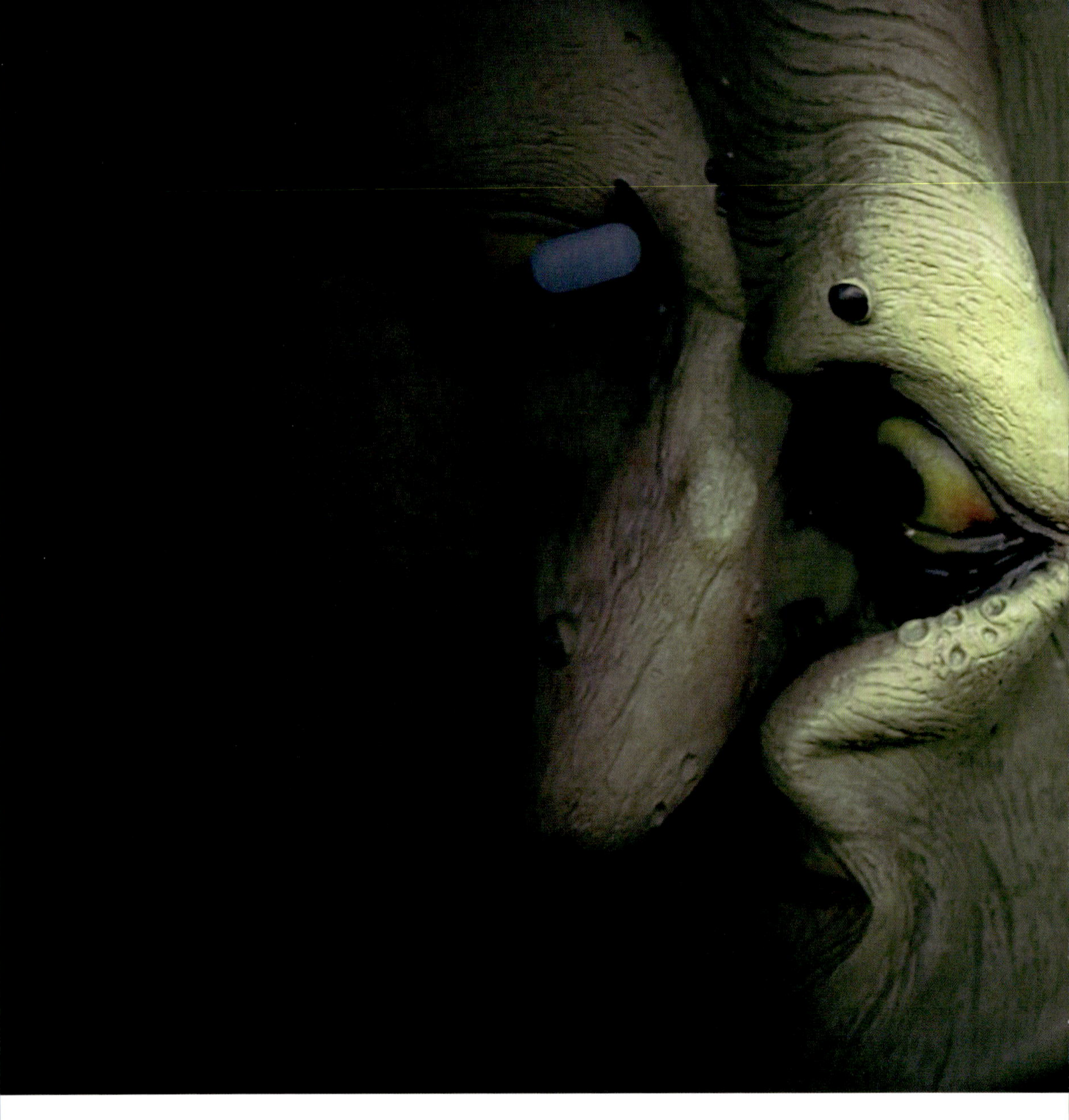

James Richards, still from *Qualities Of Life: Living in the Radiant Cold*
2022

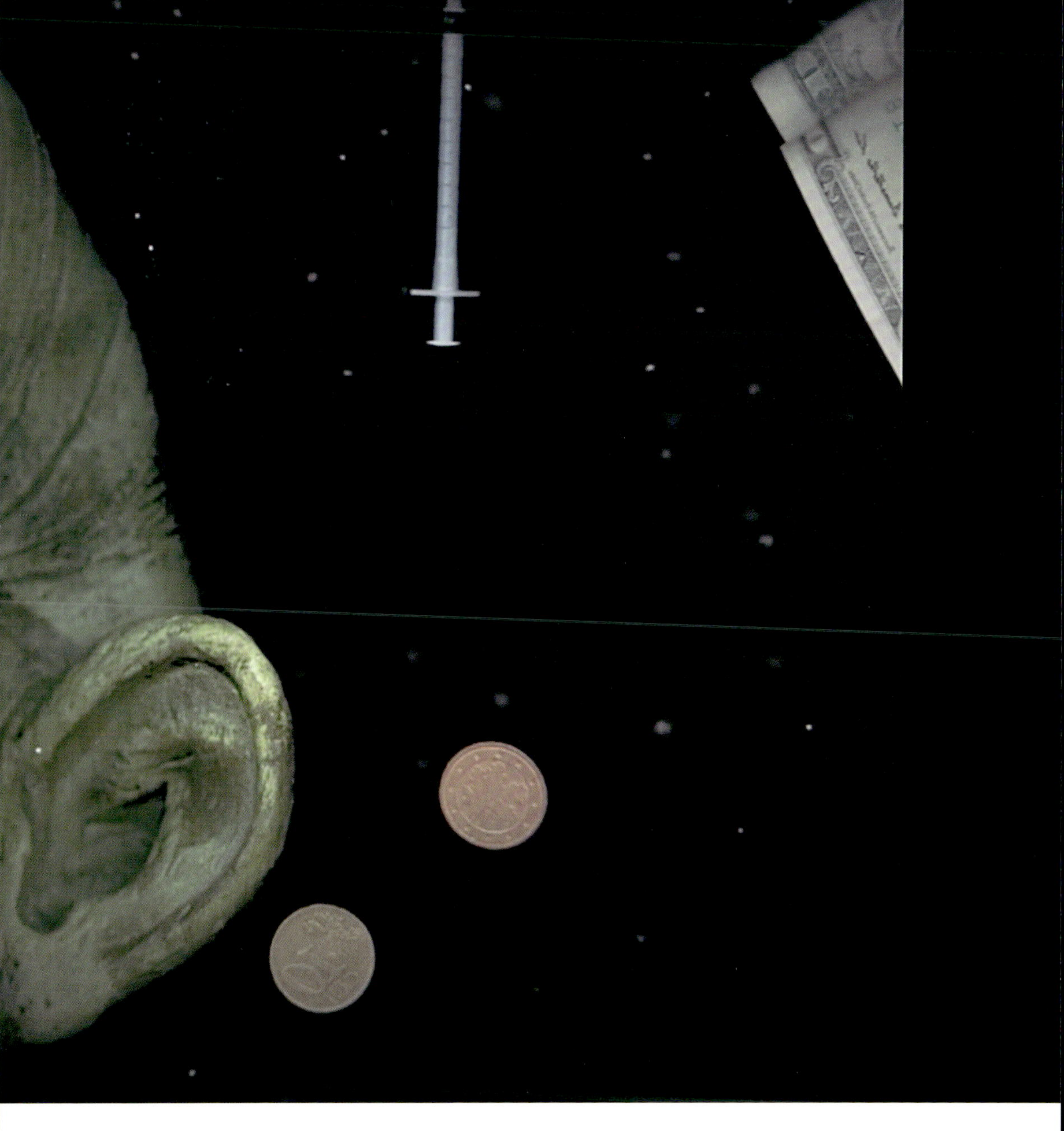

Untitled (Words, Images, Inspirations)

Mire Lee

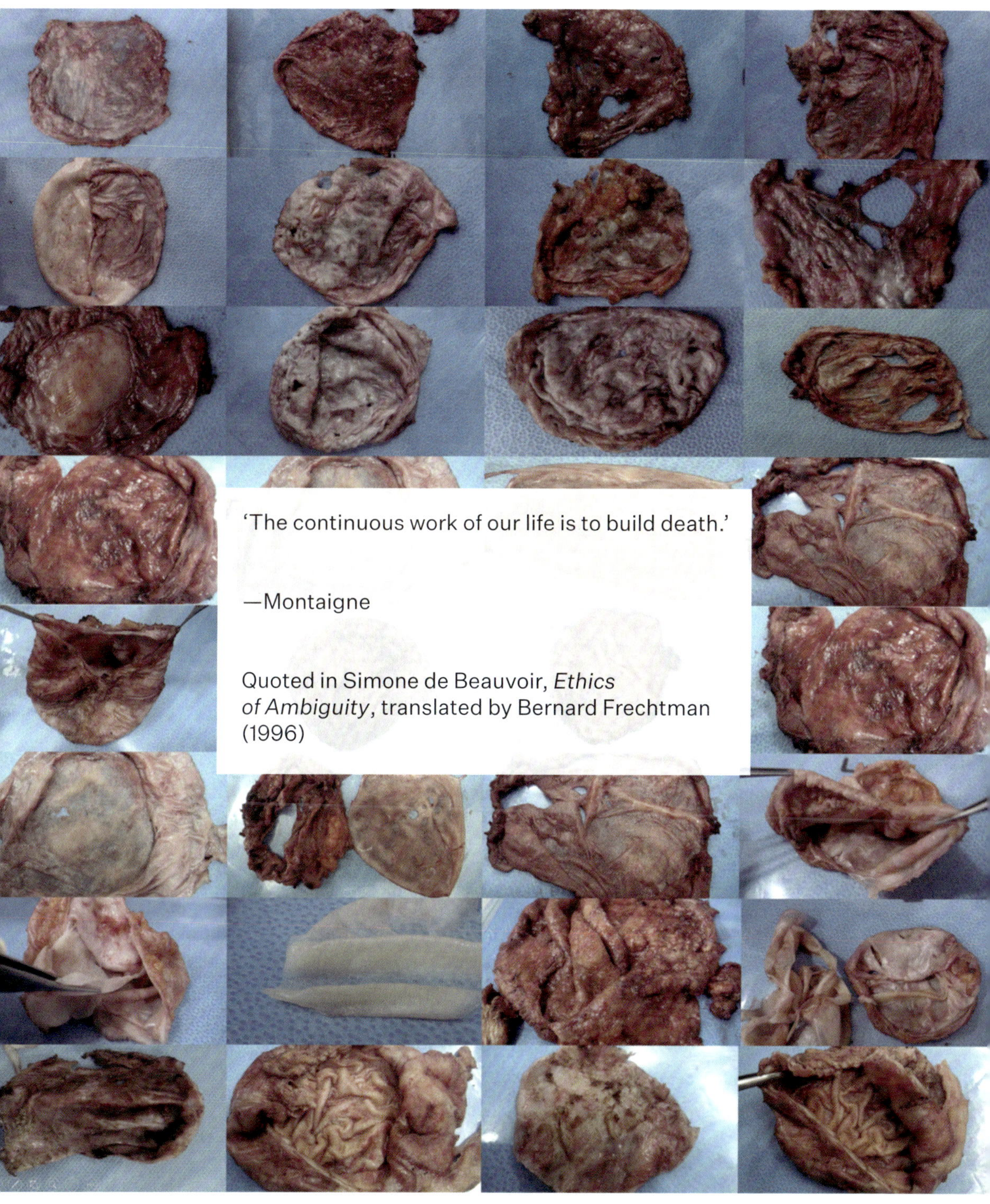

Breast skin tissue during breast surgery

'*Slow death* is not primarily a gloss on the lives of quiet desperation that Thoreau attributed to men in capitalist society, although the phrase *soul killing* has been used often enough to describe the attritions of bourgeois sociality that one might say something about the many sacrifices people make to remain in proximity to mirages of sovereignty. Nor is it in the melodramatic idiom that Baudrillard uses when he refers to 'slow death' as the double execution of the capitalist subject by the sacrificial violence of being in labor and an always-increasing seduction to consumer overexcitement. Nor is the phrase an existential way of talking about living as such, on the way to dying. Nonetheless, even this list of rejected exempla suggests something important about the space of slow death that shapes our particular biopolitical phase; mainly, people do live in it, just not very well.

For ordinary workers this attrition of life or pacing of death where the everyday evolves within complex processes of globalization, law, and state regulation is an old story in a new era. Likewise, the world continues to pulsate with counter exploitive activity, in a variety of anarchist, cooperative, anti-capitalist, and radical antiwork experiments. People are increasingly using the time they do not have— what with the exigencies of the reproduction of life—to refuse to maintain the vampirism of profit extraction that exhausts the body and saturates the infrastructure of even the most benign and impulsive everyday pleasures. But for most, potentiality within the overwhelming present is less well symbolized by energizing images of sustainable life and less guaranteed by the glorious promise of bodily longevity and social security than it is expressed in regimes of exhausted practical sovereignty, lateral agency, and, sometimes, counter absorption in episodic refreshment, for example in sex, or spacing out, or food that is not for thought.'

—Lauren Berlant, *Cruel Optimism* (2011)

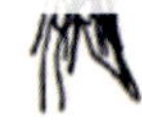

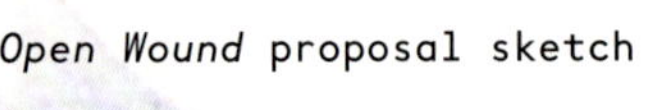

Open Wound proposal sketch

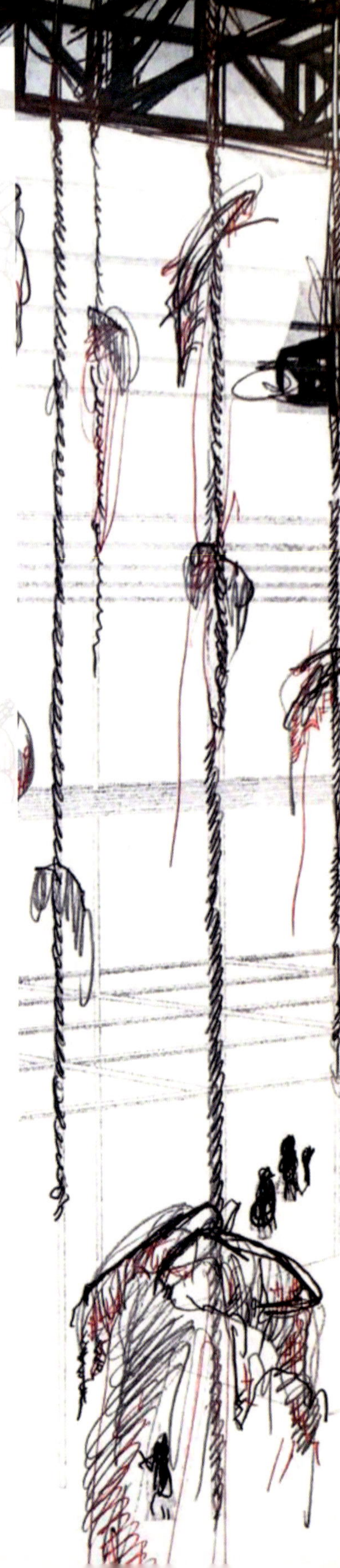

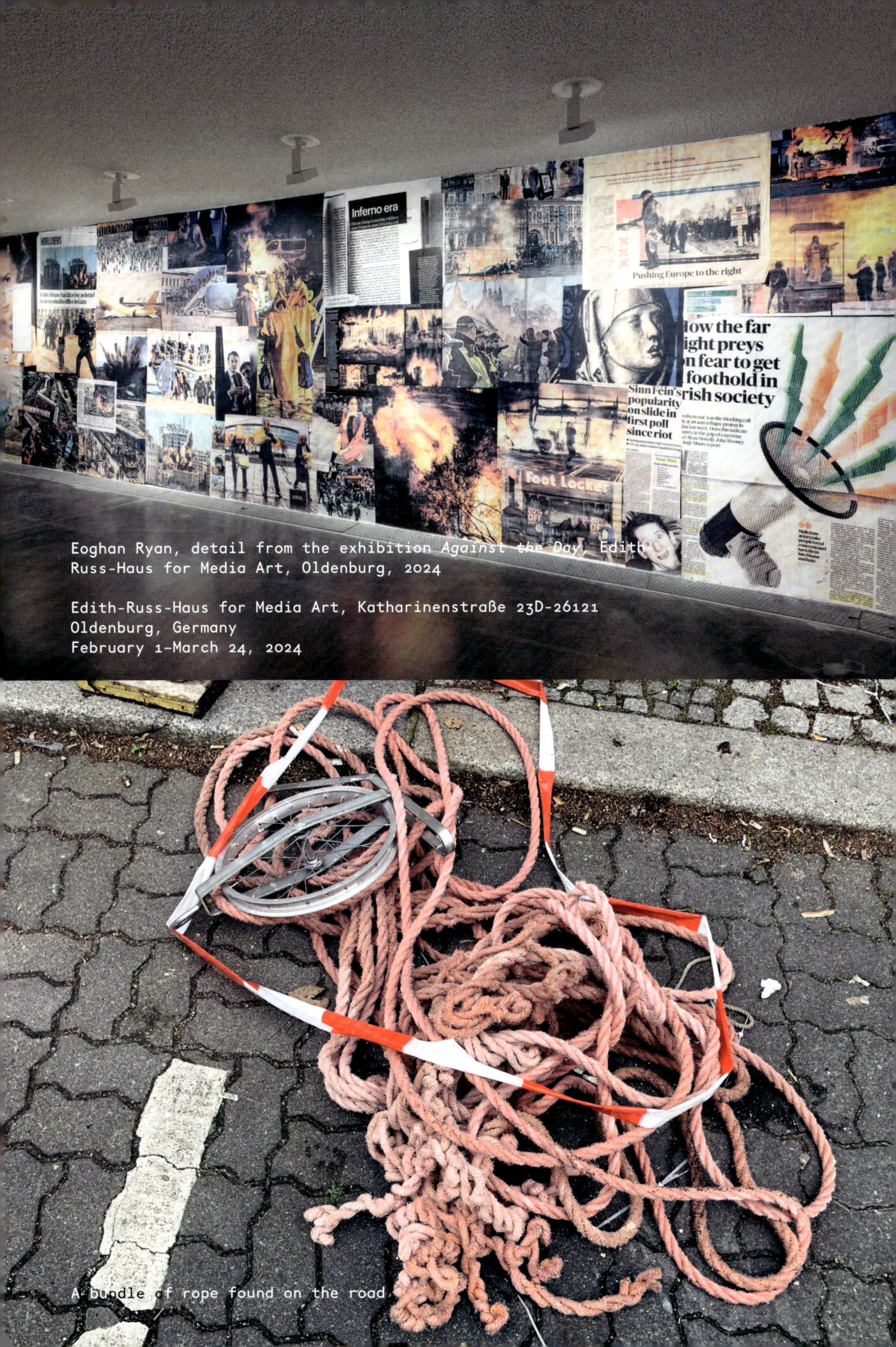

Eoghan Ryan, detail from the exhibition *Against the Day*, Edith-Russ-Haus for Media Art, Oldenburg, 2024

Edith-Russ-Haus for Media Art, Katharinenstraße 23D-26121 Oldenburg, Germany
February 1–March 24, 2024

A bundle of rope found on the road

'In a crisis we need to provide a concept of structure for transitional times: I call it transitional infrastructure. All times are transitional. But at some crisis times like this one, politics is defined by a collectively held sense that a glitch has appeared in the reproduction of life. A glitch is an interruption within a transition, a troubled transmission. A glitch is also a claim about the revelation of an infrastructural failure.

…

To attend to the terms for transition is to forge an imaginary for managing the meanwhile within damaged life's perdurance, a meanwhile that is less an end or an ethical scene than a technical political heuristic that allows for ambivalence not to destroy collective existence.'

—Lauren Berlant, *On the Inconvenience of Other People* (2022)

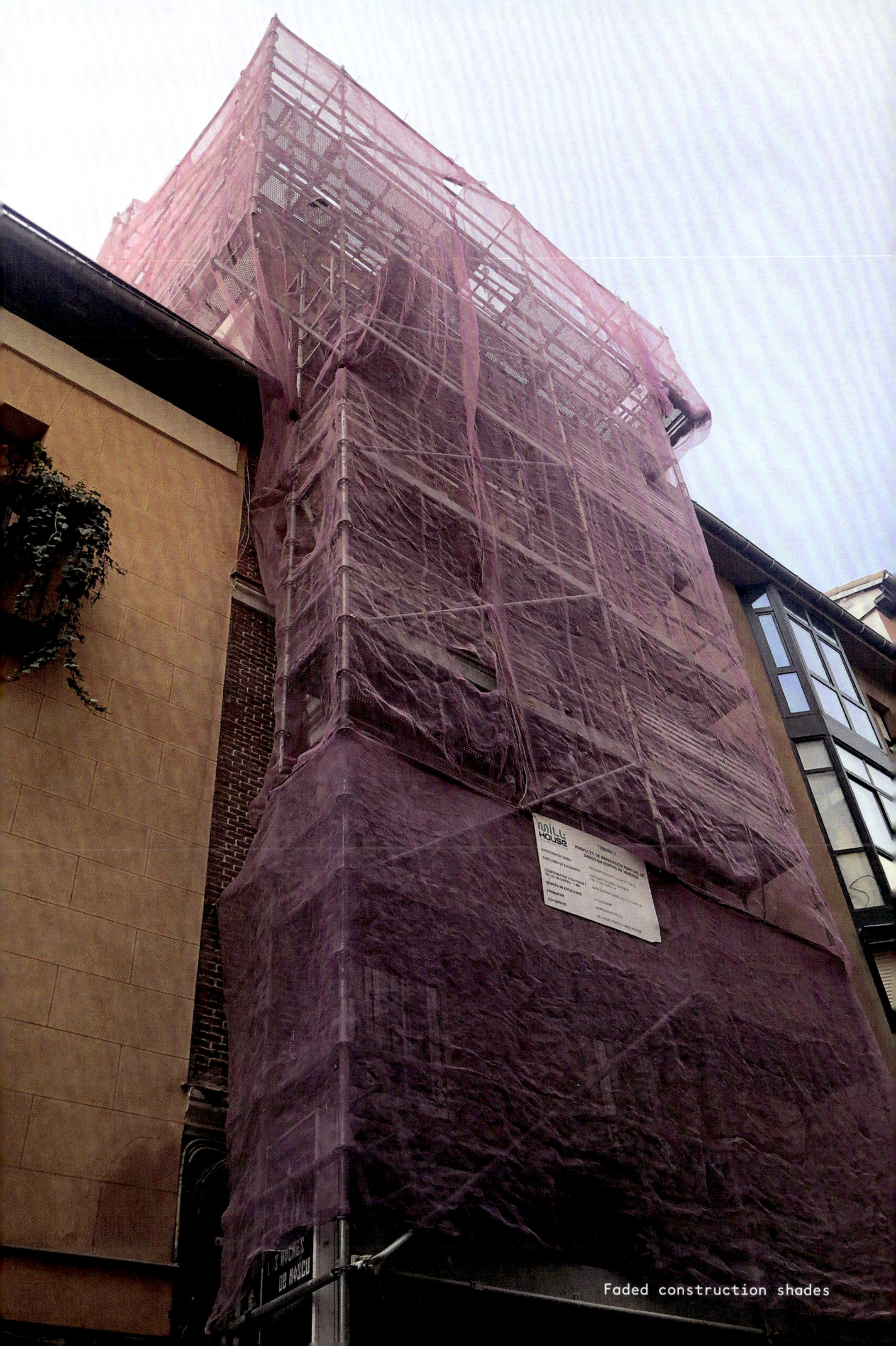

Faded construction shades

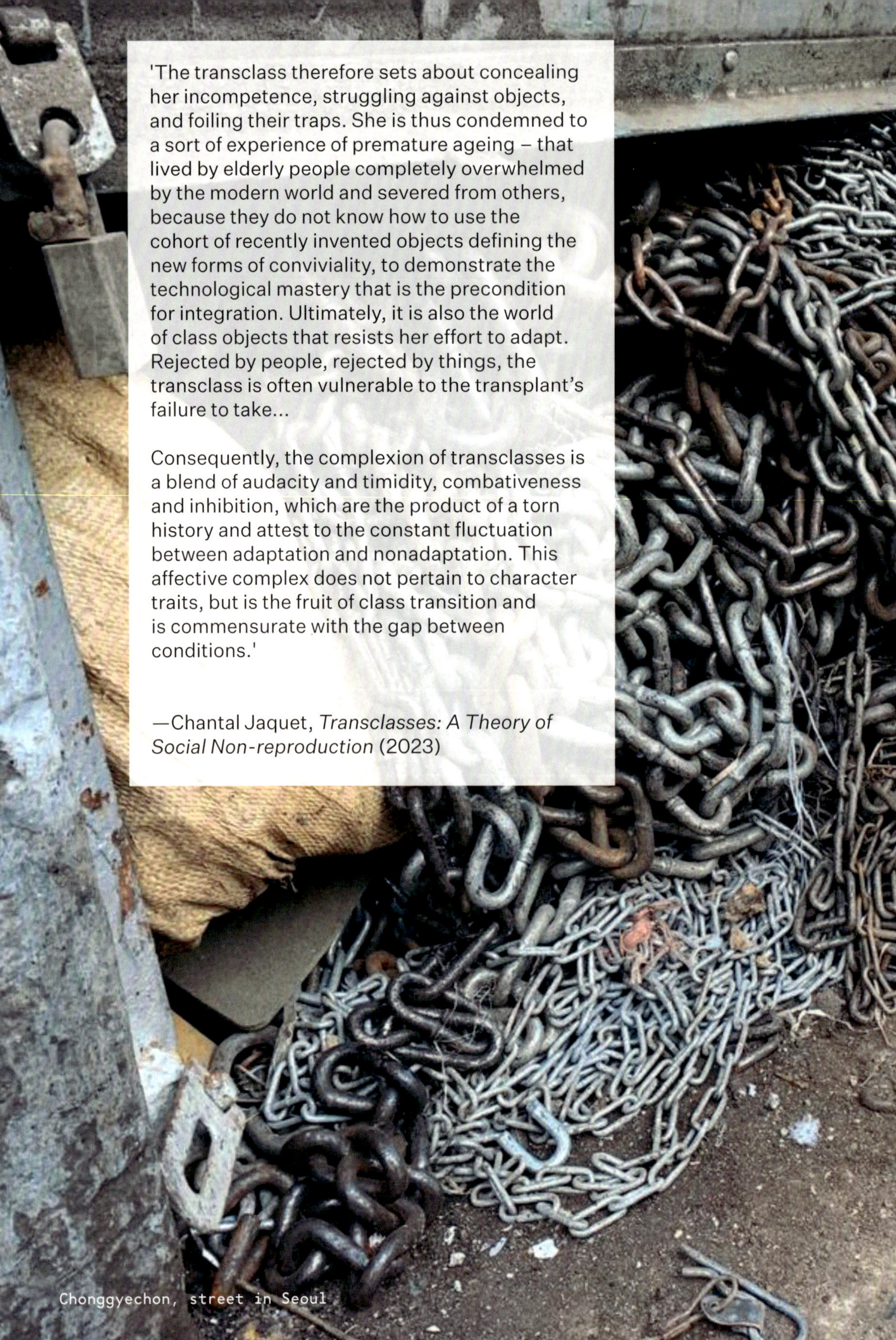

'The transclass therefore sets about concealing her incompetence, struggling against objects, and foiling their traps. She is thus condemned to a sort of experience of premature ageing – that lived by elderly people completely overwhelmed by the modern world and severed from others, because they do not know how to use the cohort of recently invented objects defining the new forms of conviviality, to demonstrate the technological mastery that is the precondition for integration. Ultimately, it is also the world of class objects that resists her effort to adapt. Rejected by people, rejected by things, the transclass is often vulnerable to the transplant's failure to take…

Consequently, the complexion of transclasses is a blend of audacity and timidity, combativeness and inhibition, which are the product of a torn history and attest to the constant fluctuation between adaptation and nonadaptation. This affective complex does not pertain to character traits, but is the fruit of class transition and is commensurate with the gap between conditions.'

—Chantal Jaquet, Transclasses: A Theory of Social Non-reproduction (2023)

Chonggyechon, street in Seoul

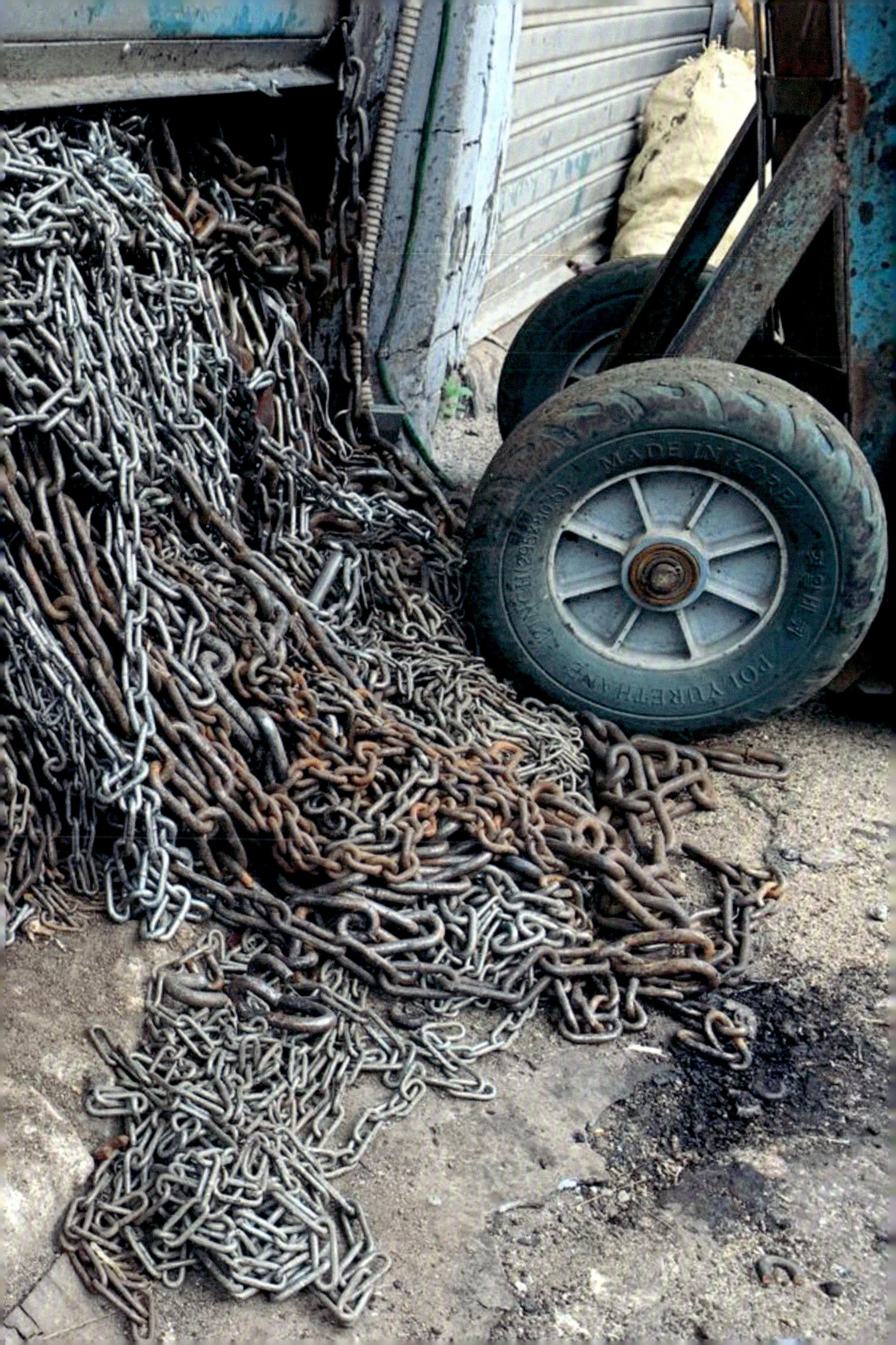

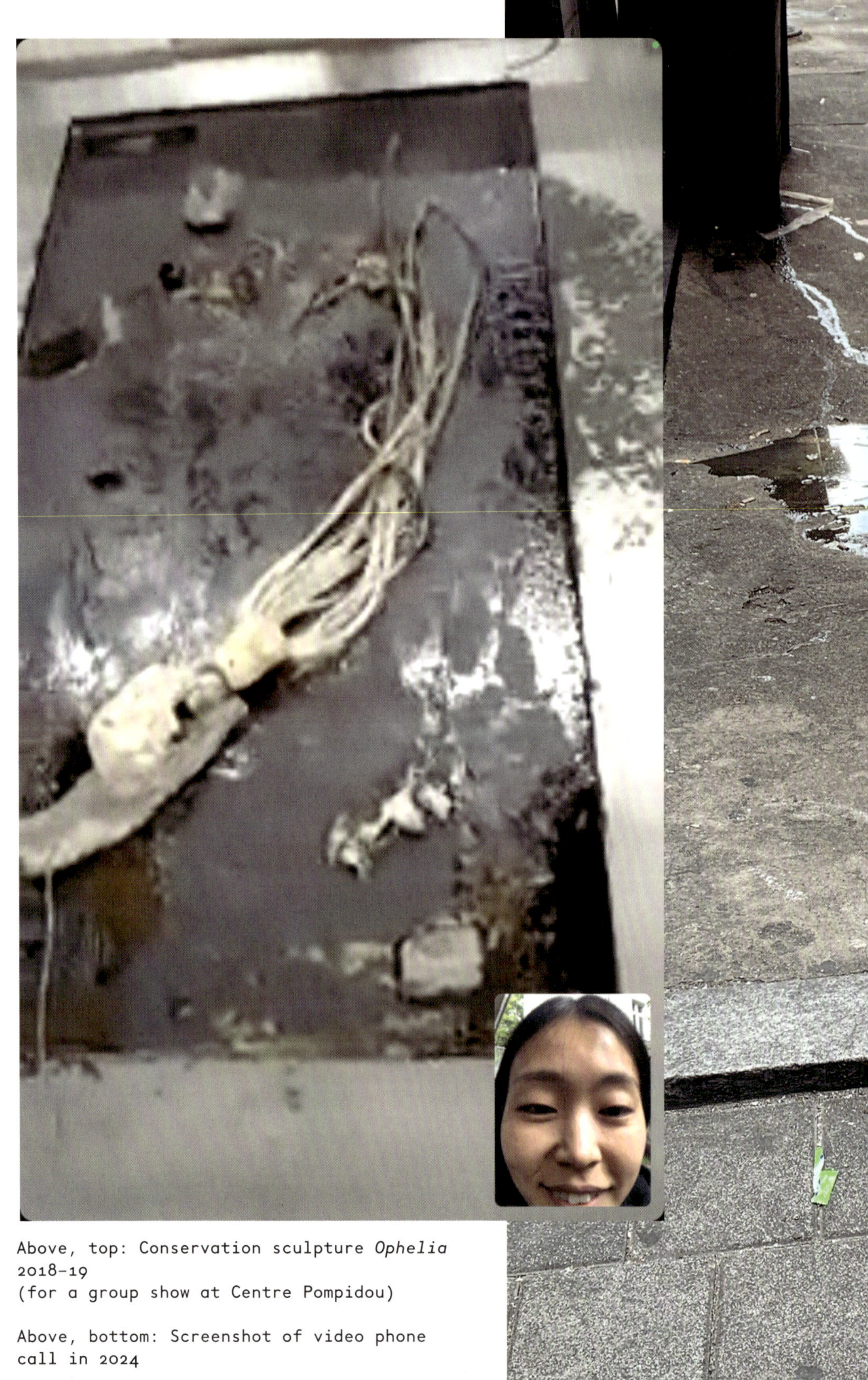

Above, top: Conservation sculpture *Ophelia*
2018-19
(for a group show at Centre Pompidou)

Above, bottom: Screenshot of video phone
call in 2024

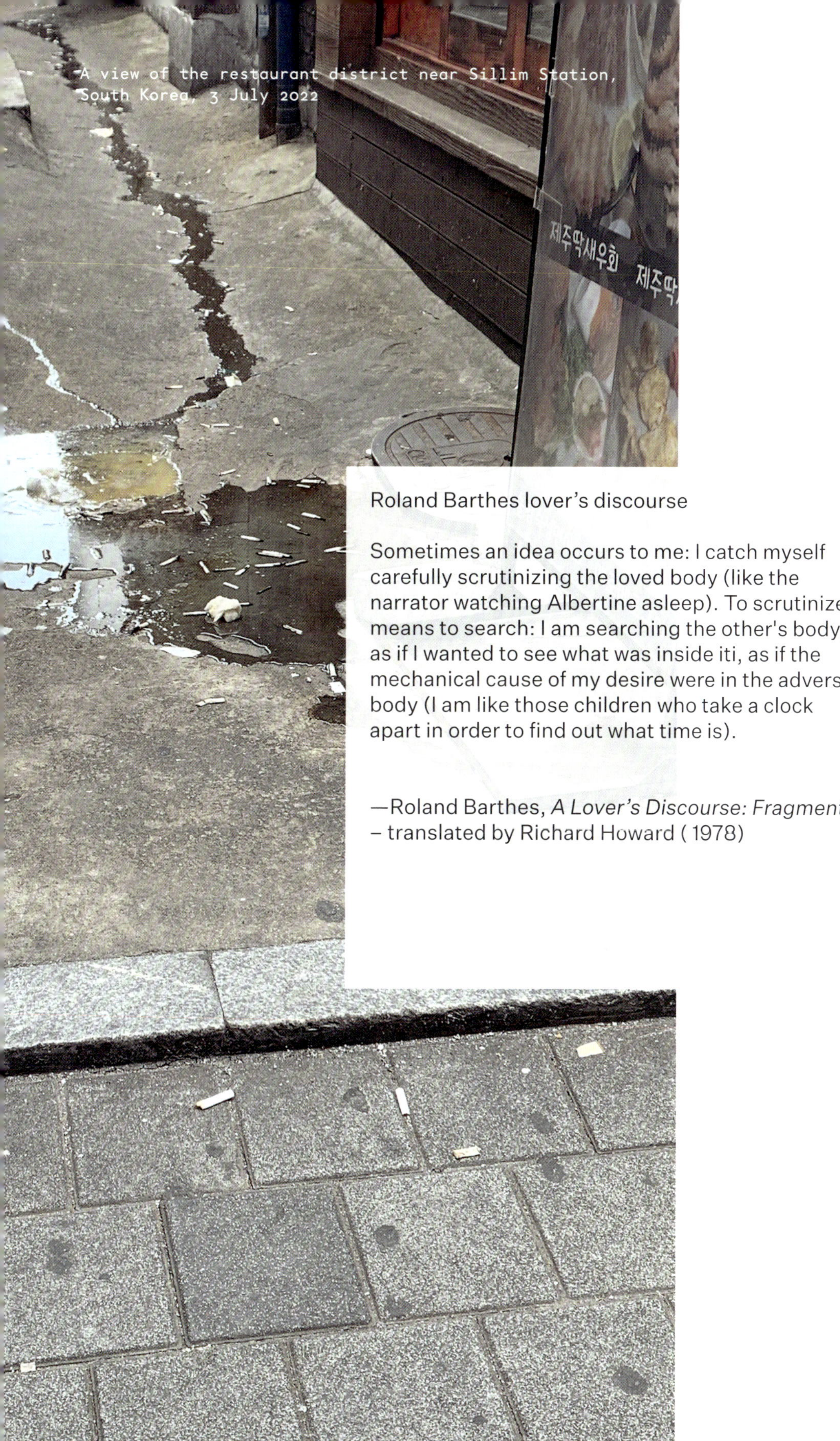

Roland Barthes lover's discourse

Sometimes an idea occurs to me: I catch myself carefully scrutinizing the loved body (like the narrator watching Albertine asleep). To scrutinize means to search: I am searching the other's body, as if I wanted to see what was inside iti, as if the mechanical cause of my desire were in the adverse body (I am like those children who take a clock apart in order to find out what time is).

—Roland Barthes, *A Lover's Discourse: Fragments* – translated by Richard Howard (1978)

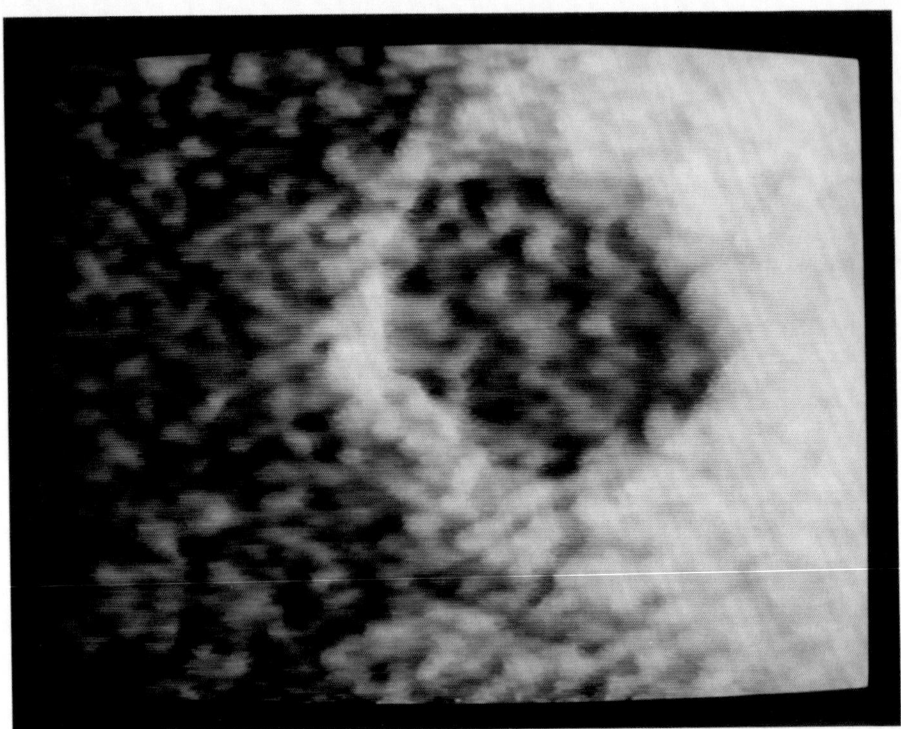

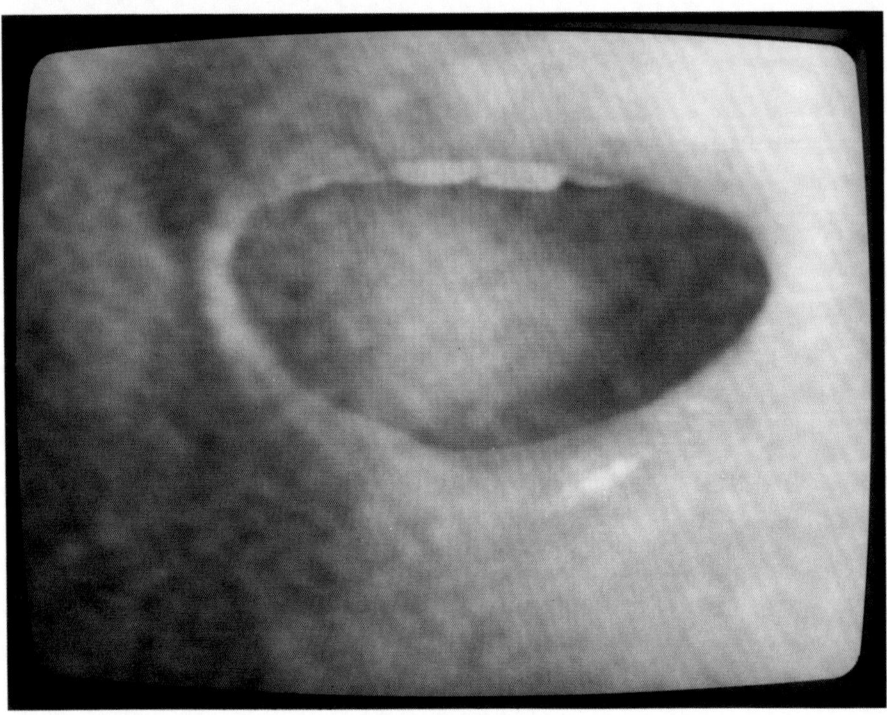

Theresa Hak Kyung Cha, *Mouth to Mouth* 1975;
single-channel videotape with sound (of Korean vowels)

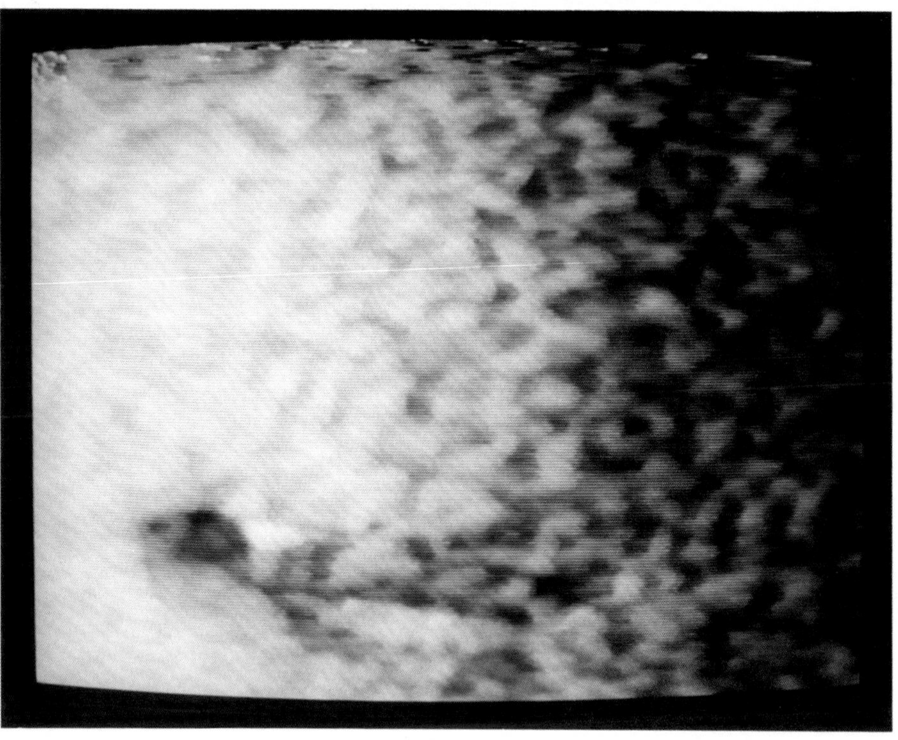

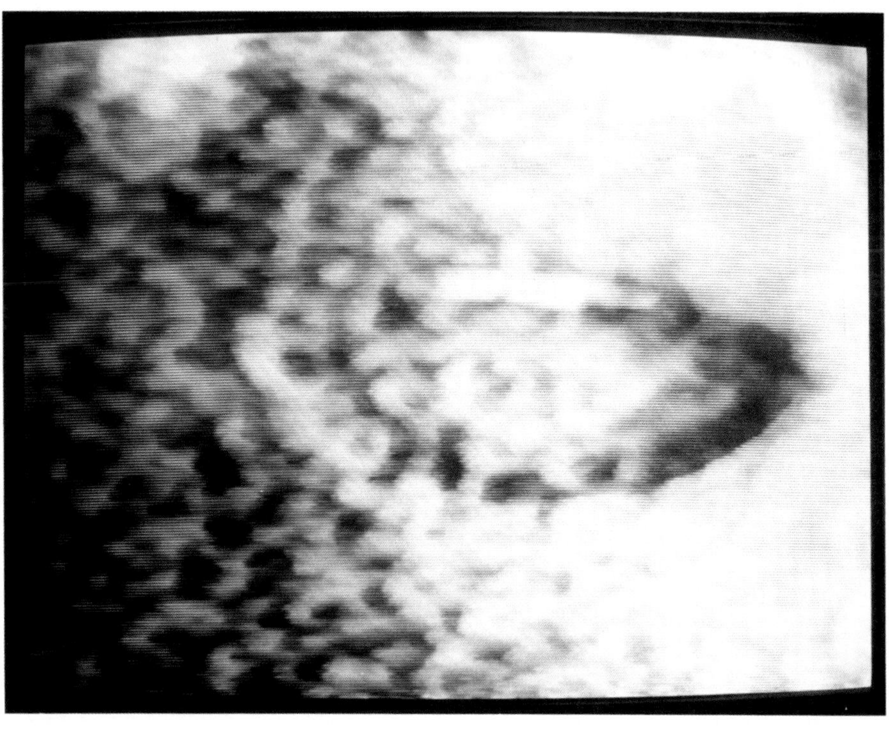

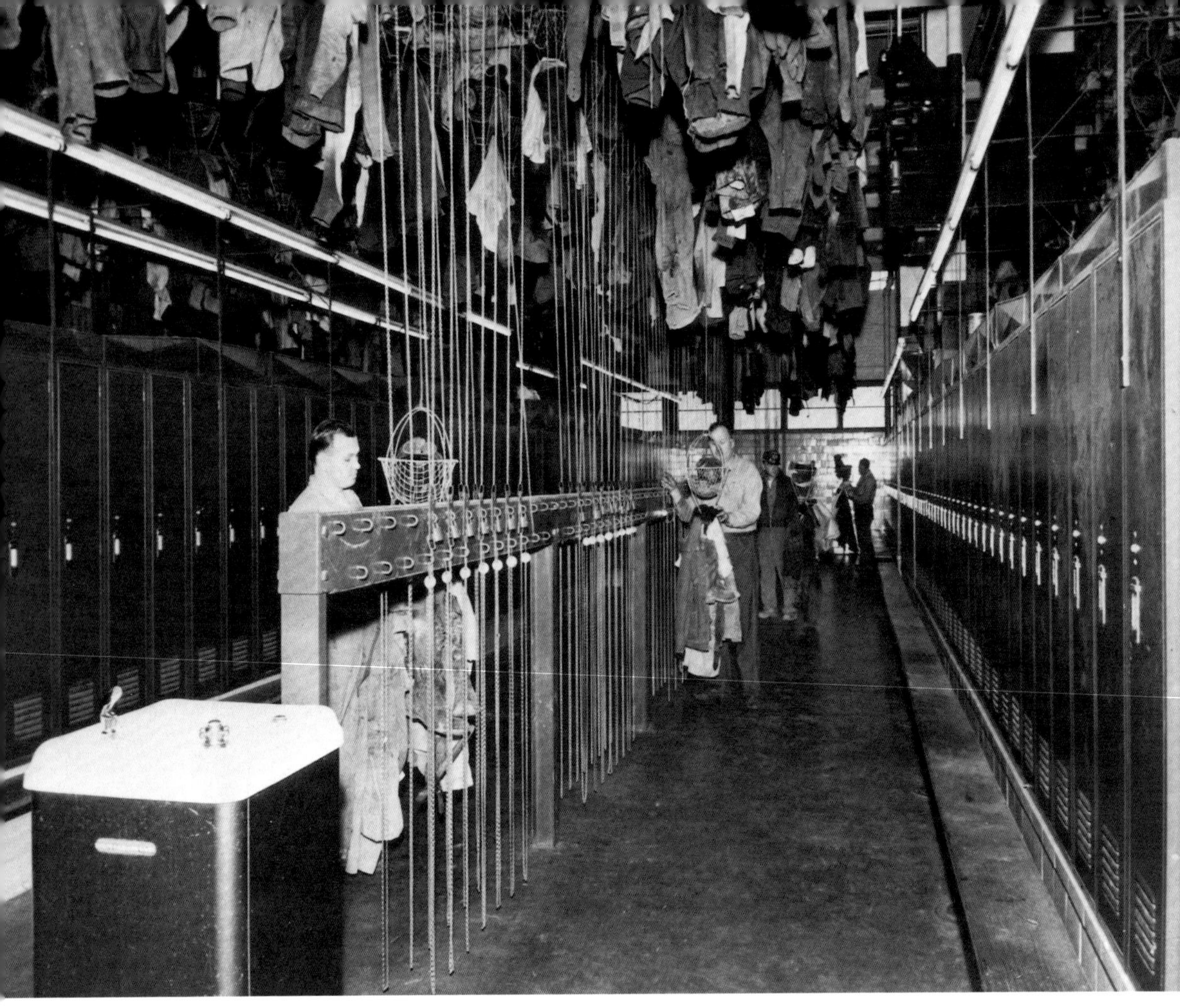

Above: Miner's Locker Room, Pittsburgh Consolidation Coal Company
Inspection Trip

Right: Miners changing clothes in the wash and change house,
Wyoming, 1946

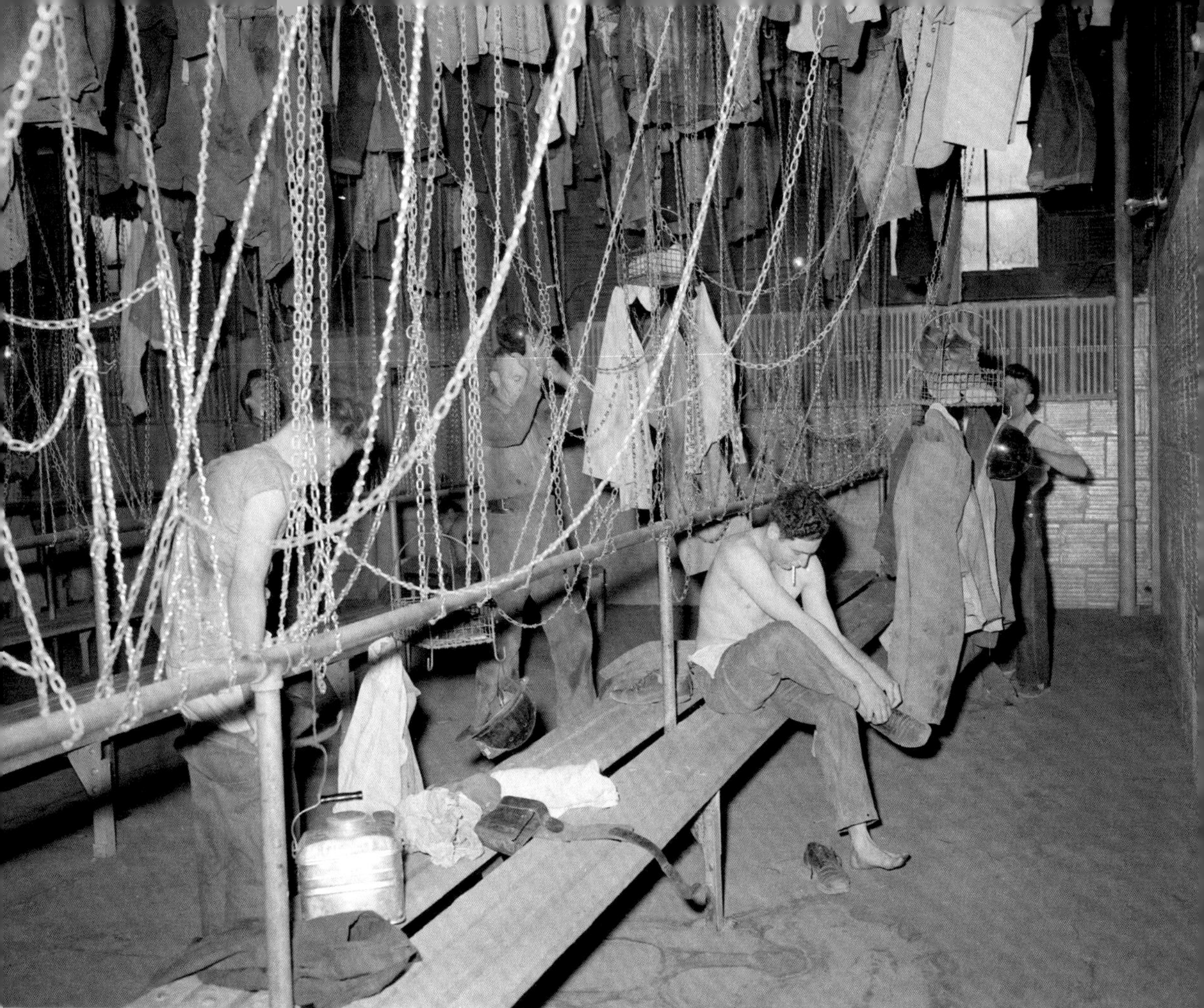

'The personal is political because there is
no personal.
There is no private realm to retreat into.'

—Mark Fischer, *Remember Who The Enemy Is*,
K-punk

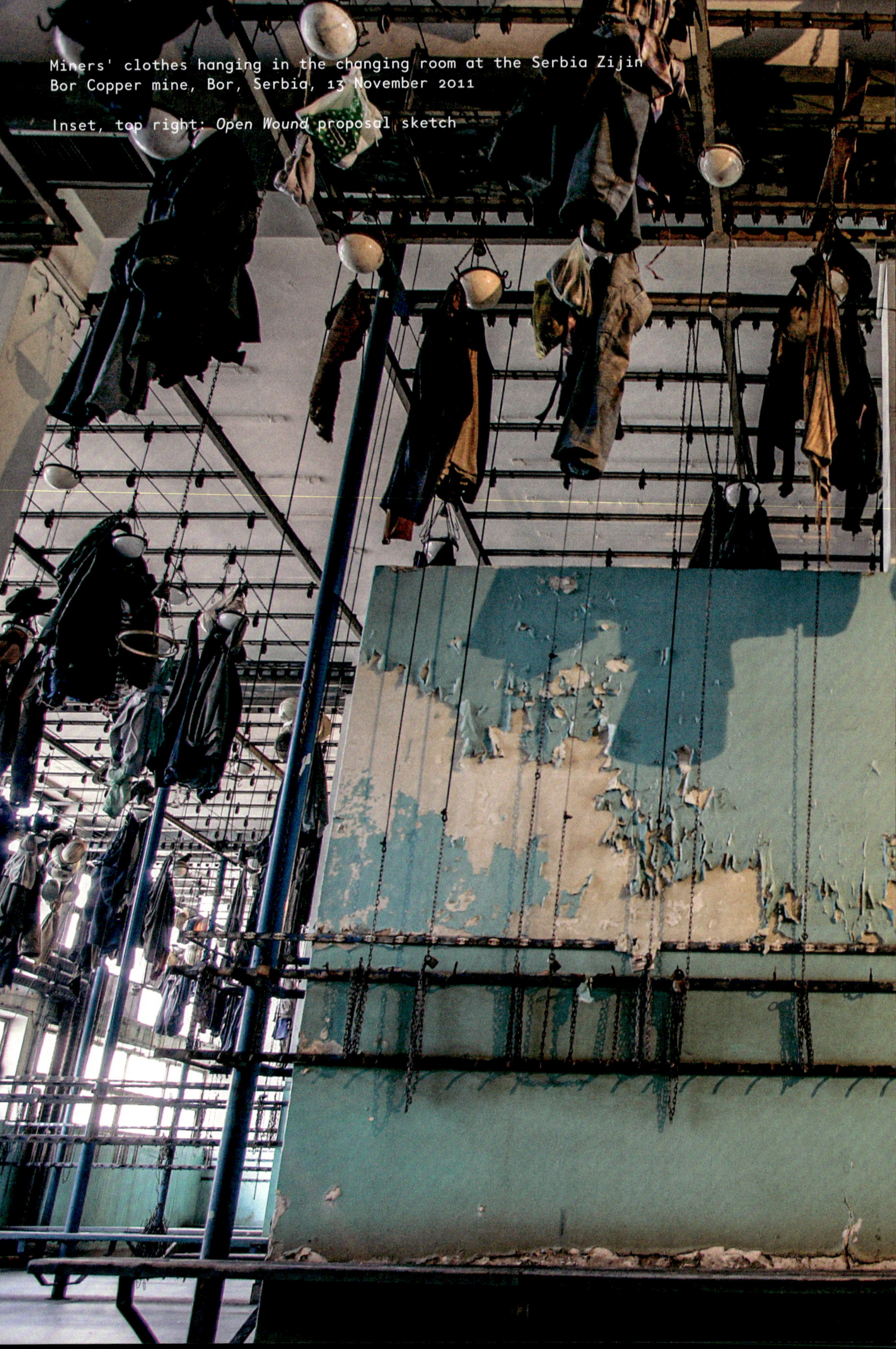

Miners' clothes hanging in the changing room at the Serbia Zijin
Bor Copper mine, Bor, Serbia, 13 November 2011

Inset, top right: *Open Wound* proposal sketch

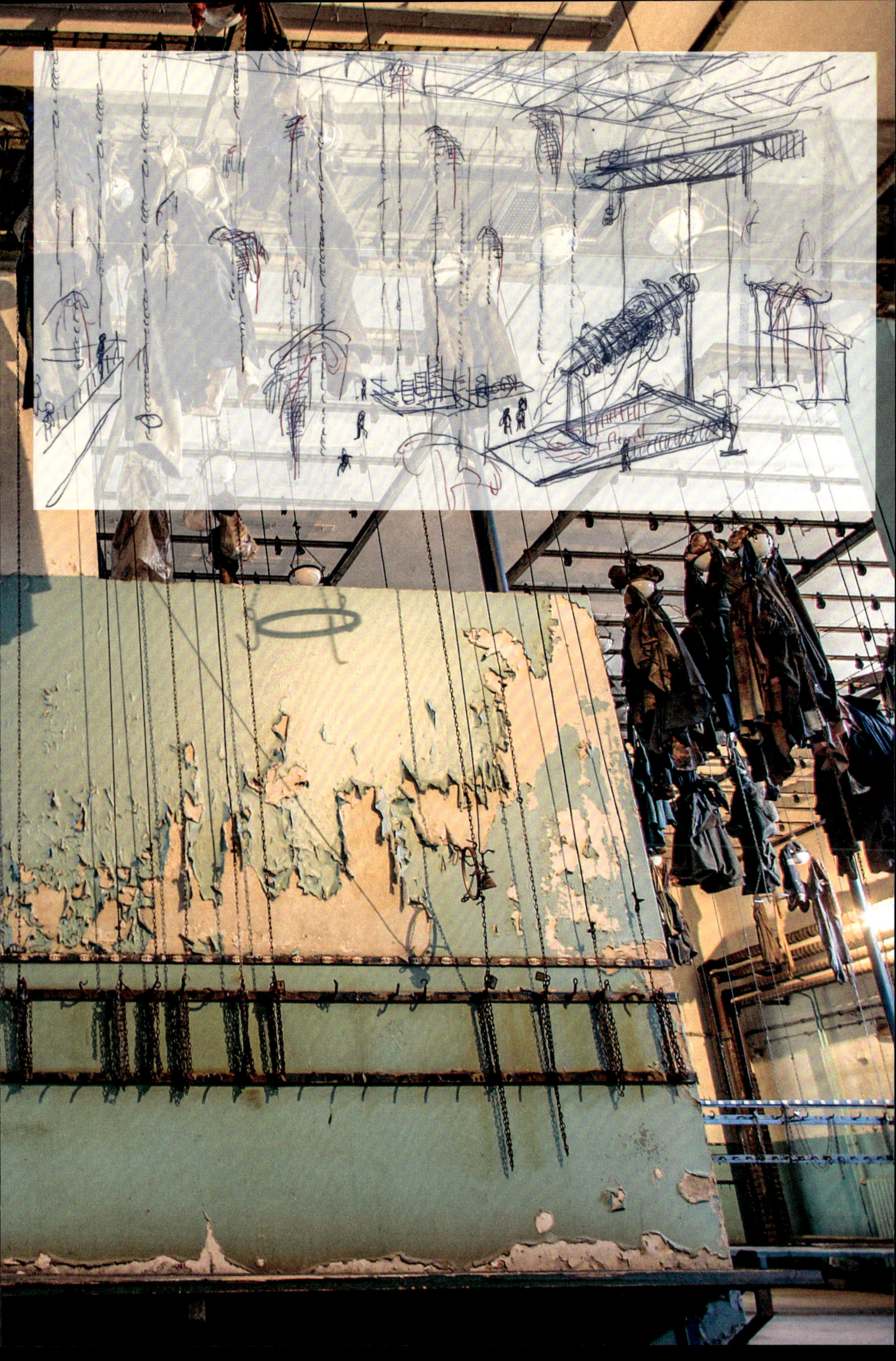

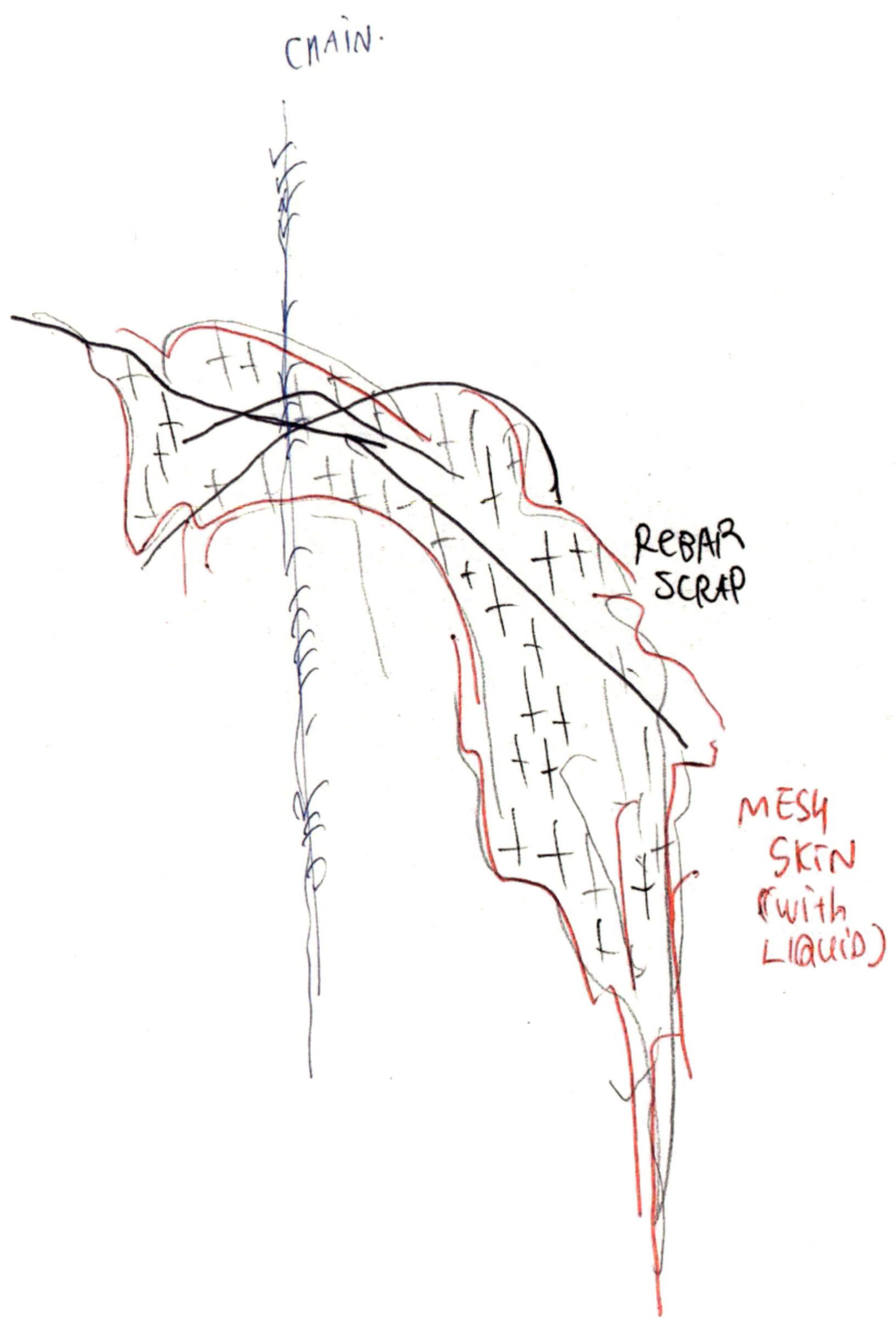

CHAIN.
REBAR
SCRAP
MESH
SKIN
(with
LIQUID)

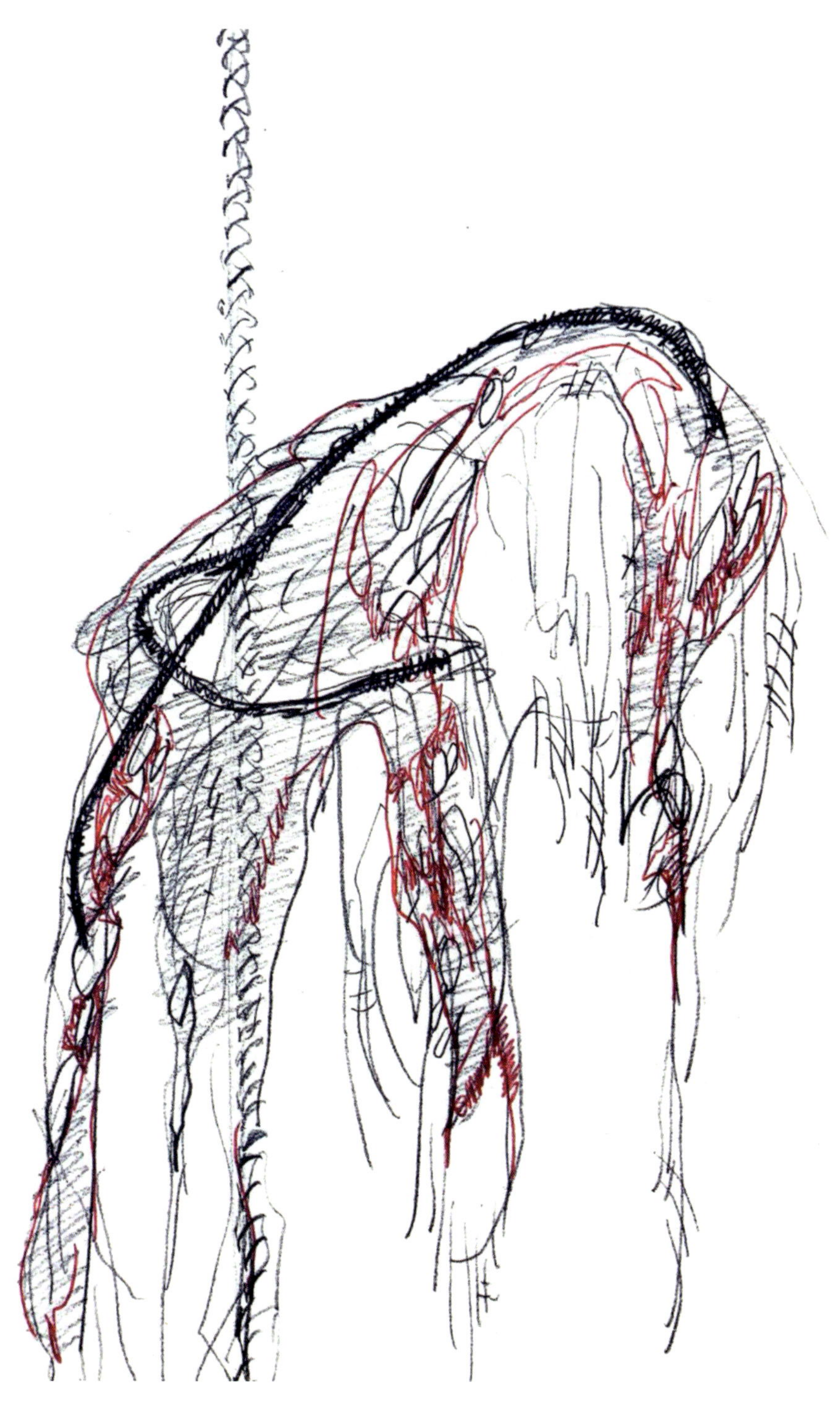

Open Wound proposal sketches

'The present moment is made possible by
the fantasy of you, laden with the X qualities
I can project onto you, given your convenient
absence.'

Lauren Berlant, *Cruel Optimism* (2011)

Left: Found graffiti

Below: Prototype of *Hysteria, Elegance, Catharsis; words were never enough*
2019
Process picture, left overnight with power on in the studio

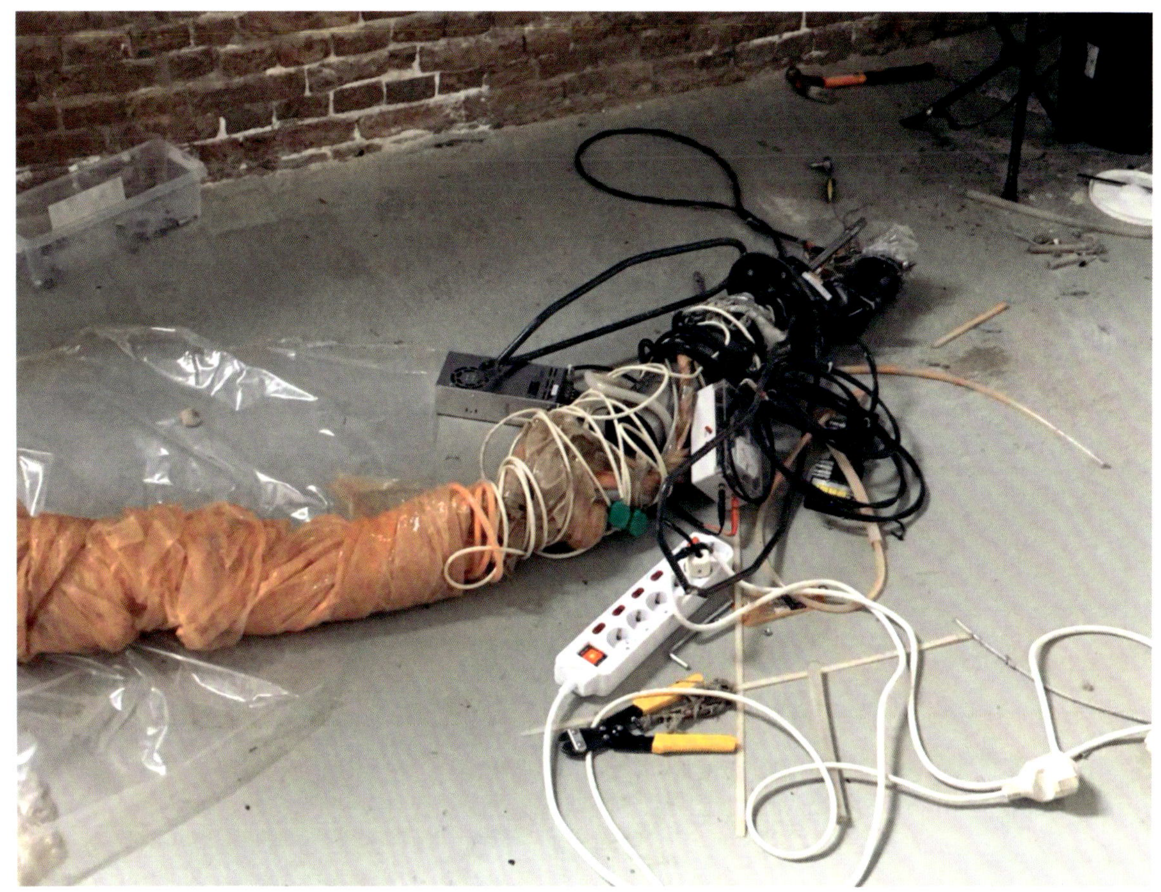

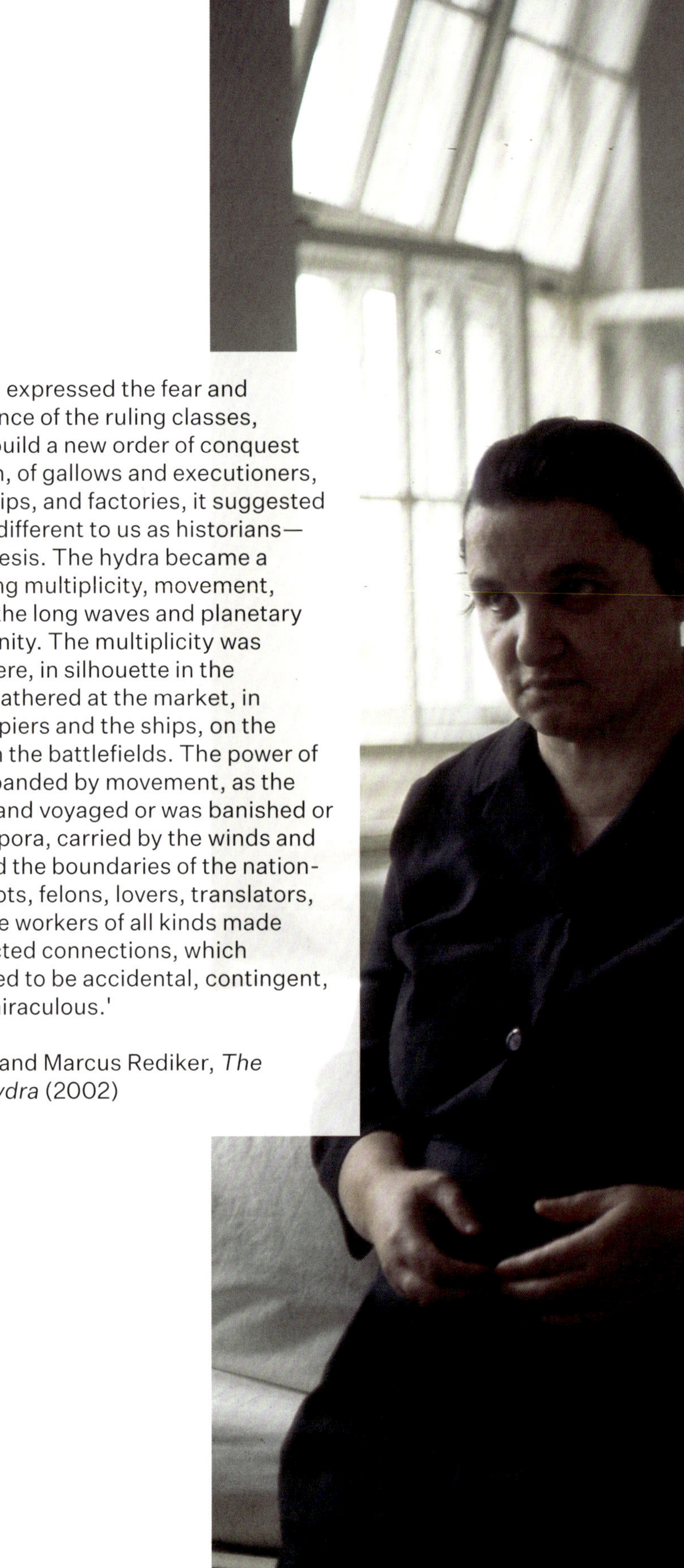

'If the hydra myth expressed the fear and justified the violence of the ruling classes, helping them to build a new order of conquest and expropriation, of gallows and executioners, of plantations, ships, and factories, it suggested something quite different to us as historians—namely, a hypothesis. The hydra became a means of exploring multiplicity, movement, and connection, the long waves and planetary currents of humanity. The multiplicity was indicated, as it were, in silhouette in the multitudes who gathered at the market, in the fields, on the piers and the ships, on the plantations, upon the battlefields. The power of numbers was expanded by movement, as the hydra journeyed and voyaged or was banished or dispersed in diaspora, carried by the winds and the waves beyond the boundaries of the nation-state. Sailors, pilots, felons, lovers, translators, musicians, mobile workers of all kinds made new and unexpected connections, which variously appeared to be accidental, contingent, transient, even miraculous.'

Peter Linebaugh and Marcus Rediker, *The Many-Headed Hydra* (2002)

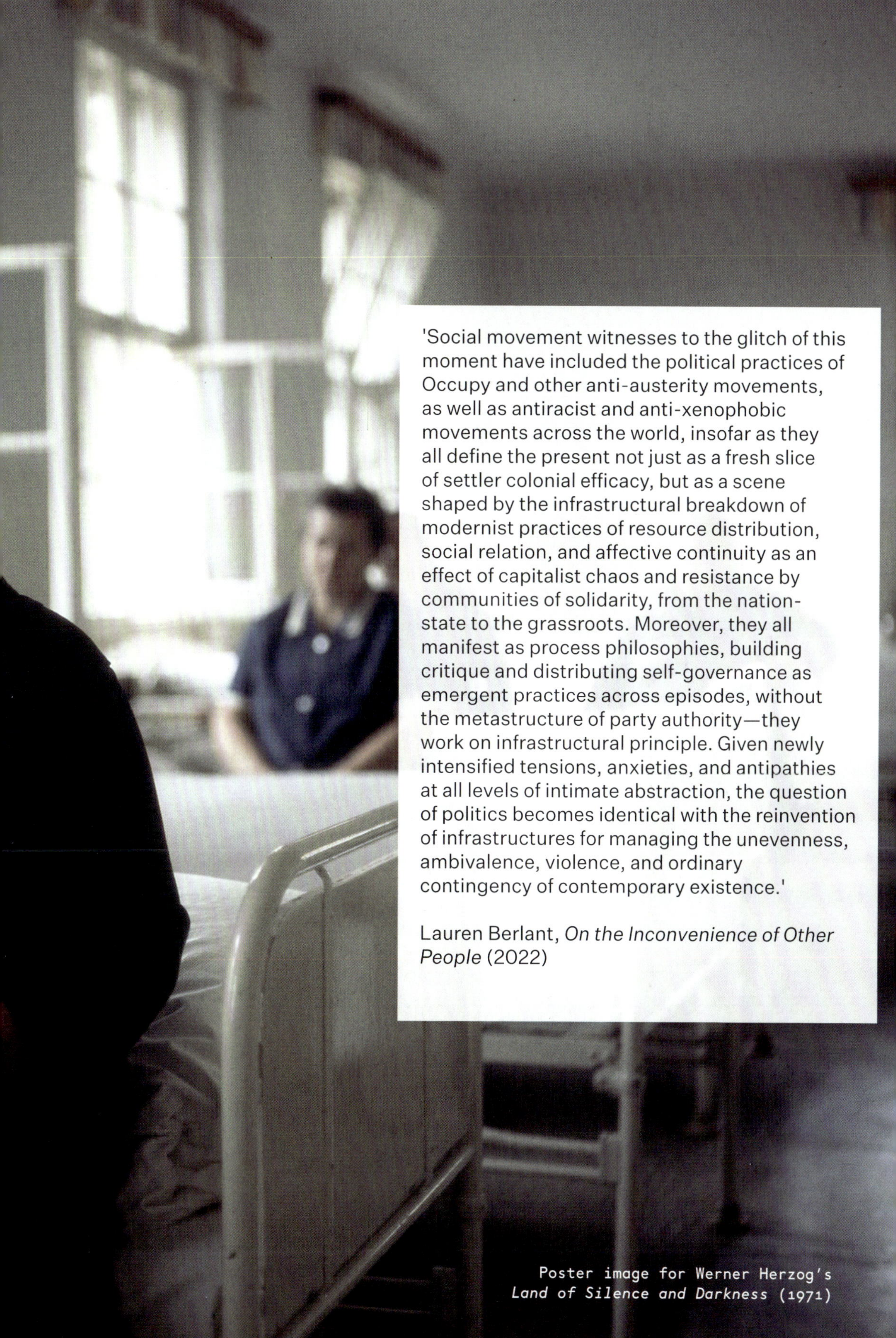

Poster image for Werner Herzog's
Land of Silence and Darkness (1971)

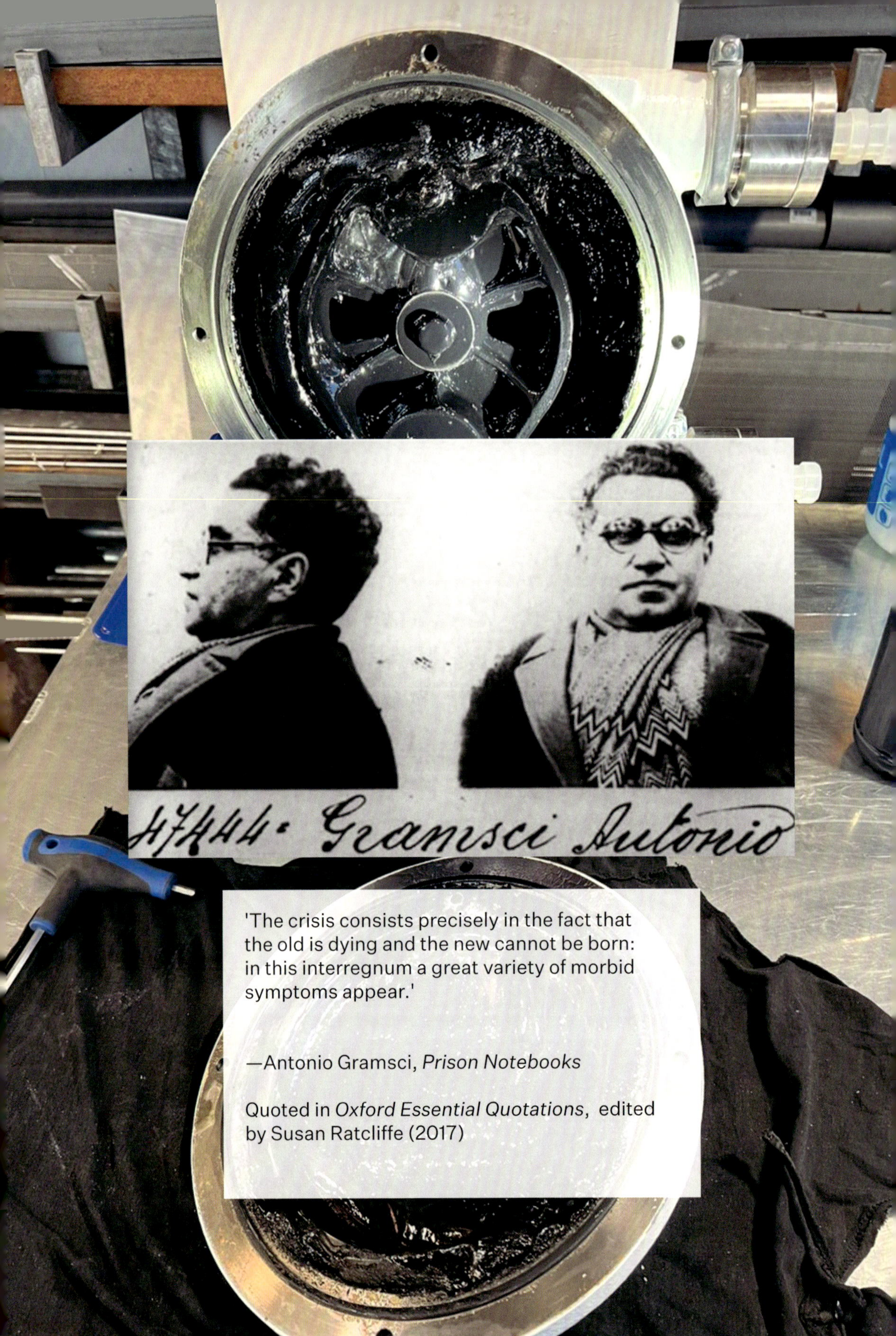
47444 Gramsci Antonio

'The crisis consists precisely in the fact that the old is dying and the new cannot be born: in this interregnum a great variety of morbid symptoms appear.'

—Antonio Gramsci, Prison Notebooks

Quoted in Oxford Essential Quotations, edited by Susan Ratcliffe (2017)

I'M SMARTER THAN THIS FEELING, BUT AM I?

I watch your film about fisting: orifice as cave,
as grave, as starlit wormhole dug in space.
You're obsessed by interiority.
By the drunk shipwreck of it. By our inside rivers
so alien, we might as well call them Sweden or Pluto or 1973
and what's the difference, all of them are out of reach.
I know we're both smarter than this feeling
because we have talked about desire and her little games.
I cry easily as I watch. You're old school.
You want what O'Hara wanted, I think, which is a kind of boundlessness
that won't kill anyone. Edging. You don't believe in bodies.
Everyone is dust, condensed by circumstances.
You see what I was before I was a was. An am.
What's your thing with smut, I ask.
You say it's not smut, it's a love story.
To be taken apart is as important as being put together.
Near-annihilation reminds you of a limit
and ask yourself, who do you trust at your limit?
At a party last night in Chinatown, I invent you
walking through the door. It is warm and I smoke
a cigarette on the balcony. Everyone is a producer
and talking about Kathy Acker and what would I say
if I could? That I want our years to keep meeting.
I don't want 1973 or a failed planet or even Sweden.
Instead of saying this, I ask about your film.
We put the art between us because the art exists
and we do not. This is called sublimation.
We puppet our meat in the grey twilight
of the real world and I pretend
I'm not speaking to Time.

Left, background: The inside of a peristaltic pump, opened for maintenance
Left, centre: Antonio Gramsci, prison mugshot, 1926

Above: Megan Fernandes, *I Do What I'm Told: Poems* (2023)

'In his refusal of economic determinism
Gramsci writes, "Mechanical historical
materialism does not allow for the possibility of
error, but assumes that every political act is
determined, immediately, by the structure,
and therefore as a real and permanent (in
the sense of achieved) modification of the
structure"(2000: 191). For Gramsci, ideology
has as much to do with error or failure as with
perfect predictability; therefore a radical
political response would have to deploy an
improvisational mode to keep pace with the
constantly shifting relations between dominant
and subordinate within the chaotic flow of
political life. Gramsci views the intellectual
function as a mode of self-awareness and
an applied knowledge of the structures
that constrain meaning to the demands of a
class-bound understanding of "common sense."

Queer studies offer us one method for imagining,
not some fantasy of an elsewhere, but
existing alternatives to hegemonic systems.
What Gramsci terms "common sense" depends
heavily on the production of norms, and so
the critique of dominant forms of common
sense is also, in some sense, a critique
of norms. Heteronormative common
sense leads to the equation of success with
advancement, capital accumulation, family,
ethical conduct, and hope. Other subordinate,
queer, or counterhegemonic modes of
common sense lead to the association of
failure with nonconformity, anticapitalist
practices, nonreproductive life styles, negativity,
and critique.'

—Jack Halberstam, *The Queer Art of Failure*
(2011)

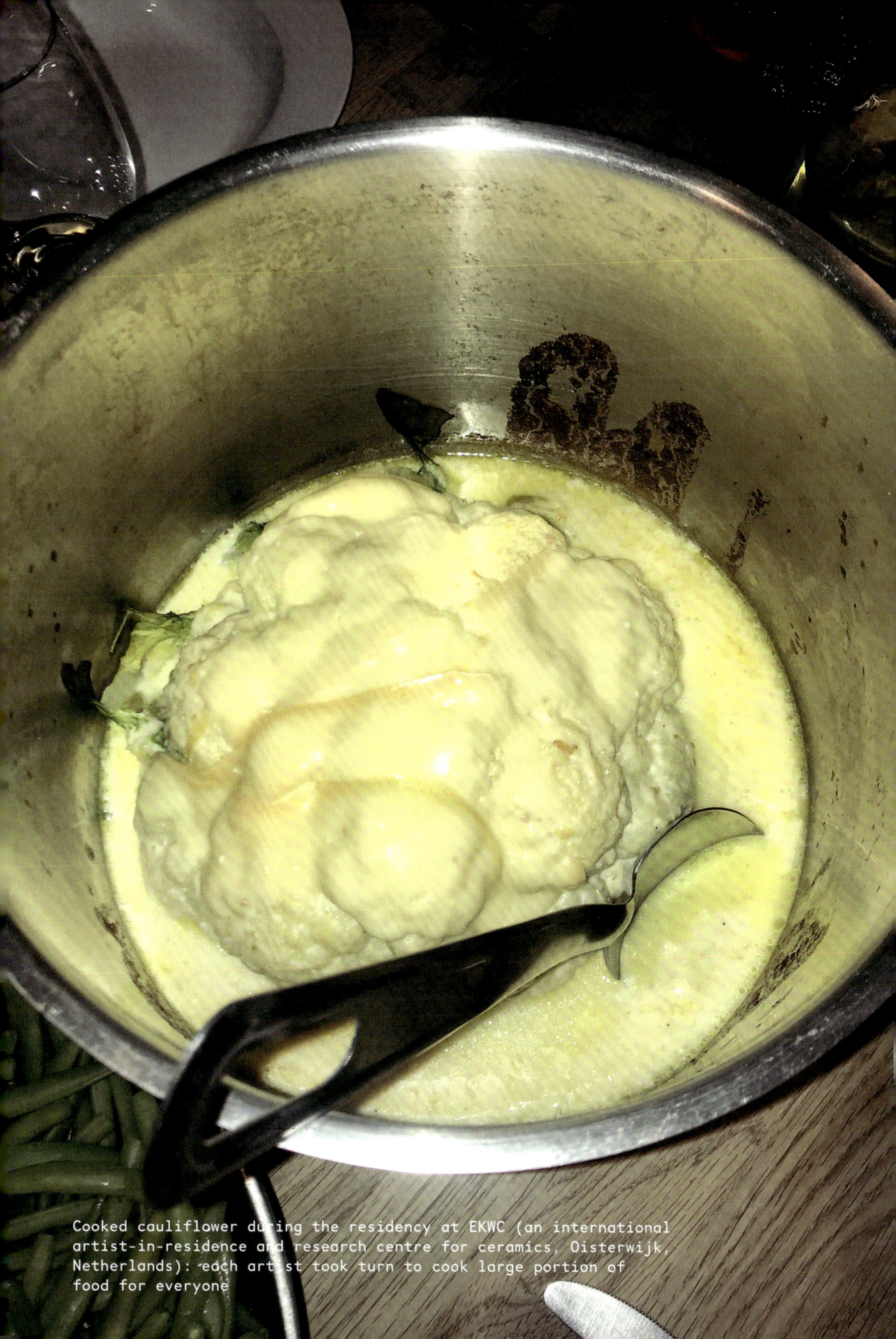

Cooked cauliflower during the residency at EKWC (an international artist-in-residence and research centre for ceramics, Oisterwijk, Netherlands): each artist took turn to cook large portion of food for everyone

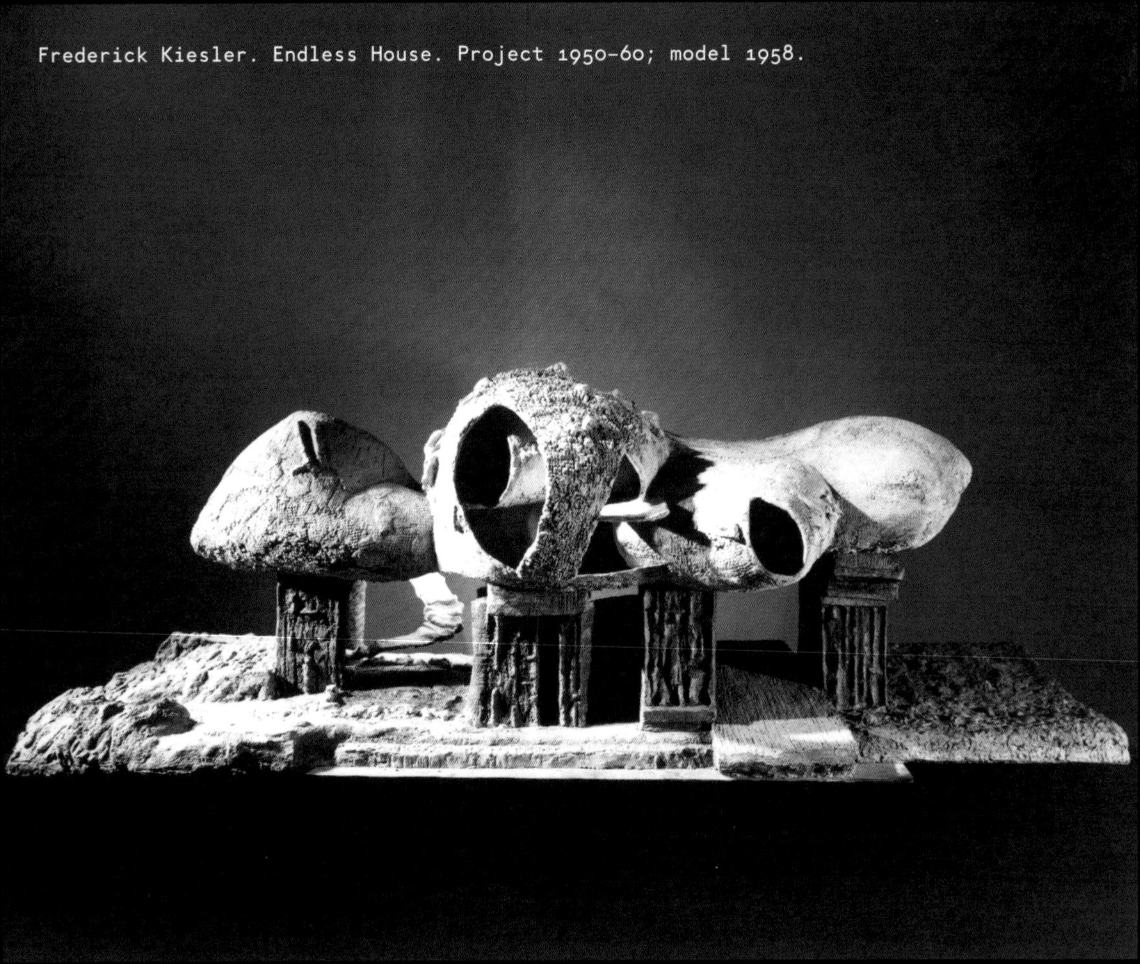

Frederick Kiesler. Endless House. Project 1950–60; model 1958.

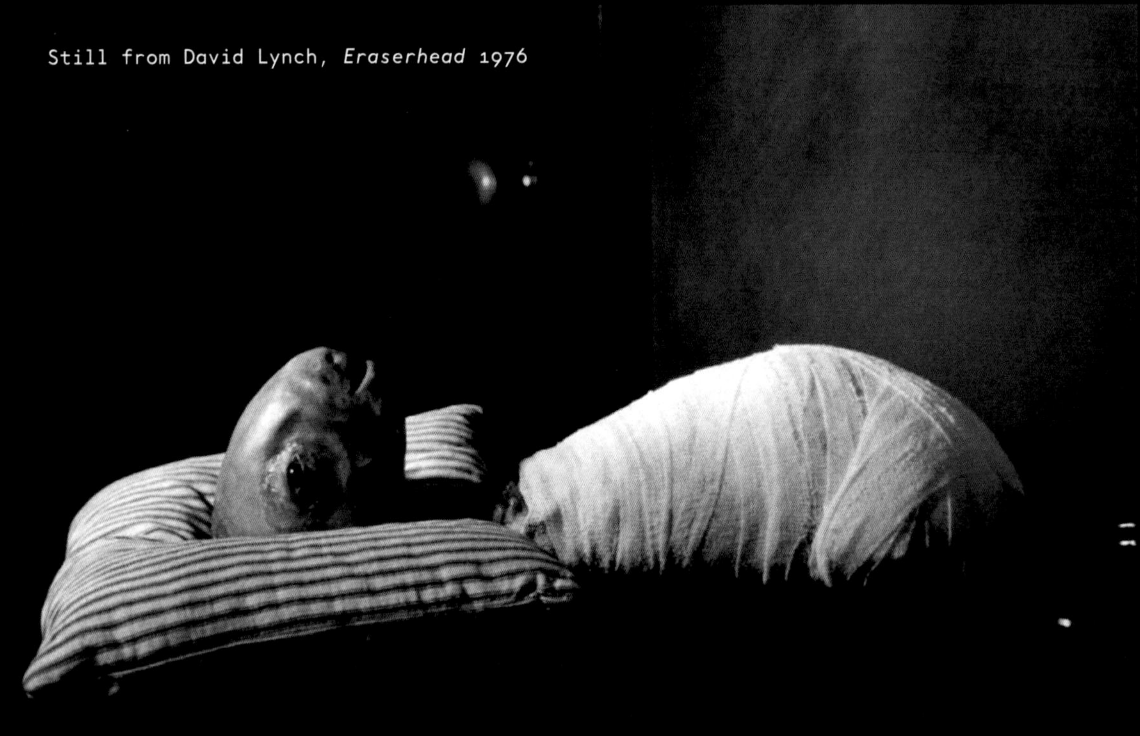

Still from David Lynch, *Eraserhead* 1976

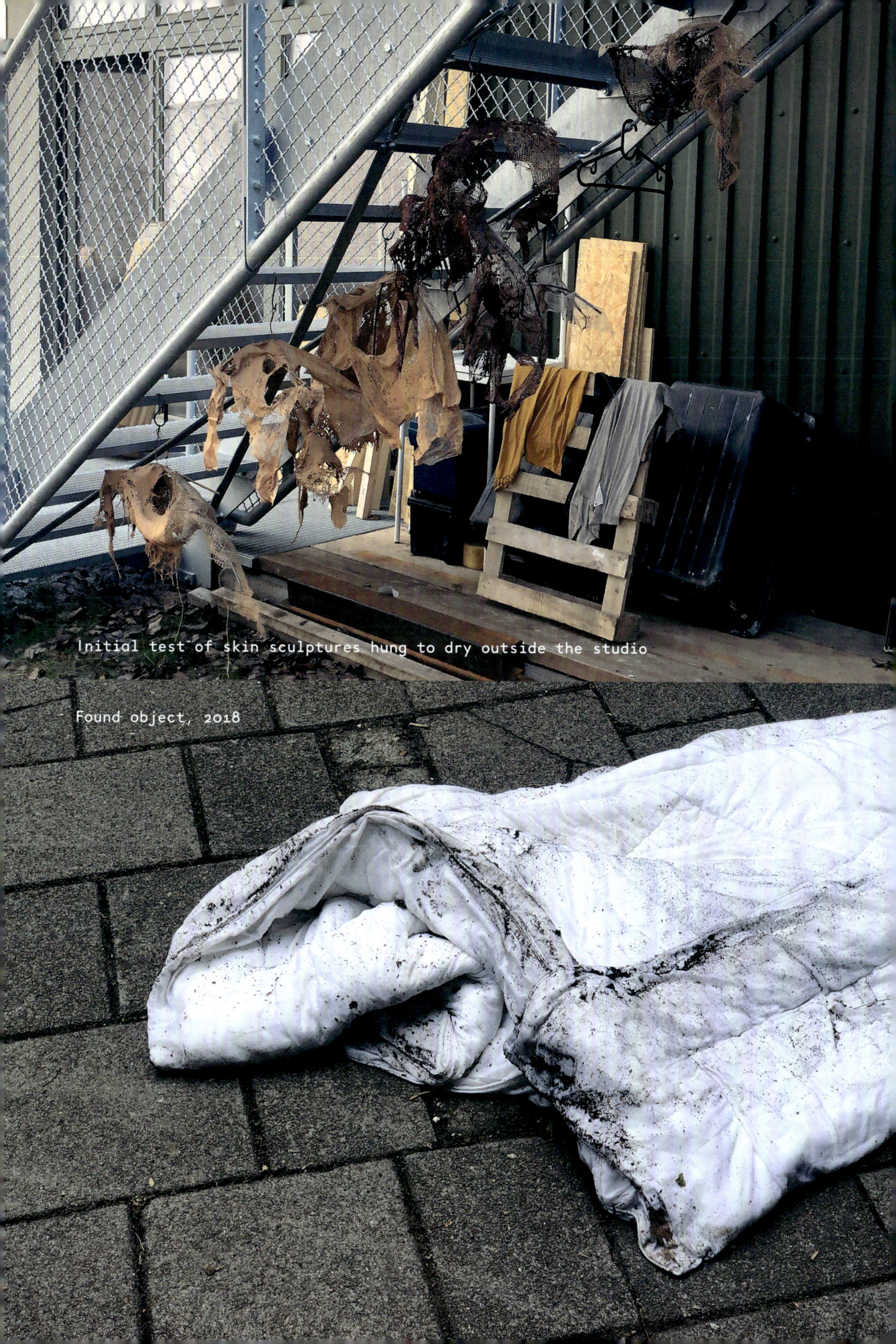

Initial test of skin sculptures hung to dry outside the studio

Found object, 2018

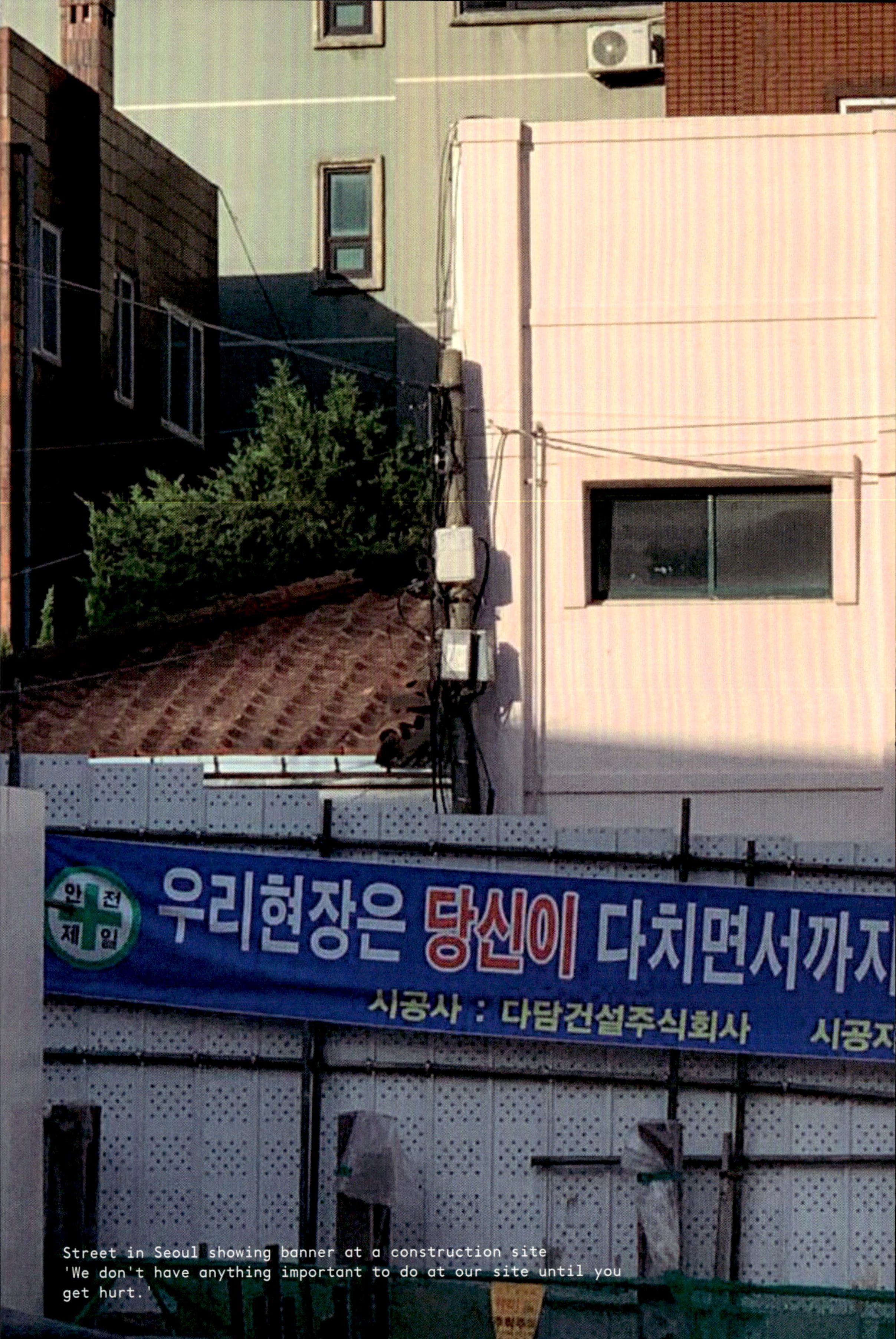

Street in Seoul showing banner at a construction site
'We don't have anything important to do at our site until you
get hurt.'

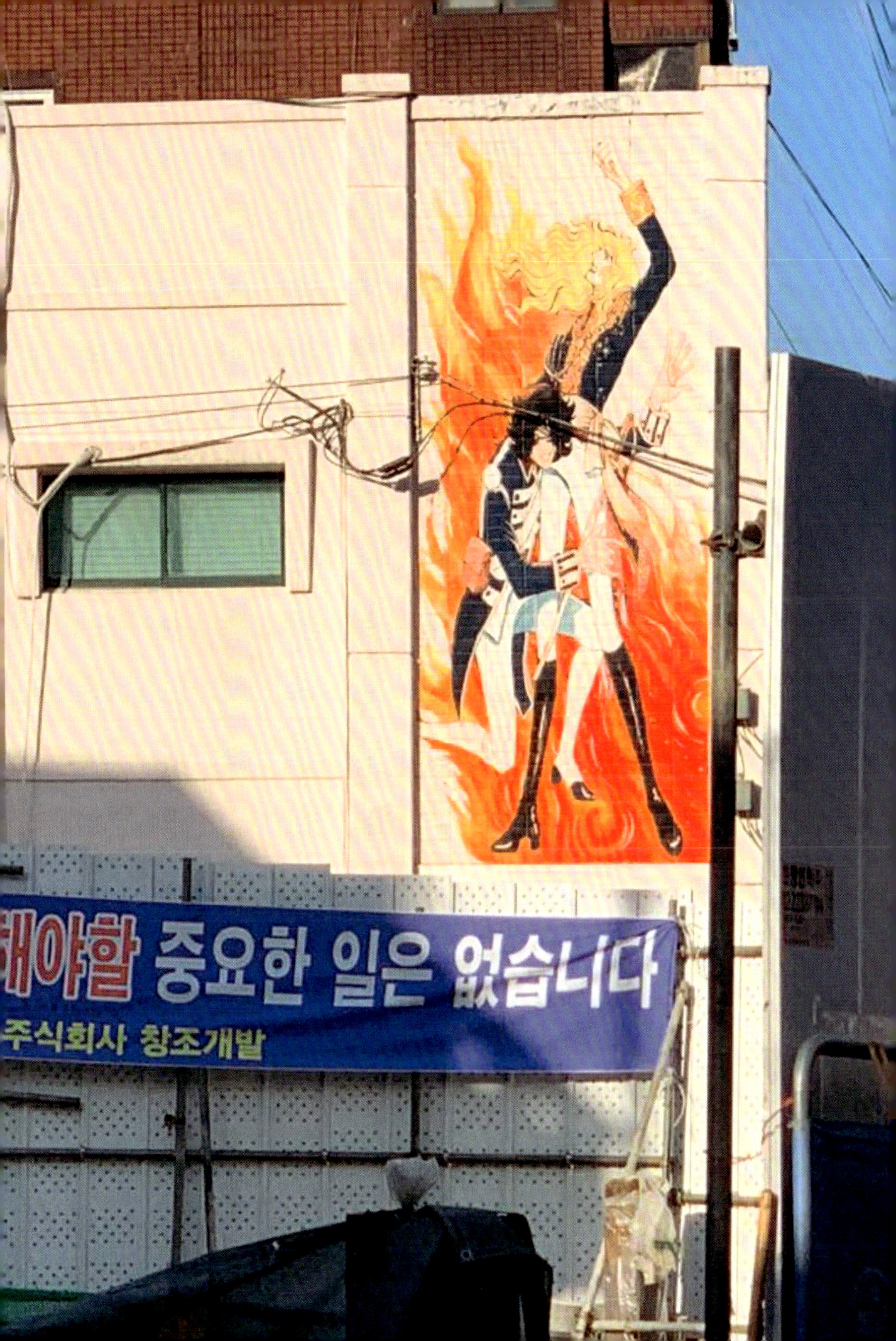
해야할 중요한 일은 없습니다
주식회사 창조개발

Below: A street in Seoul, handwriting over worn-out advertisement:
'Where will my circles go in the fourth(辰年=The Year of the
Dragon, 2024) and fifth(巳年=the Year of the Snake, 2025) year?'

Right: A broken ceramic sculpture that fell during an exhibition

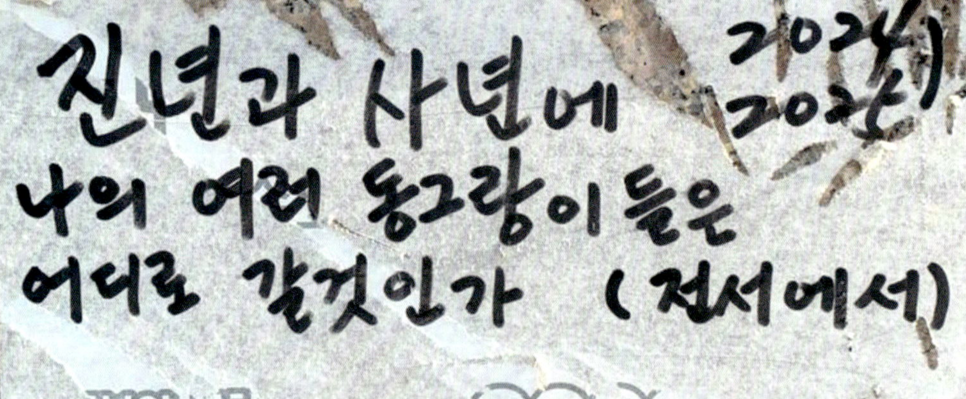

진년과 사년에 2024)
나의 여러 동그랑이들은 2025)
어디로 갈것인가 (전서에서)

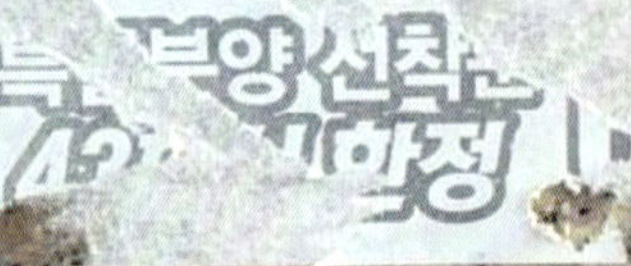

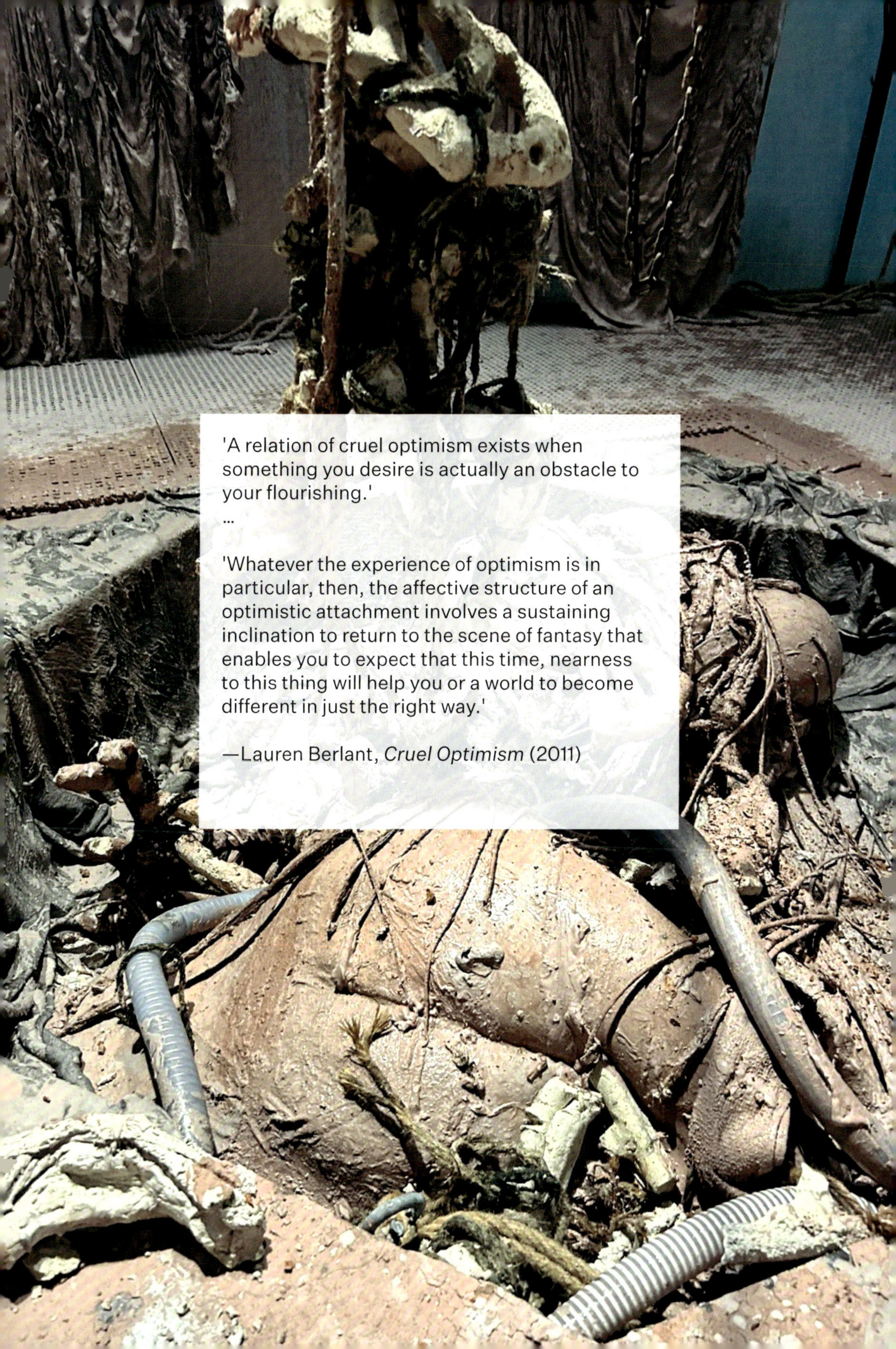

'A relation of cruel optimism exists when something you desire is actually an obstacle to your flourishing.'
…
'Whatever the experience of optimism is in particular, then, the affective structure of an optimistic attachment involves a sustaining inclination to return to the scene of fantasy that enables you to expect that this time, nearness to this thing will help you or a world to become different in just the right way.'
—Lauren Berlant, Cruel Optimism (2011)

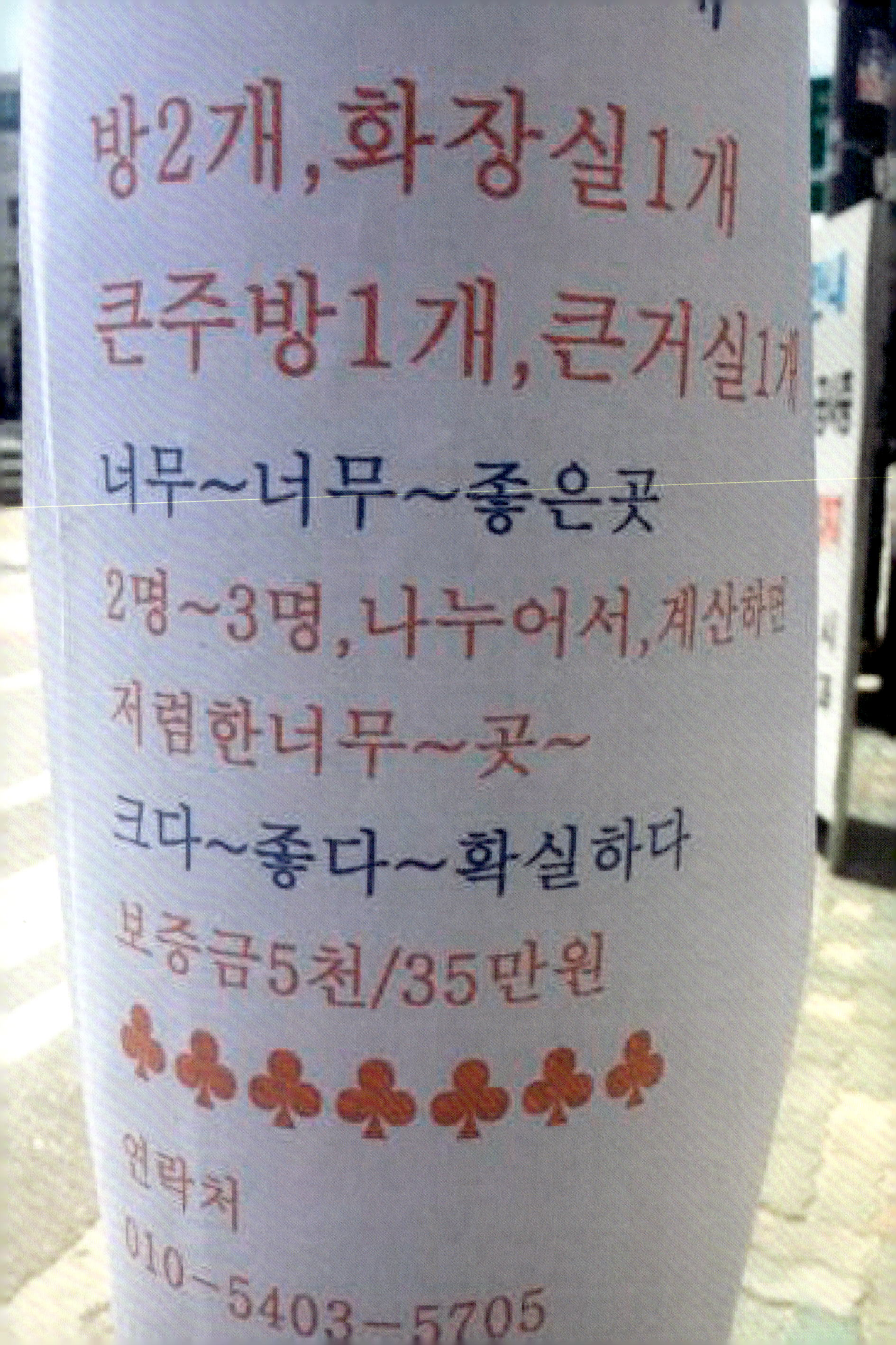

방2개,화장실1개
큰주방1개,큰거실1개
너무~너무~좋은곳
2명~3명,나누어서,계산하면
저렴한너무~곳~
크다~좋다~확실하다
보증금5천/35만원
연락처
010
-5403-5705

Rental advertisement in the street in Seoul

2 rooms, 1 bathroom, 1 large kitchen, 1 large living room
Too ~so~ nice to be true
If divided by 2 or 3 people
Too~ cheap~ place
big~good~sure
Deposit 5,000/monthly rent 350,000 won

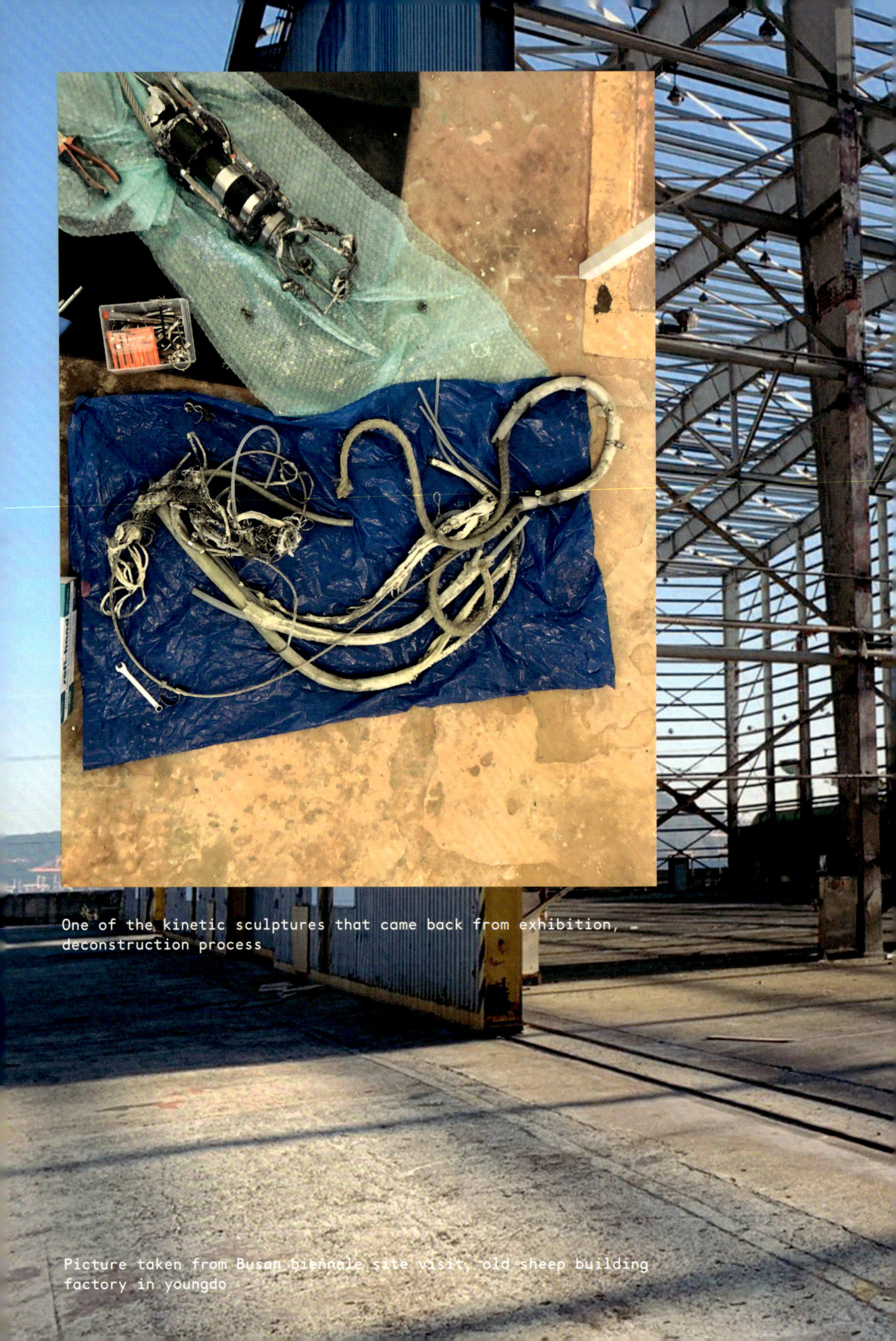

One of the kinetic sculptures that came back from exhibition, deconstruction process

Picture taken from Busan biennale site visit, old sheep building factory in youngdo

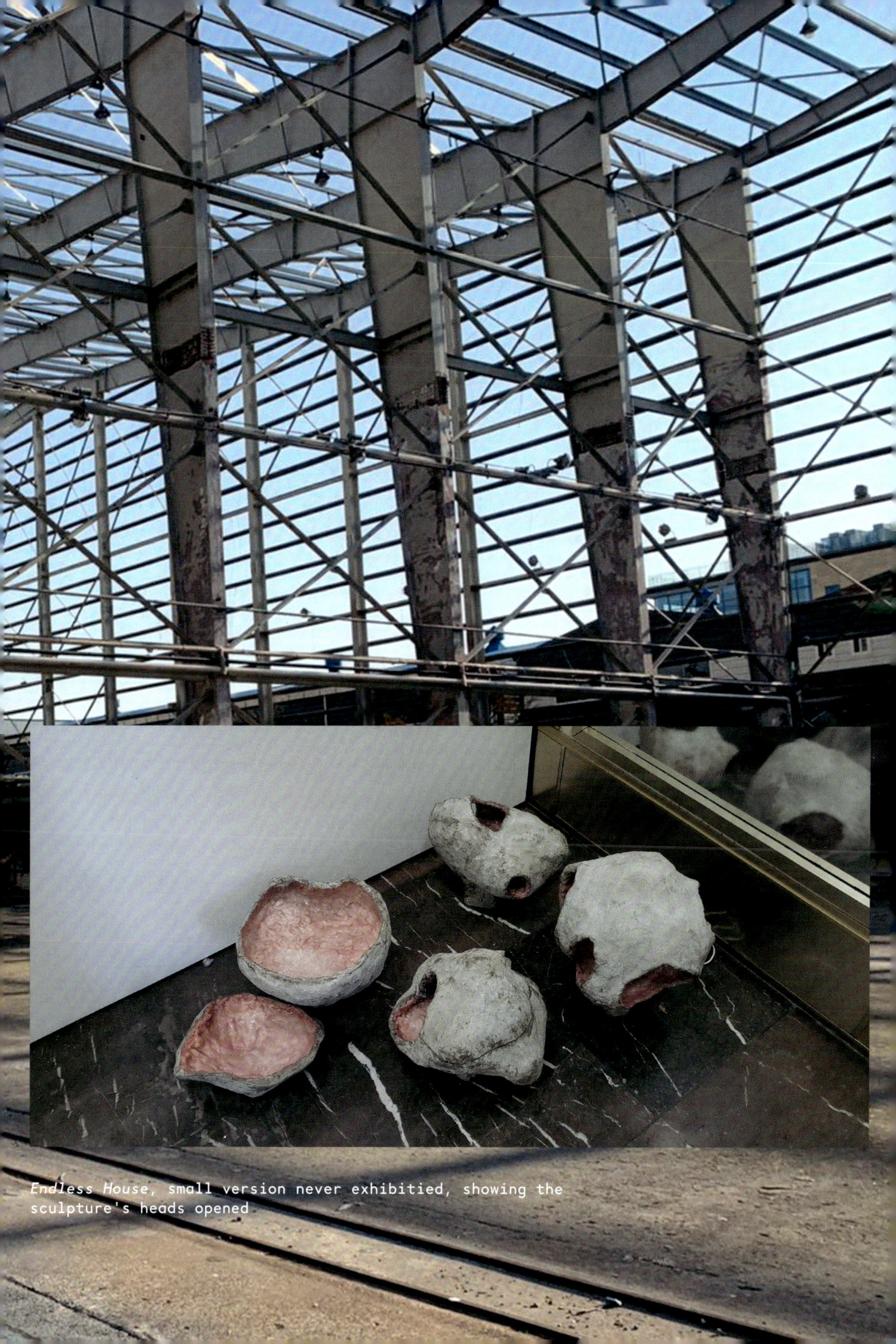

Endless House, small version never exhibitied, showing the
sculpture's heads opened

A sculpture hung outside and forgotten for months

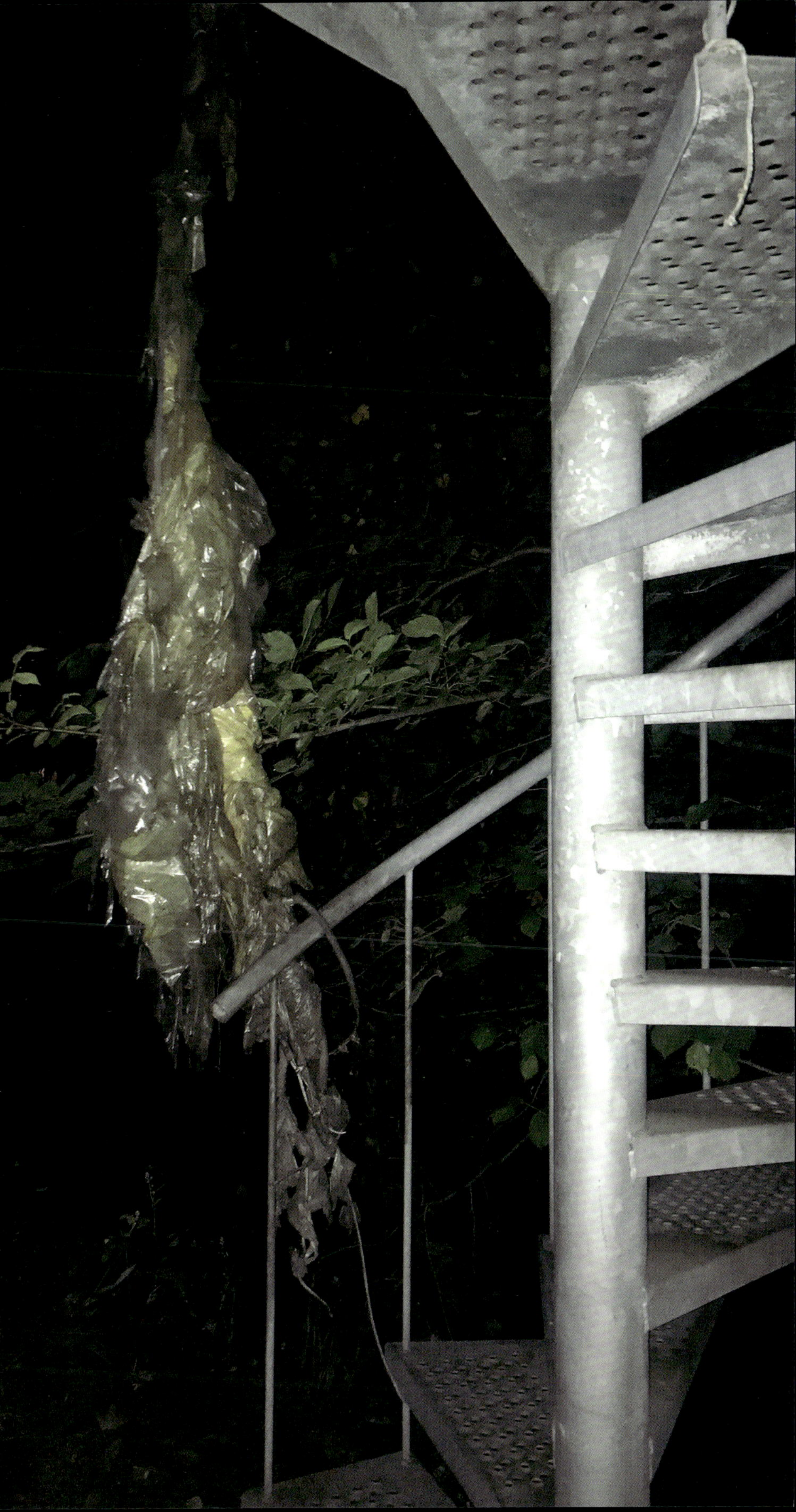

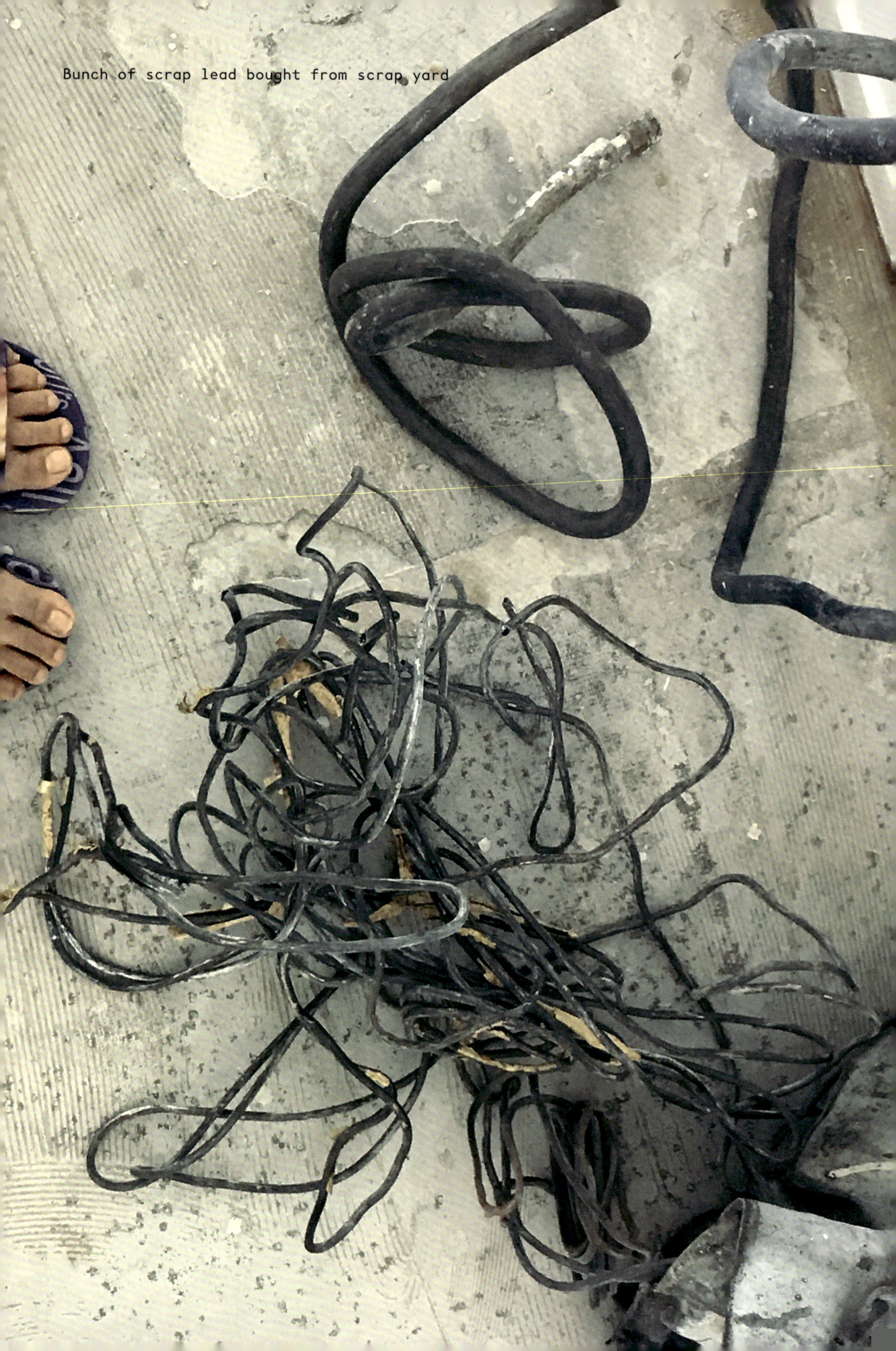
Bunch of scrap lead bought from scrap yard

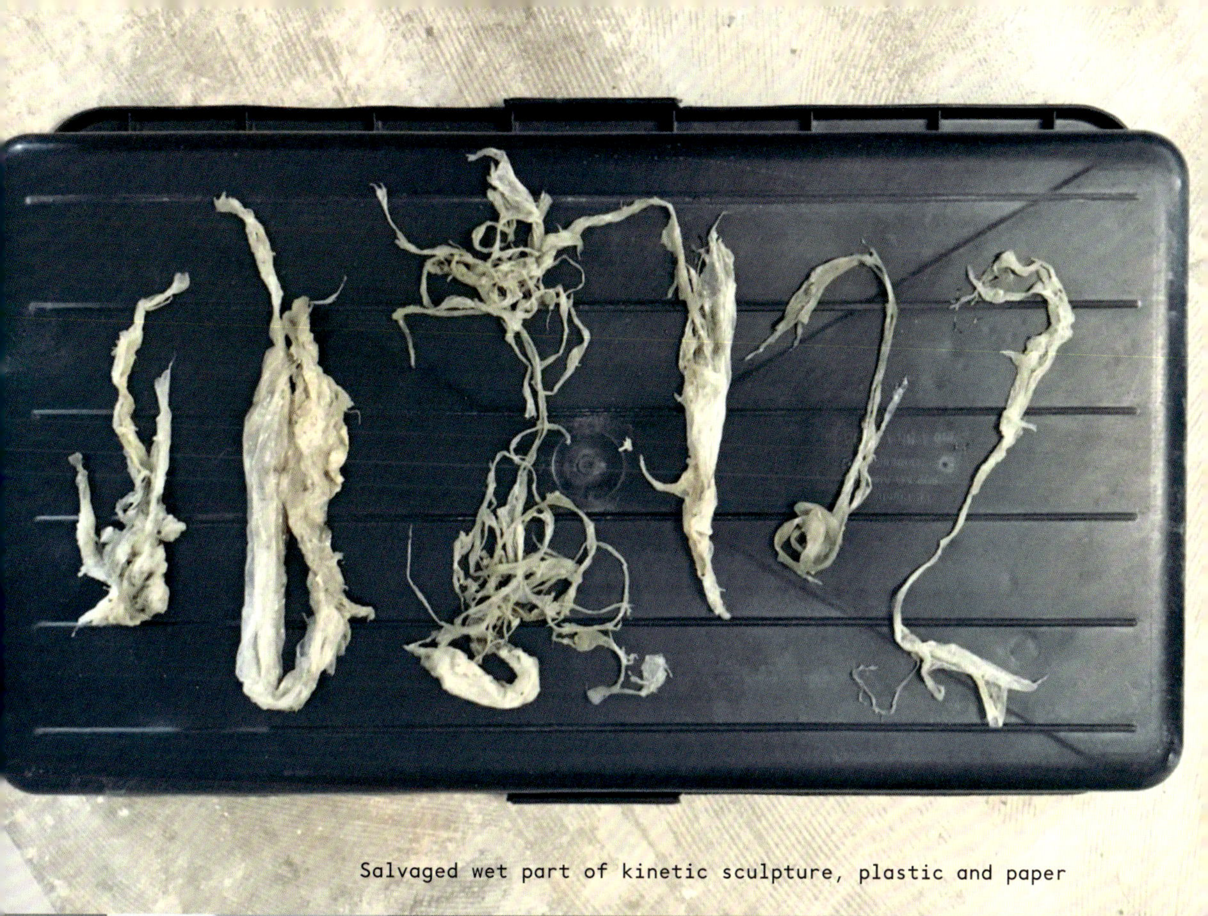

Salvaged wet part of kinetic sculpture, plastic and paper

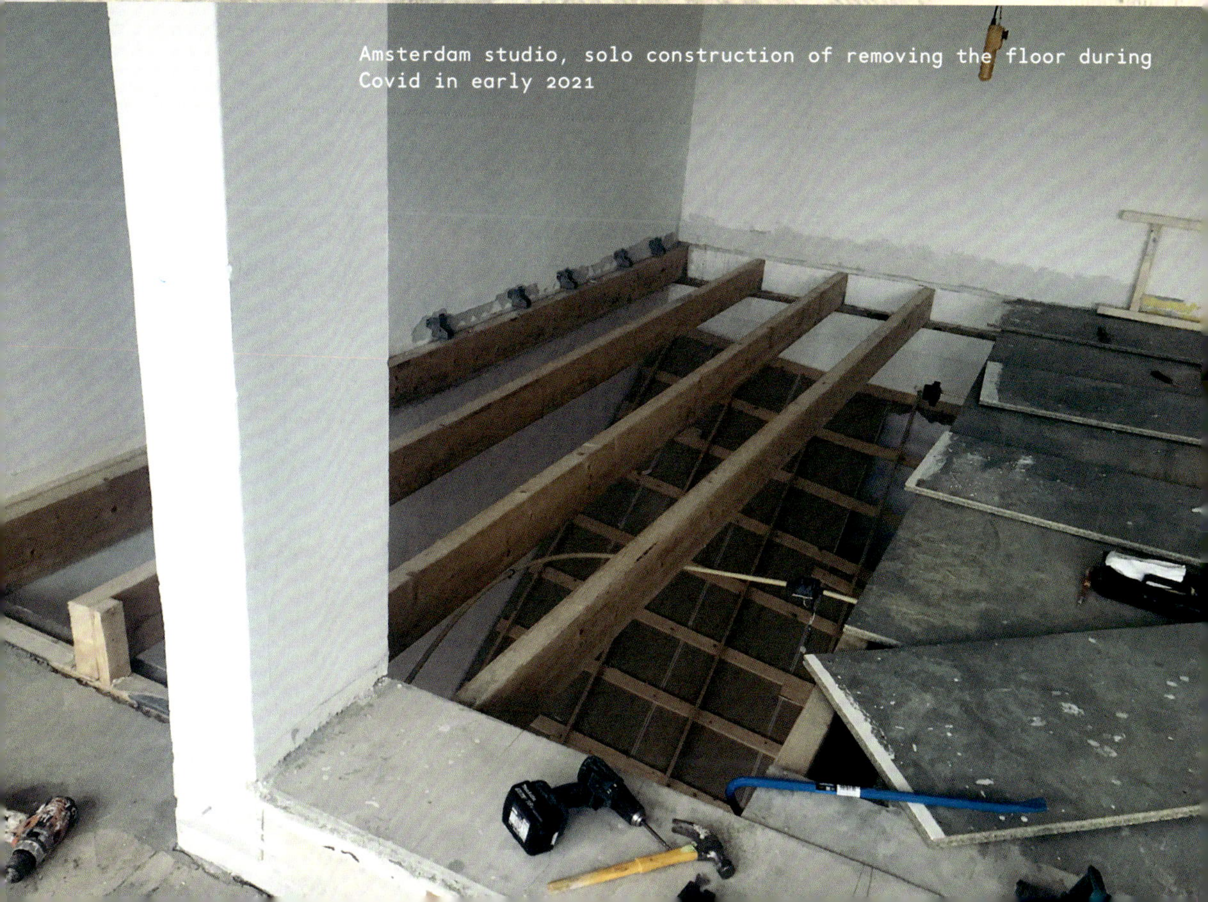

Amsterdam studio, solo construction of removing the floor during Covid in early 2021

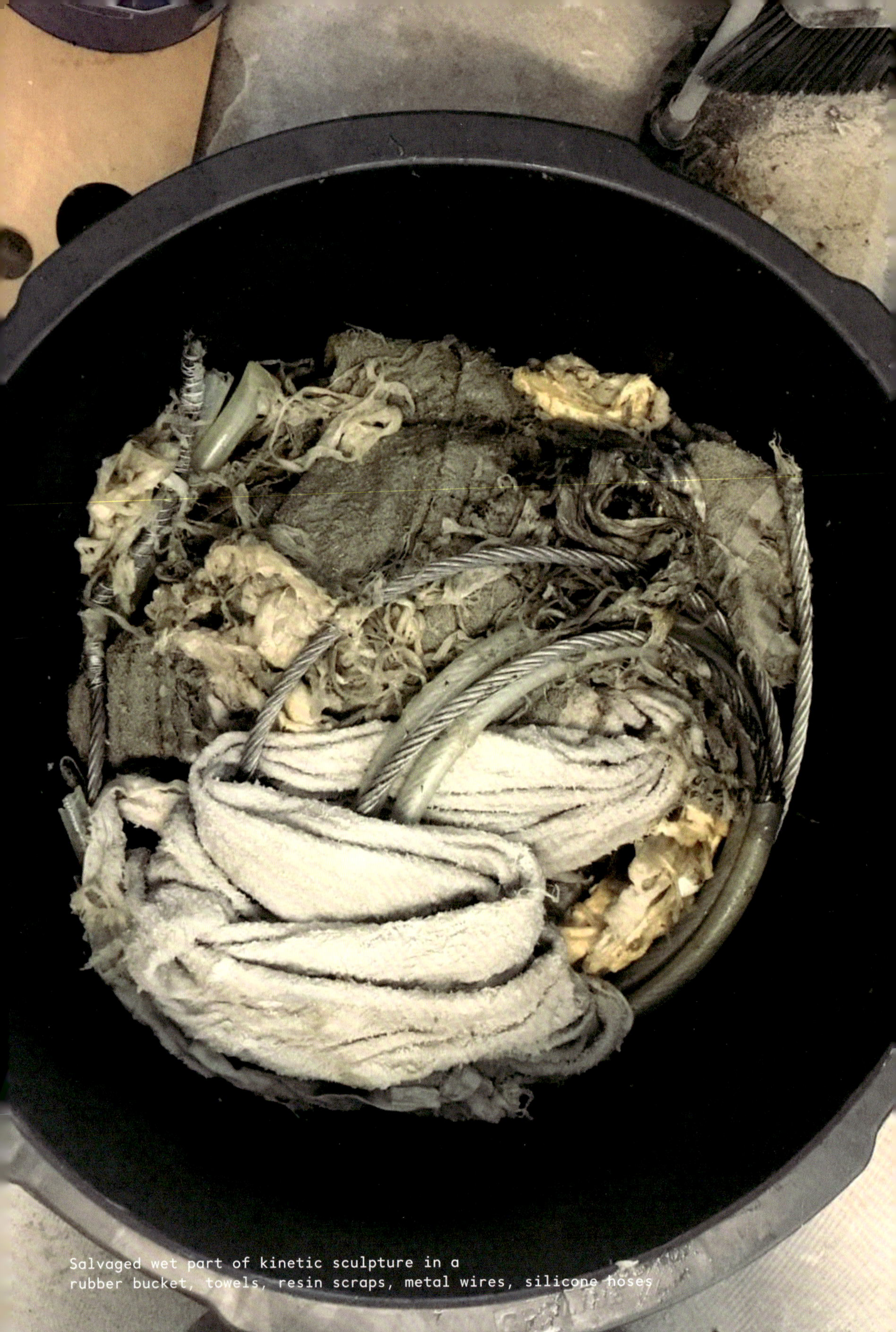

Salvaged wet part of kinetic sculpture in a
rubber bucket, towels, resin scraps, metal wires, silicone hoses

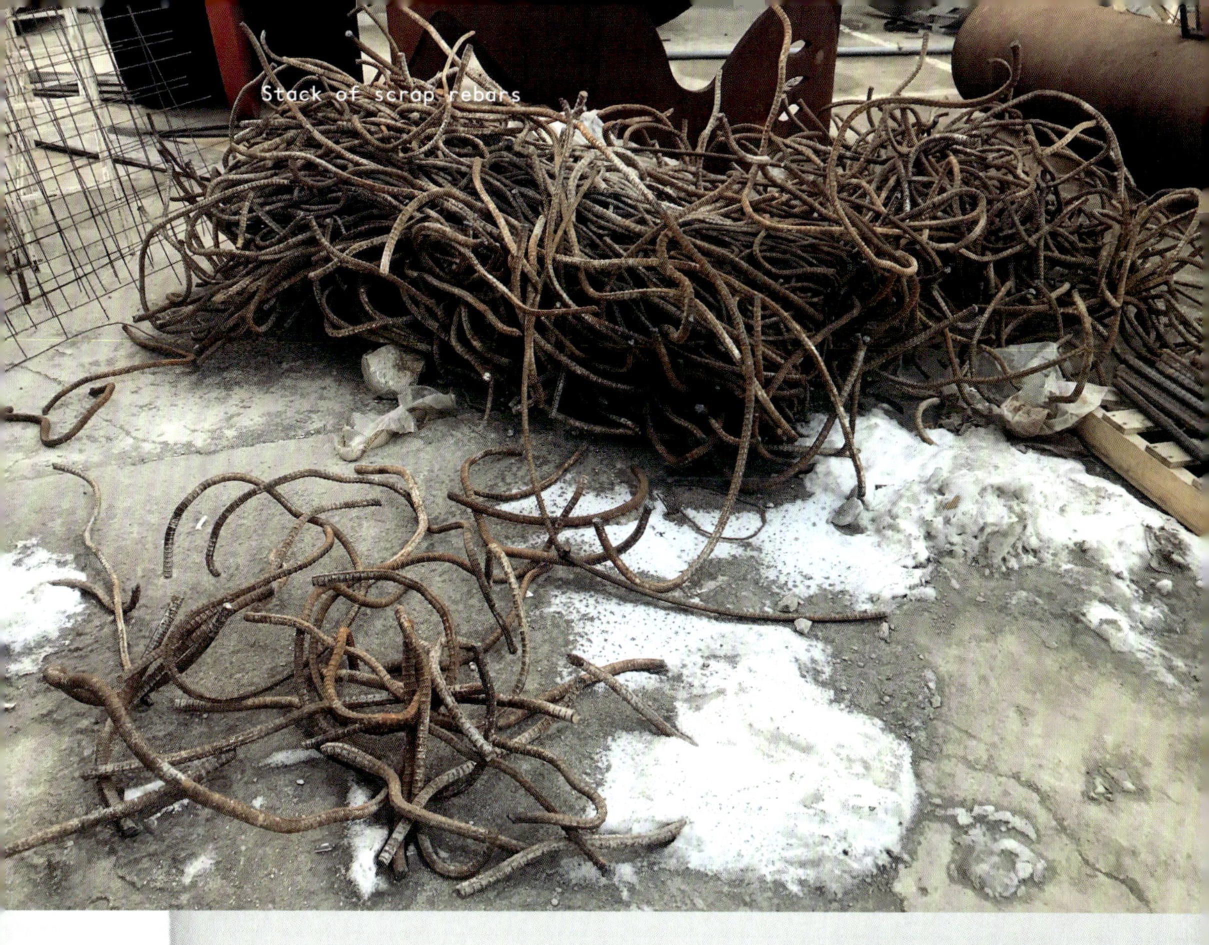

Stack of scrap rebars
strugglers
mugglers
ufferers
eee
Detail of
Babi Badalov - Casco exhibition

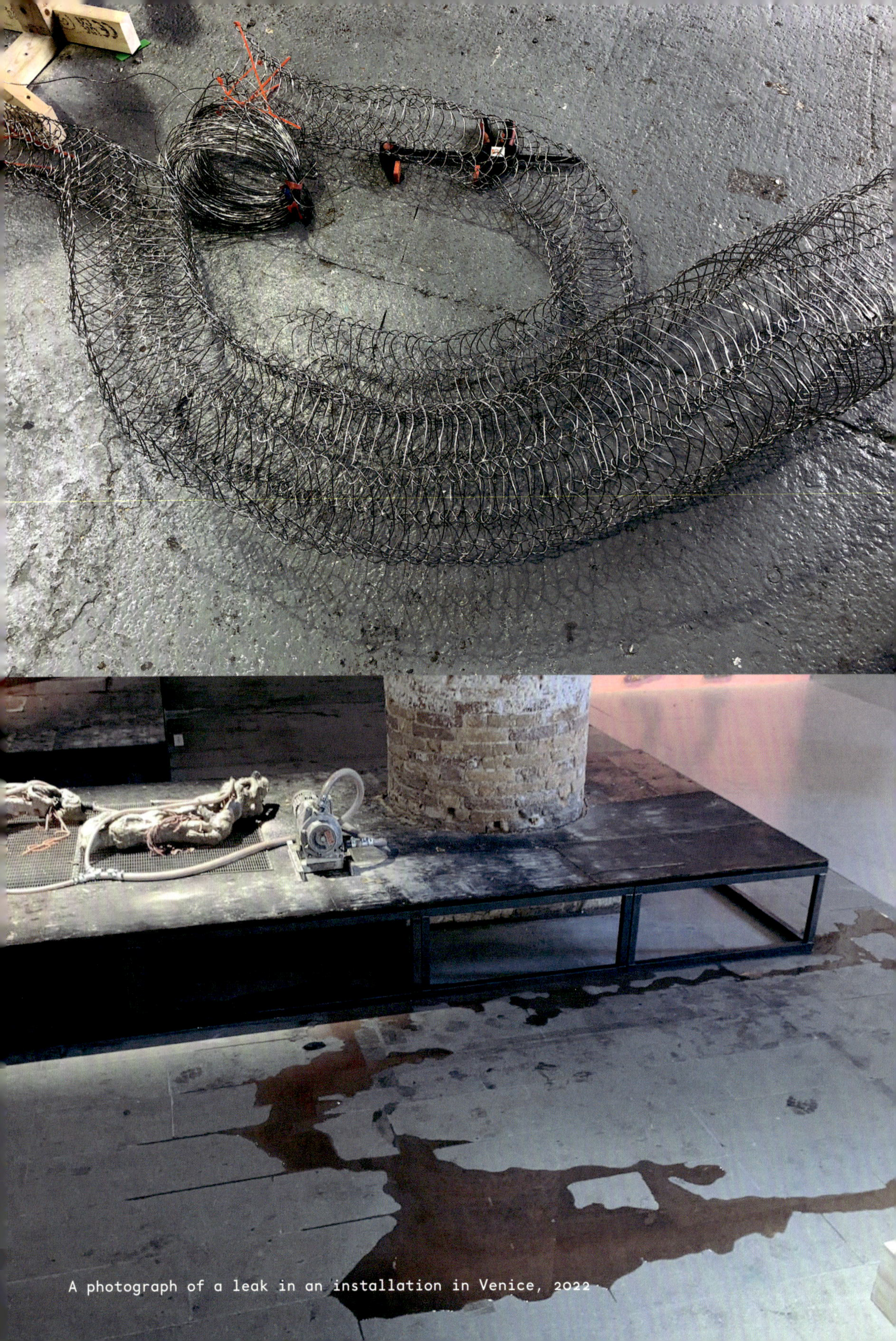

A photograph of a leak in an installation in Venice, 2022

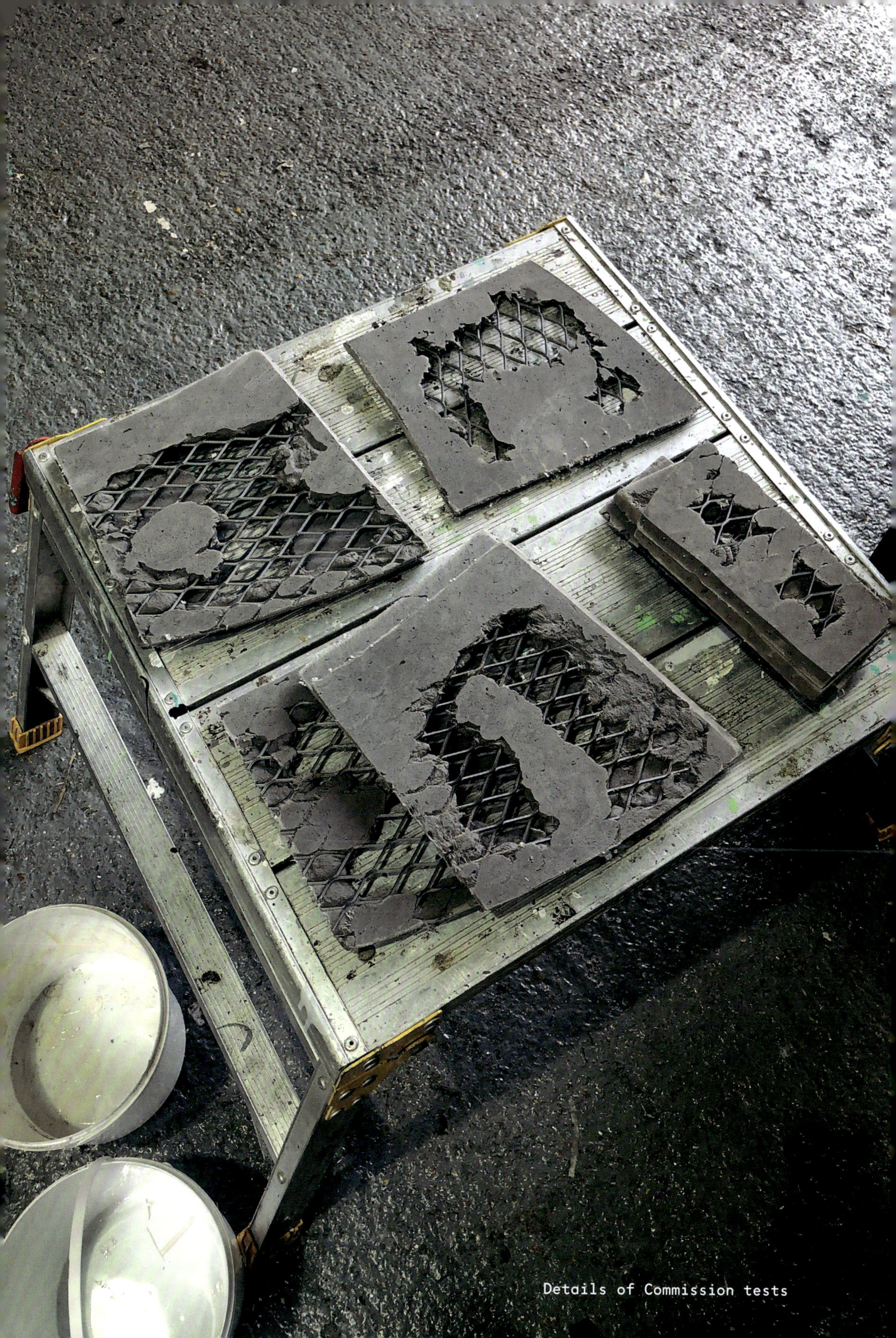

Details of Commission tests

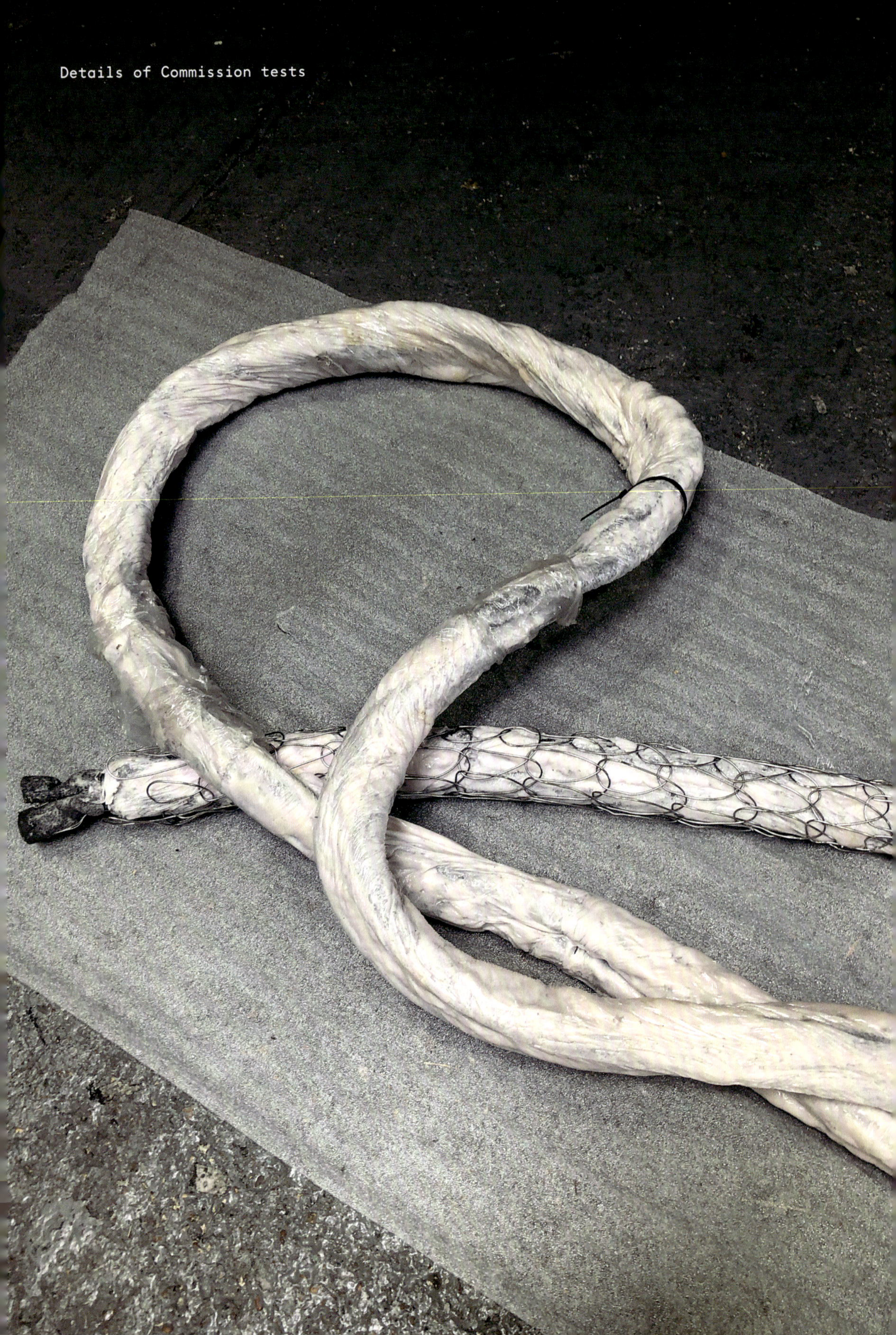

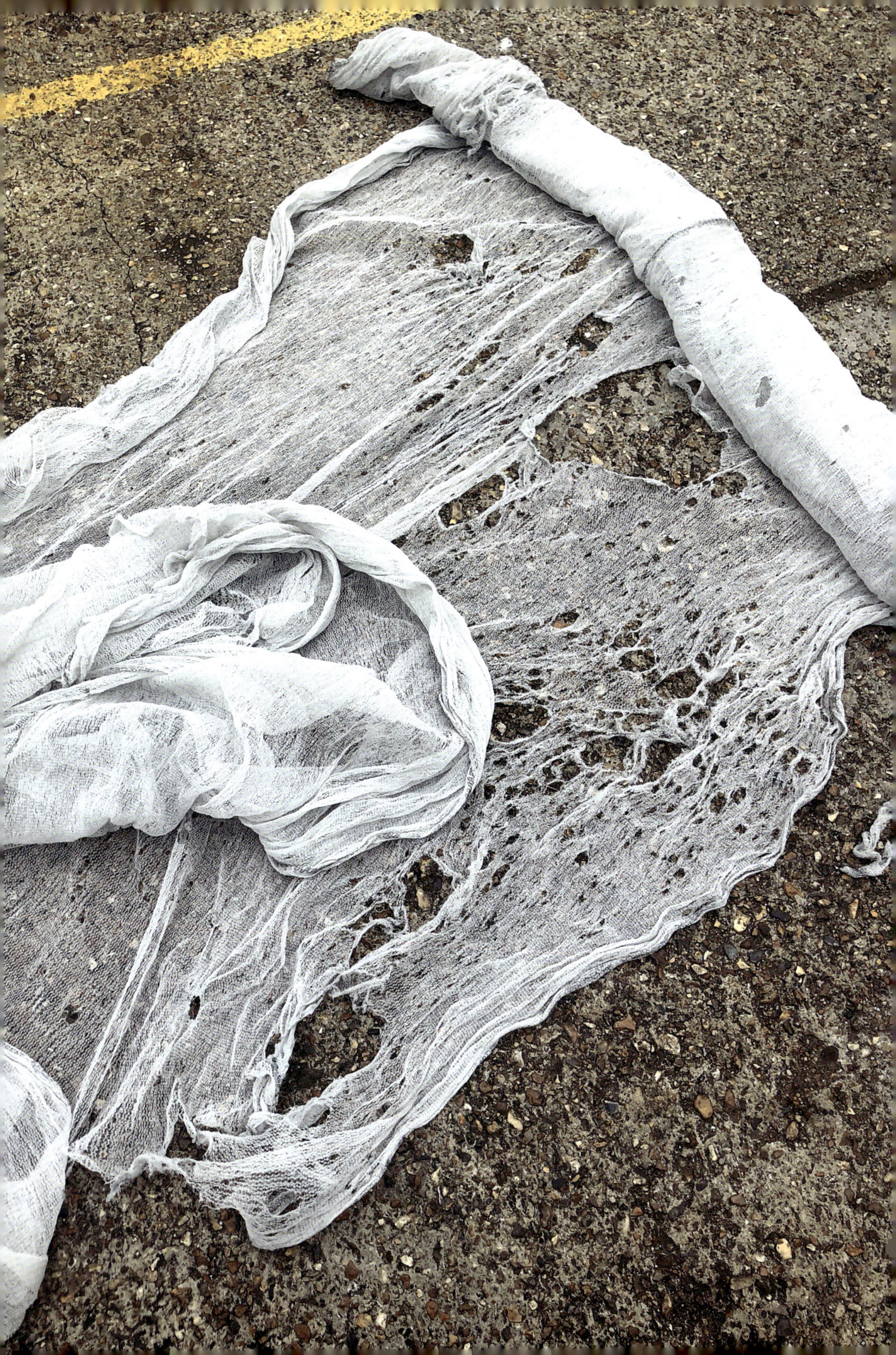

Mire Lee
in conversation with Alvin Li and Bilal Akkouche

May 2024, Tate Modern, London

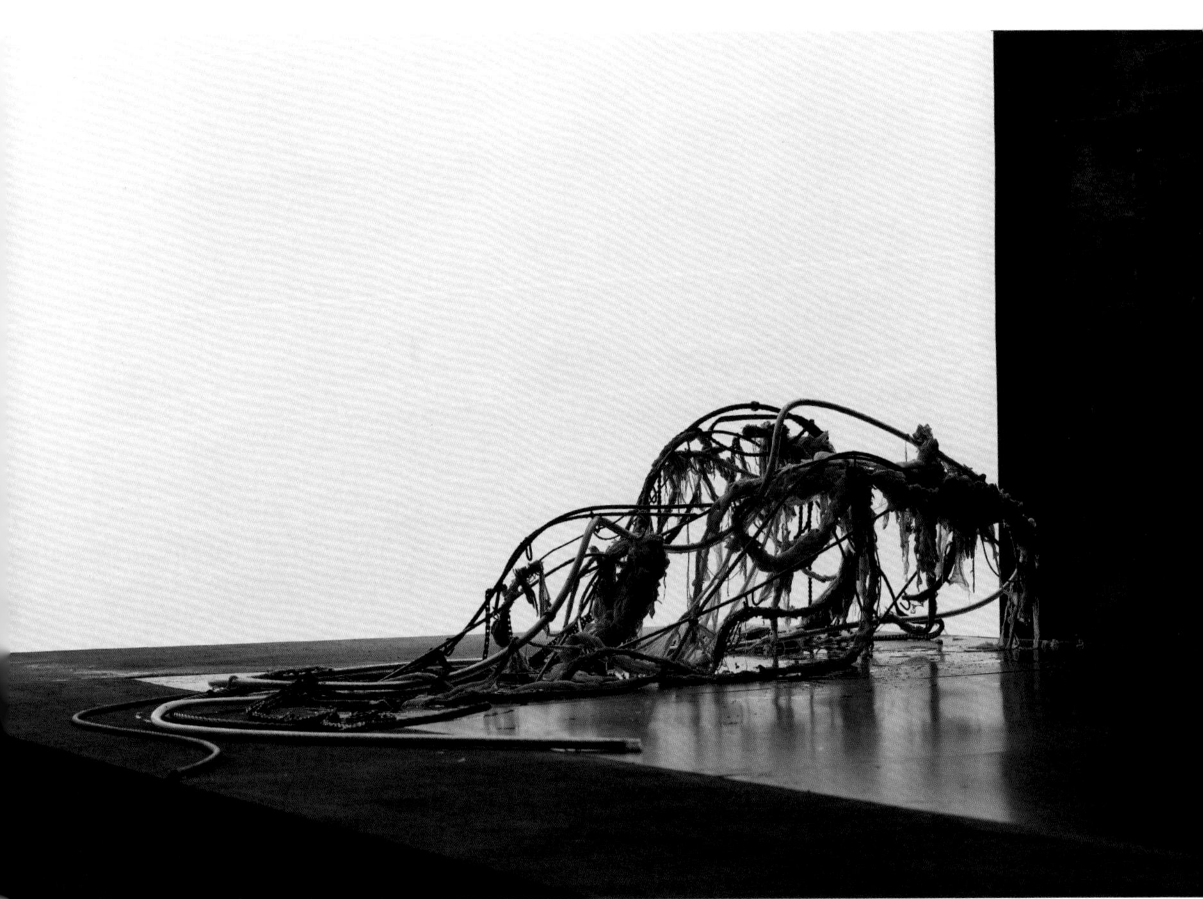

Hysteria, Elegance, Catharsis; the islands 2017 (detail); series of different
sculptures in mixed media, dimensions variable

Alvin Li: You once said you didn't want to become an artist. How did you end up studying sculpture at Seoul National University?

Mire Lee: Korea has a very competitive educational system – it's also a very brutal and rigid one. As you come to the end of school, it is as if the entire life and career ahead of you depends on just one exam, on one single day. I studied just like any other Korean student, but on the actual day of the exam, I failed at math.

I then had only a very short period of time to decide what to do. It was still possible for me to go to a good university if I applied for art – in Korea, arts students have low exam scores. On top of that, the sculpture department was the least popular. So, I decided to apply there and sit an entrance exam for art school.

Back then, Korea had a really distorted art education, which was imported from Japan, and which Japan in turn had imported from France. I think it's changed a lot now, but at the time when I sat the exam for sculpture school, you had a live model who would turn through ninety degrees, a quarter turn, every five minutes, and you'd take a bunch of clay and start making the head, same as what you see. We also had to make the head of Caesar, Brutus, Voltaire ... And I loved it. Not just that, but I was good at it. The whole system of studying in middle school and high school had been so oppressive, but touching clay and making something was genuinely a joy. I felt like I could do it forever just because it was so much fun.

AL: You took a class on kinetic art when you were studying sculpture, and something about the roughness of the technology made you realise that this might be for you.

ML: Yes. This had to do with a desire to be wild or wanting to create something that could shock myself. It was the crudity I was interested in.

There was still something that I wanted to have for myself that I felt wasn't quite possible with drawing or sculpting. I found a deep undefinable satisfaction in doing motor-related things – not because I was interested in the engineering side of it, nothing like this. It was the joy of accidental crudity I was able to create myself that got me really into machinery works.

AL: What were some of the early experiments? What did they look like? I remember you saying that for one of your sculpture graduation classes, you made a silicone mould of someone.

ML: Of myself! I made a cast of my body in silicone, and then I took it out as it was like a skin and put a motor at the back so that it would dance. I also always wanted to make big works. I was a tomboy as a kid, and I think generally a lot of this comes from growing up in a patriarchal Korean society, and how there was always a tendency to attach positive values to masculinity. And also, because my mum raised me alone, and she was a self-made woman. So, I think I always had this thing about wanting to be tough.

AL: Can you talk a little about literary or theoretical influences on your work?

ML: I used to write a lot, but when I left Korea, my life shifted into being less language-centric in general. I was no longer speaking in my mother tongue, and I wasn't writing that much, and now I'm also reading a lot less. I feel it's a disaster, really. But as a teen I read a lot of French existentialist philosophies, a lot of Sartre, and then I was very into Nietzsche and Bataille. In my twenties, through my friend Rita, I got into queer theory and affect theory – the likes of Jack Halberstam, Paul Preciado and Sianne Ngai. I also loved reading a bit of psychoanalysis. I'm very influenced by the poet Kim Eon Hee, too, and if there's one thing I'm proud of with my recent art doings it's that I think I somehow initiated a lot of conversations around Eon Hee's work.

Bilal Akkouche: Let's talk about your time in Amsterdam, where you had a residency at the Rijksakademie in 2018–19. How was it there? Were you influenced by the other artists you met on the course? And moving away from Seoul to Amsterdam, how was that transition?

ML: If I think about it now, there were so many 'first times' in Amsterdam. Something about identity politics registered with me for the first time in the diverse environment at Rijksakademie, which they spend great effort fostering by inviting artists from underrepresented parts of the world. In comparison, Korea was very homogenous. Growing up in Asia, I witnessed a lot of idealisations of Western culture and of whiteness itself. But at Rijks I think I felt this acceptance or protection, especially from fellow minority artists – a kind of solidarity. I felt like something was surrounding me, or there was some sort of blanket over me.

AL: Did you start working with liquids while at Rijks? And how was the whole process?

ML: My work with liquids started while still in Seoul. First, it came from starting to use motors in my work and the technical necessity of having to lubricate things, and from there I started to find the materiality interesting. Before coming to Rijks, I had my first big installation, *Andrea, in my mildest dreams*, at the 2016 Seoul Mediacity Biennale, in which I pumped silicone onto multiple plexiglass trays above a group of plaster sculptures and let it fall like rain. If I think about it now, Beck Jeesook, the curator of that edition, really took a risk in giving a commission of this size to such a young and unexperienced artist as I was.

AL: So, the use of kinetics and liquid happened around the same time?

ML: Yes. How I would make kinetic things in Seoul was by going to this one famous long street called Cheonggyecheon, which is part of the real, mostly ungentrified Seoul, and is full of makers and industries. In one corner you would only have rubber products, in the next you would only have bolts and nuts, then pumps and motors, and then electronics and computers. All these individual vendors, and all of them with expertise in their one small section of industry. People used to joke that if all the shop owners in Cheonggyecheon got together, they could easily build a rocket. So, what you can do is you can go there with your idea and start visiting the shops and asking the shop owners: 'How can I do this? What should I buy?' And they'll tell you where to go and what to buy. I'd go there if I had an idea and start buying things to put together. That's how I used to make kinetic or machinerybased works, and it was very, very crude. I failed a lot, and I made a lot of malfunctioning works.

BA: Could you speak a bit about your desire to utilise both soft and hard materials in your kinetic works?

ML: Firstly, since I was always trying to make largescale works, and to make big works on a low cost, I naturally deployed a lot of construction materials, which I also felt familiar with from growing up in Seoul.

In addition, I was always interested in eroticism, or, should I say, pornographic materials in general. So, it was a good match when I started to use lubricant or a kind of liquid.

I also loved working with liquid because it was such a technical challenge all the time. As a sculptor, the first thing you need is a firm grip. As soon as you have a little bit of slime on your hand, everything starts slipping out. So, the labour

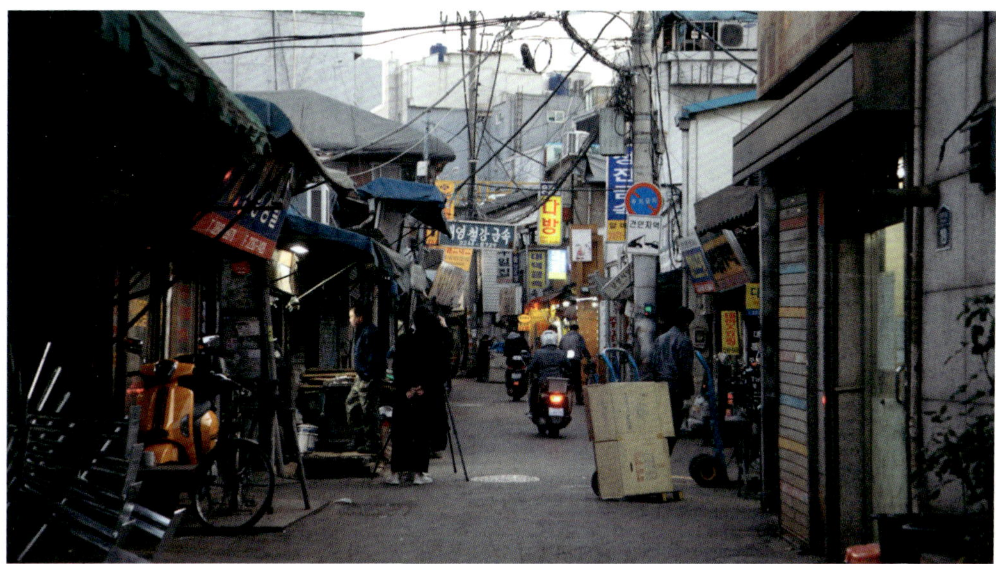

Yipjeong-dong Alley, Cheonggyecheon Street, Seoul

process becomes stupid and counterintuitive, which of course is the main purpose of lubricant – it sets things free from being firmly held. It was annoying at first, but I eventually grew attached to this base struggle.

BA: You clearly enjoy that idea of testing yourself with different materials, trying to find solutions or working through things. It sounds like that process is very much integral to your work, the selection of a more difficult option in relation to materials, one that will take more time to perfect – or maybe not even perfect, but for it to work in some capacity.

AL: And it sounds like there is a degree of submission, or masochism, involved. To step outside one's subjectivity.

ML: It's a little bit like this: sculpture making, or making itself, is really a comfort zone for me. Working with your hands and body has this quality of letting you forget all the other things, because in the process there is a non-linguistic chaos and then a following harmony, within which you can blissfully submerge yourself. It's always also an escape zone. When it comes to my own projects, I sometimes suspect I tend to come up with ideas that would obviously cause lots of problems because the prospect of solving them gives me a sense of purpose and comfort.

I've always thought I'm not very curious, as a person. I think I'm more 'thirsty' than curious. Curiosity is cerebral: you want to know how this works, and you want to take it apart and see inside it. I've never had this kind of impulse. For me, it was always more a feeling like waiting for something that could shake me, even if I couldn't really tell what it would. I notice people tend to think I'm a very technical or scientific person, but I'm not at all.

BA: Can you talk a little about the mixture of intentionality and the accidental in your practice? In some of your sculptures, you're utilising so many different materials at the same time that, a lot of the time, you

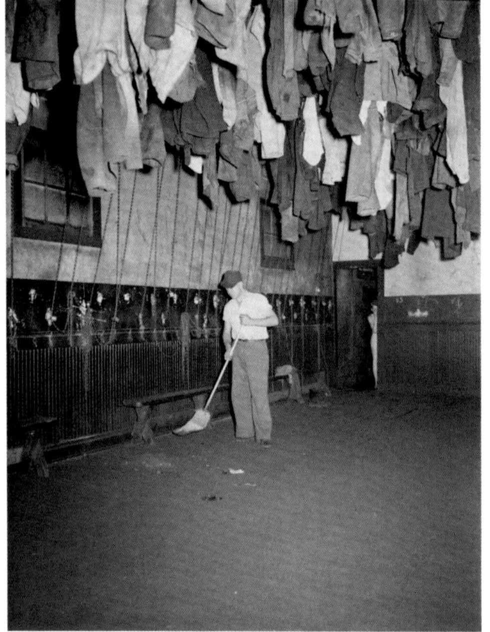

Changing room in the washhouse for white miners, Southern Coal Corporation, Bradshaw Mine, Bradshaw, McDowell County, West Virginia

can't actually control every aspect – I'm thinking, for example, of the smell in some of your installations, which is not something you can control or even want to control. You also spoke before about failure and incorporating that into your practice.

ML: More and more I really like this quality of the unpredictable. I wouldn't even say it's about art – I think it's maybe something to do with ageing, because I think you're less and less surprised as you get older. Artmaking is a very domesticated version of the unpredictable – so, it doesn't matter if my liquid is blue, brown, green. But in general, I'm interested in being submissive to something I didn't plan for, and I want to pursue that, I think, in an overall way, not just in making.

AL: Can you share how your ideas for the Turbine Hall evolved into the final proposal?

ML: The very first proposal involved a lot of scaffolding, as well as getting rid of the bridge in the middle. I had an idea that the space could be like the inside of a body of a big machine or a big creature, which made me think of scaffolding as a skeleton. And then I also liked the spatiality of the Turbine Hall, which is already an interior, but more like that of an animal, because a person stands erect, and animal's body is horizontal.

I started thinking about it as an industrial womb – something at once both animalistic and industrial, all heavy steel and metal. Gestating, the womb would produce skin-like matters that gradually fill the space, in the air.

The first problem was: how to keep them in the air? I thought about using scaffolds –something I've used before – to hang the skins. Then my technical advisor Stephan Kudernas, who I met at Rijks, saw the drawings and sketches and introduced me to the design of miners' changing rooms, where wet clothes would be hoisted upwards on pulleys to dry out. That vertical movement felt like a perfect reference point. At the same time, you and I were talking, Alvin, about the performativity of my practice, which you observed as something important in my work over time but which has remained unexplored. So, we became interested in tipping the balance to spotlight that performativity by bringing the production and maintenance actions out into the Turbine Hall, and then by spreading the hanging of the skin sculptures throughout the exhibition period to add another durational, live element.

The whole process was very exciting. I really love working with limitations of materiality or architectural quality, and I really like to adapt and change.

BA: I am really interested in you talking about the performative aspect or the durational aspect, since this will be the first time that you place that aspect front and centre, rather than in the periphery. It augments what I find so unique in your work, which is its need for the human touch to maintain itself, or for the work to continue. It is also as if you want to be able to continue working on it, even in the space, during the exhibition. Where does that desire to create a work that needs that kind of care come from?

ML: On one hand, it's something to do with the laborious process of my practice. I never really come up with an idea unless I'm working. The process itself is the work for me – not the finishing or displaying of the work. For this project, considering the Turbine Hall is such a big stage, I also like how the durational component disrupts the monumentality. Intuitively it's very against my nature not to have the final work in its most impressive light when it is unveiled, but now I believe it comforts me and balances its completeness.

BA: Could you speak more about the notion of machine as body in relation to some of the working parts that we'll

see in the commission?

ML: What I am interested in machines is human emotions, dreams and affects around the machine as well as the stupidity of machines and humans, and finally nostalgia and melancholia around technology.

In this sense, I'm more interested in old-school machines – those very robust machines whose shape has a direct resemblance that lets you see its function. The structure of the peristaltic pump, for instance, resembles an intestine, because it works in a similar way to animal guts, and so it has the U-shaped hose part which pushes the substance in and discharges. So, from what it looks like, you can perhaps guess what a machine does. It's almost like when some birds have a long beak because they eat from a certain shape of plant. The shape and the function are interrelated.

But that kind of relationship between appearance and functionality is more characteristic of modern, old-school machines, whereas nowadays our contemporary devices are minimal and more geometrical. Oftentimes, you don't know what a device does – it's just a flat oval, a sleek shape. What I've always liked, then, is the kind of machine that cannot hide because it's doing such a robust physical activity. And then those machines, I think, inevitably resemble a body, or parts of a body – when we look at our bodies and see that our organs look like this because they must digest, or food must pass through them and so on.

BA: That makes me think how insane it would be if we humans saw each other as our body parts, underneath the skin – how in awe of each other's structure we would be. And in fact, your work kind of exposes those inner makings that we're so conditioned to cover up. Not only are our body parts covered by skin, but what's perceived as best design for laptops, phones, new technology is how well hidden the functioning parts are. So, in a way, your work is beautiful in the sense that it opens our minds to thinking around the inner working of things.

AL: Or how they don't work, be it a body, a machine or a system. Your work often evokes a kind of inertia, stagnation or breaking down. Systemic glitches.

ML: I think this inertia is related to my interest in melancholia and nostalgia. It is also about the time of decline – after the heyday of Fordism or industrialism, for instance – or the mood of a deserted construction site, or of a planned city like Chandigarh or Brasília. It's not just the idea of emptiness, but also of futility, when something has started to wither.

AL: And yet, from the very beginning, you were interested in the commission being in a state of becoming. It nods to Turbine Hall's industrial past, while also raising questions about the productive capacities (or lack thereof) of the museum, or our current system at large. Can you speak a little about your decision to activate this symbolically charged space as a site of labour and production?

ML: When we see something monumental, I believe we also subconsciously experience the violence that lies behind its creation. We somehow feel how much effort the workers have made, and how as individuals they become anonymous, absorbed into the collective of executing this monumental project, especially in relation to an existence of the master behind the plan – an architect, artist, a dictator ... I think this is a part of why monumentality makes us emotional. It took me some time to realise the significance of this sentimentality to me, and the desire to make monumental works, which I had all along, is more about evoking this melancholia than creating a spectacle.

AL: I guess the sense of violence you're describing is also revealed by the suspended skins, these not-yet-human half-

forms. Can you say a little bit more about your thoughts around the skin? I'm also curious why you think of them as skins instead of flesh.

ML: In my work I've thought a lot about the threshold between what is considered normal and acceptable, and what is deemed disabled, deformed or grotesque. I've always been interested in skin because it is something that registers otherness. In this case, given the project's architectural indebtedness to the design of miners' changing rooms, the skins are also about the tension between individuality and collectivity.

BA: Yes, there's something very personal to them: the changing room was a place of safety, and you were able to use your own locking key and lift things up out of the reach of other people.

ML: It reminds me a little bit of how students or soldiers who must wear uniforms make little changes to the uniforms to be more unique.

BA: At the same time, like you said, it was also a space, in a sense, of solidarity or collectiveness. I like the idea that, at times, you leave behind your individuality before you take part in labour.

ML: Yes. I find that to be heartbreaking but at the same time beautiful about industrial labour.

BA: Speaking of the beauty of heartbreak and tragedy, do you mind telling us about your fascination with the idea of the expensive gift?

ML: It is about realising that the desire to give your loved one as expensive a present as possible is something not superficial, but actually one of the most genuine things that you can do in our capitalist society. It really hurts to spend a lot of money, that's what makes the expensive gift an expression of love. This is very tragic, of course.

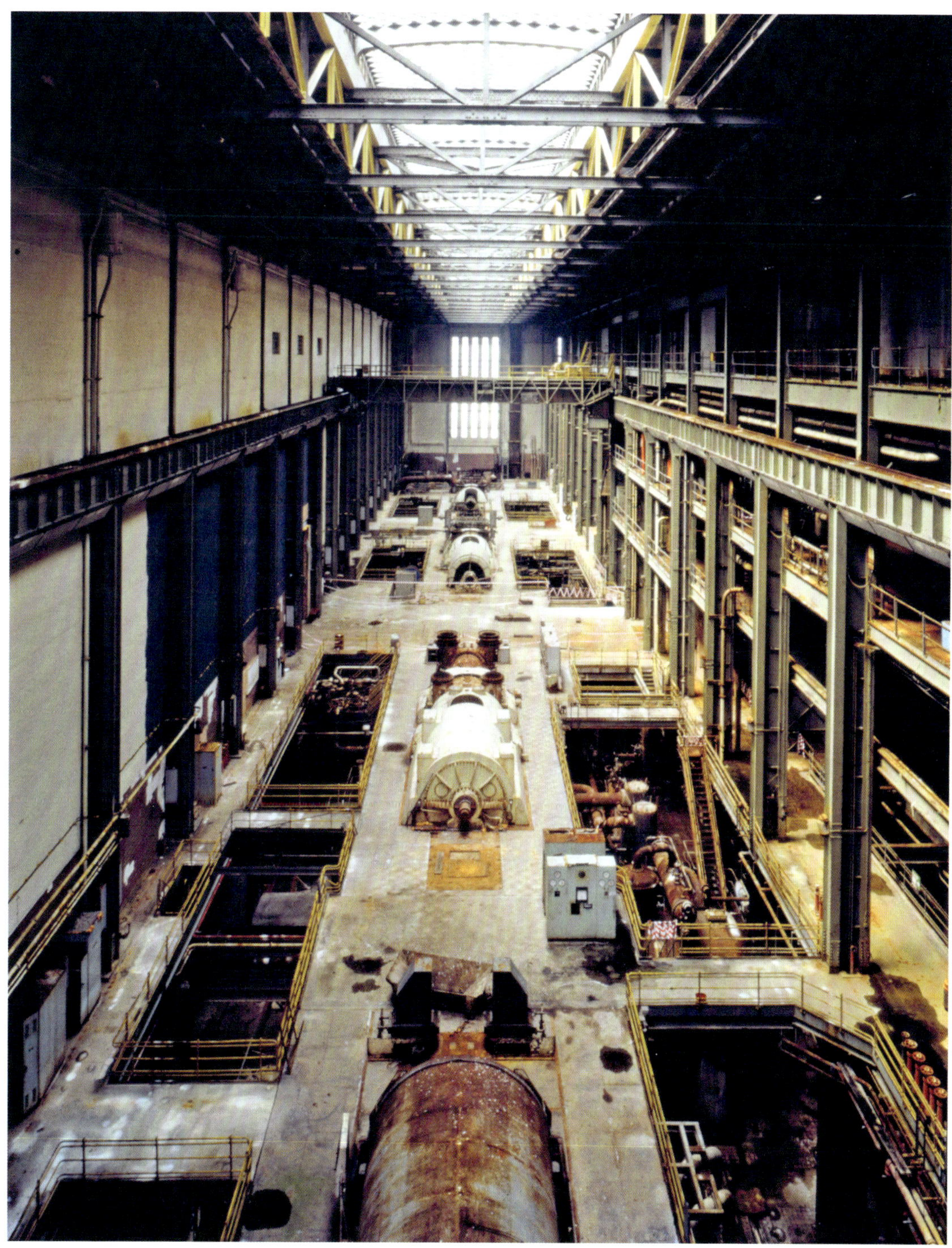

The Turbine Hall before the power station was transformed into
Tate Modern

What's more tragic is the story Mark Fisher tells in *Capitalist Realism* about the owner of the cheap jewellery brand who made a joke about how their product was actually 'total crap', and then their brand just collapsed. Because everybody knows it's trash, but it's the only kind of jewellery that poor people can afford, and when you give it to your loved one, they know it's trash too but it's still so good. It's like a shared consciousness – we've all collectively just decided to pretend it's not trash. But then if someone reveals it, breaks the spell of the open secret, then it's over. That whole story left a deep impression on me, because I think this shared belief, this shared consciousness, works in a very similar way with the expensive gift, too. It's a very strong or intense human impulse to build this collective idea of value together. It doesn't solve a problem or bring about a change, and yet I think that shared consciousness, elevates us or transforms us. And I think that's what art can do, too.

Where I'm going with the expensive gift story may be that while dreaming itself is a universal thing, something raw and infinite and unlimited, everyone's dream is dressed and shaped in class and where they belong to. It's shaped, in other words, by their limitations.

AL: It's important, I think, to see Mark Fisher's anecdote as a remark on the importance of self-narrativisation or fictionalisation for living with precarity and disparity. Looking this brutality of inequality right in the eye could be so crushing that there would be no way for us to live on.

You once mentioned that ultimately you would like the visitors to the commission to experience a sense of warmth and hope in the face of this uncanny spectacle, by experiencing it through a kind of veil, this collective fantasy. That's really the beauty, as well as horror, of the work.

ML: Ultimately, I guess, aesthetic experience for me is when something moves me, or when something shakes me. I think an experience of being moved is the strongest thing you can have by looking at art or experiencing art. And I think I'm naturally drawn to witnessing a human, an individual life, getting caught in a larger system.

AL: I guess that's where the openness of the work becomes so important. Your work is definitely not centred around critique and it's not exactly about empowerment. It's like this open space, it's amplifying this feeling. It may be liberating, but it could also feel unsafe.

ML: Yes. I often think about the idea of an 'open wound': a wound that never closes, meaning the subject forever lives with it. For me, this is similar to how we experience art. As a metaphor, it also allows us to think about art's power to effect change. For me, it's not about whether the artist can or cannot do anything – it's more about the wound being ever-present and hurting.

AL: What you're saying seems to touch on an ontological question. The artwork outlives the artist, and its meaning cannot be exhausted, nor fixed to a particular space and time. In his latest book Art's Properties, *David Joselit pinpoints this 'experiential inexhaustibility over time' as art's 'ontological alterity'.*

ML: I haven't read that book, but that description definitely resonates with me. As I continue to develop my work and meet different publics, I find myself coming to terms with the mechanism of how art develops and stays with an audience. The kind of change that art can bring about is quite particular, because it doesn't happen in just a second. It takes time, often over multiple encounters, but when it that change does occur, it's incredibly powerful and it changes you forever. One artist that I feel this way about is Nan Goldin. It took me almost fifteen years of witnessing how she presents her life experience inside the museum

Installation view of *Endless House: Holes and Drips* 2022, Venice Biennale 2022: The Milk of Dreams

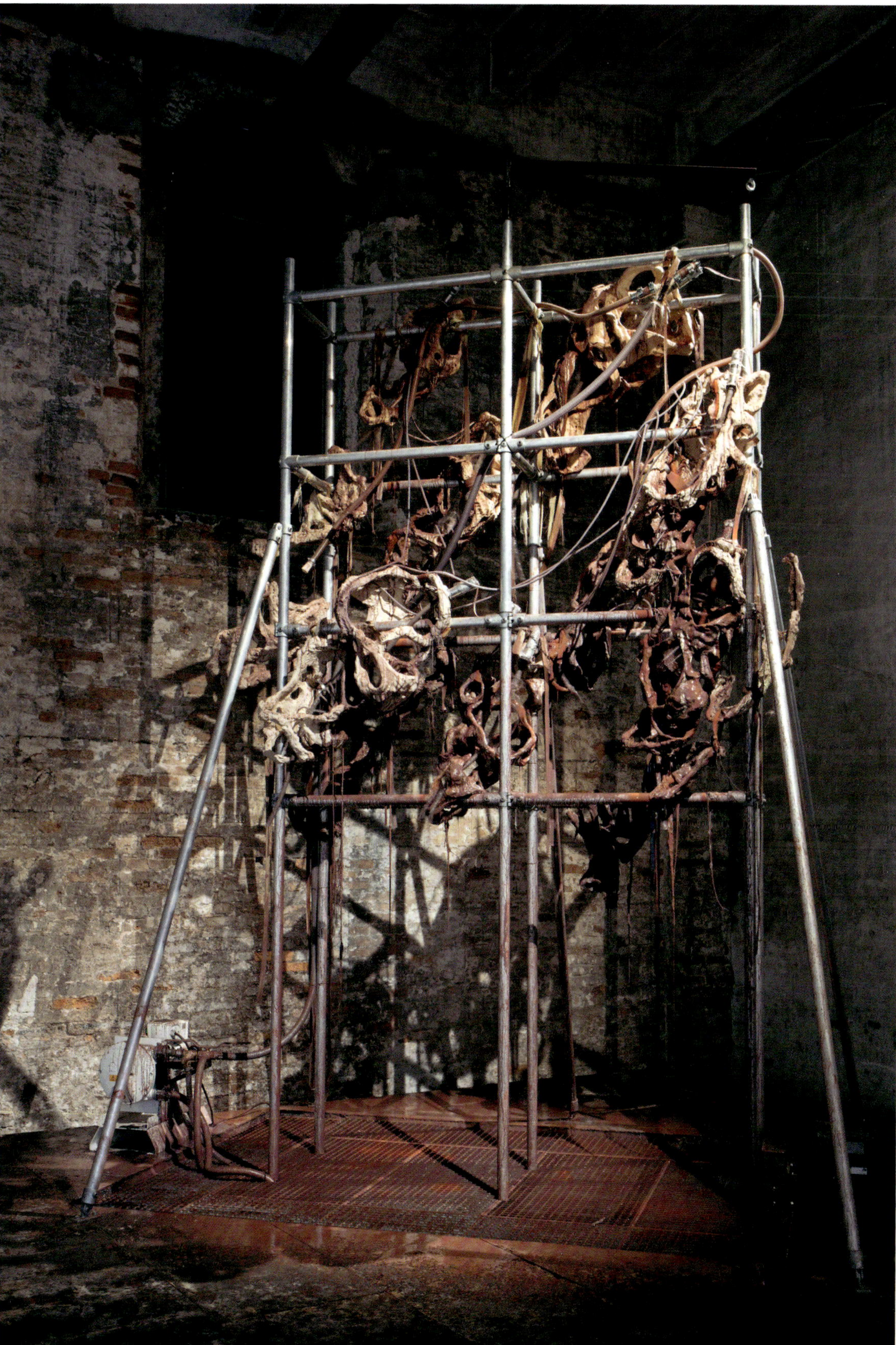

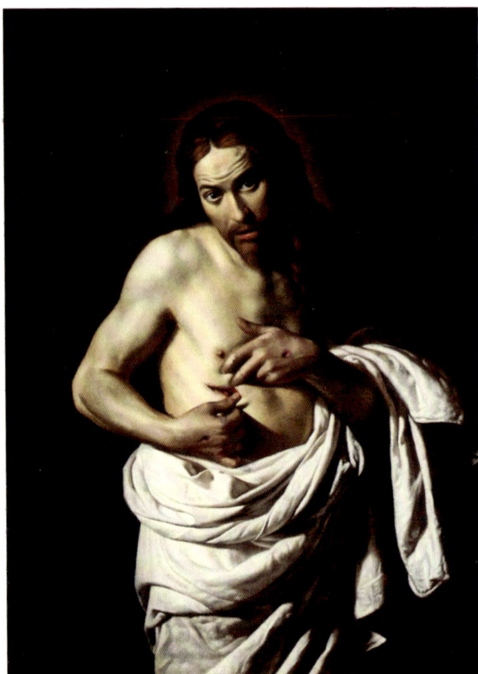

Giovanni Antonio Galli, *Christ Displaying His Wounds* c.1630;
oil paint on canvas, 132 × 99

and beyond before I felt that moment of change in
me, and it has had a profound impact on me. And
this experience might continue to evolve.

Another thing I love about the 'open wound'
metaphor is that moment of injury. Say you're
working with a knife and you have an accident,
you cut yourself. In that instant of the blade, you
might think, 'Fuck' – for a second, you don't
know how deep the cut is. Will you have to go to
the emergency room, or is it going to just need a
Band-Aid? And perhaps in this short moment, you
don't *want* to find out how deep it is. That instance
is crucial – you experience and try to understand
the risk an encounter has put you at, and how
it matters in that moment. I feel that same kind
of mixed feeling about my artistic subjectivity:
I don't entirely or immediately know what I'm
doing, I don't know if it's correct, and I feel like

I don't want to find out, or at least not now. I feel
like I will find out later, although perhaps not for
decades. Or just maybe, I will have to find out, for
sure, in the end.

*AL: Your work often appears in an institutional context
and raises many interesting challenges: how to conserve
these works? What is their lifespan? Then there is this
situational, almost self-destructive aspect of your work,
which occasions lengthy conversations between you and
curators and technicians. How have these dialogues
shifted your understanding of your work over the years?*

ML: This is increasingly influencing me now, even
governing me. Having that exposure, having those
institutional opportunities, has gradually made me
conscious that my work is not only mine. Yes, I'm
supposed to do my thing – I'm an artist, and I'm
being asked to be myself to the fullest. But what I
create then is not for me. At the same time, though,
when I am invited to show at the Venice Biennale
or the Carnegie International, I think the nature of
those events and their curatorship means I'm being
asked to have, or to share, a certain worldview.

*BA: When you situate your work in an institutional
setting or a public setting, it's like giving and taking from
the public, or putting yourself out there in a fuller sense,
but also knowing that there's going to be other people that
experience it. So, it's all about navigation.*

ML: Yes, but I personally feel like wanting to
navigate myself is completely useless. There's no
point in willing the public to perceive my work in
some certain way or other. I think their response
is not mine to orchestrate, and it would almost be
hypocritical if I wanted them to get a particular
thing from my work. Again, that makes me think
about what happens when you are given this public
exposure, and what comes as a result of it. It's a
very strong experience to feel this – one I'm still
coming to terms with, really.

AL: Institutions also evolve in dialogue with the artists and their work – it's not a one way street. From your experience, aside from what you've learned from working with institutions, are there things you've gradually realised you should never compromise on, or should deliberately push back against?

ML: To be honest, there are, of course, many different things I sometimes insist on or that I'm stubborn about, but not anything I can point to as a set of values or a belief. I sometimes feel like being in this industry and having a career as an artist is itself an almost out of body experience. In turn, it is hard for me to think about artistic integrity as something tangible, if that is what you're asking. What do I not want to compromise over, what do I want to protect about my art? I don't hold an answer to that and I kind of doubt if I ever will.

BA: Something that has helped me to read your work is a famous quote by Antonio Gramsci: 'The old is dying and the new cannot be born; into this interregnum, a great variety of morbid symptoms appear'. Gramsci was writing at a time when fascism was spreading in Italy, so his conception was that because of the capitalist world order, you had a choice between socialism and barbarism. But it feels useful to take it out of that specific context to apply to our own, and think about how your work speaks to this transitional state, where we're coming out of something that has died and we're struggling to find or build something new.

AL: I agree that Mire's work speaks so well to this transitional state. But rather than looking for or proposing something new, it seems to be saying something more existential – something closer to Donna Haraway's notion of 'staying with the trouble', or, on a perhaps more romantic note, a Sisyphean 'nevertheless'. There's something powerfully emotional and liberating about the collective awareness of enduring something terrible together.

Beyond its symbolic, experiential offer, I wonder whether we can think about the process of enacting this large-scale project, getting people with different aspirations and limitations on the same boat to make something happen, as itself a 'transitional space', a process during which a provisional infrastructure is enacted and rehearsed. Our colleague Catherine Wood once said something that forever stuck with me about how any interpersonal gesture, even just between two people, is a proto-institutional one in that it evokes a world-making potentiality. That leads me to my final question. Mire, what are some of your takeaways from working on this project, about artmaking, friendship, collaboration?

ML: When the commission was first announced, several of my British friends shared a nostalgic sentiment that the Turbine Hall was where they first encountered art as children on school excursions. After visiting Tate multiple times this year, I began to appreciate what a unique place the Turbine Hall is. Despite initial impressions of an overwhelmingly masculine interior with its towering ceiling height, it's more than just a vast space to look up at. It's a dynamic arena you can explore from various vantage points – look down on, run through – which, to my surprise, people often do – or even lie down in. It's as if you've made friends with a giant mythical creature and are wandering within its domain.

Now when I think of Turbine Hall, I think of the people before the space itself – an eclectic mix of people gazing upwards, walking through the expansive hall. As my project draws nearer, I feel a deep connection to this space, as if I'm already standing in the crowd, looking up and feeling the surreal blend of dream and distant memory. As I'm talking, the exhibition is in its final stages of preparation. Once the commission has opened, I'll likely depart the space with a sensation of standing alone in a vast crowd, where I can see everyone's faces and know we are all together in this shared experience.

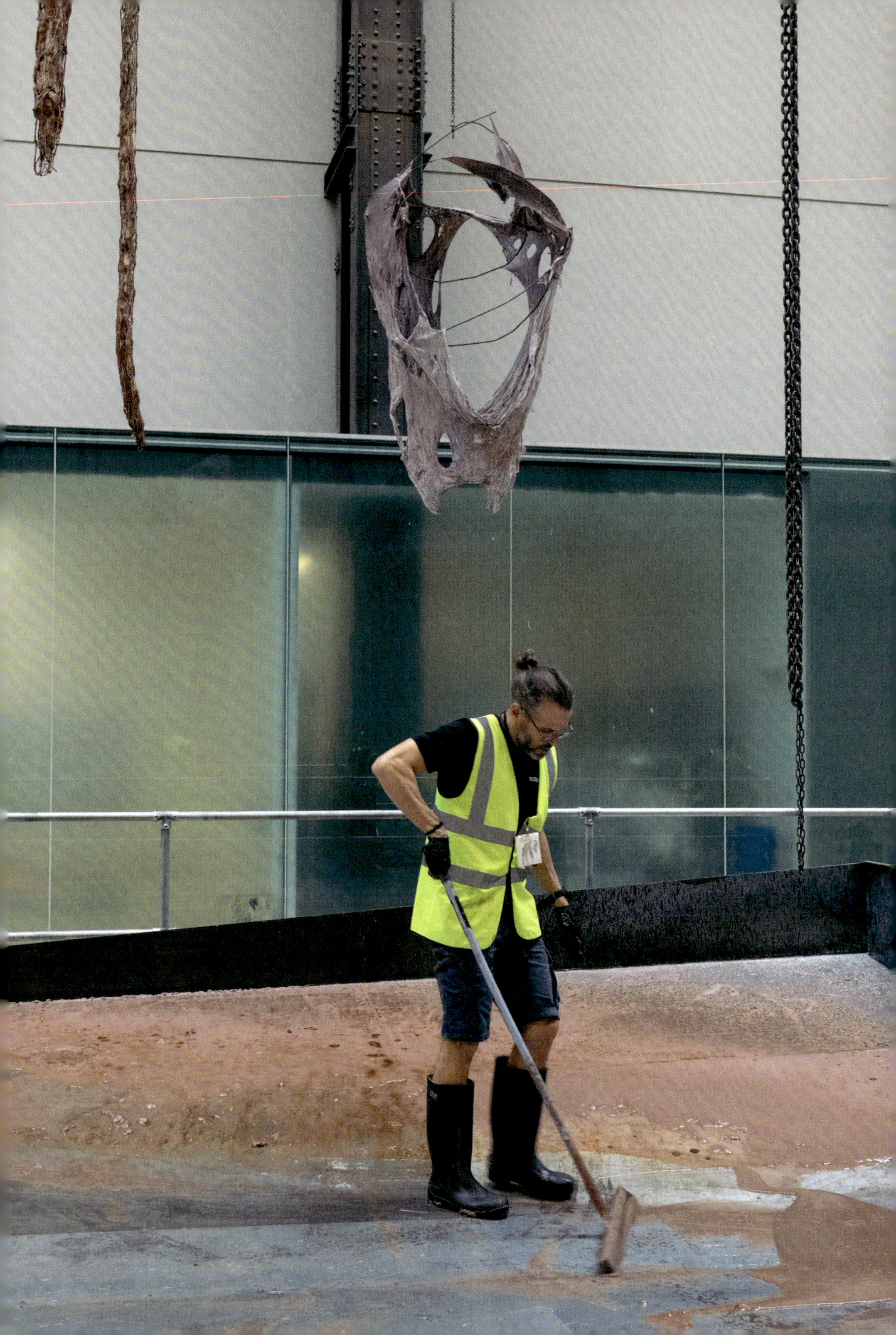

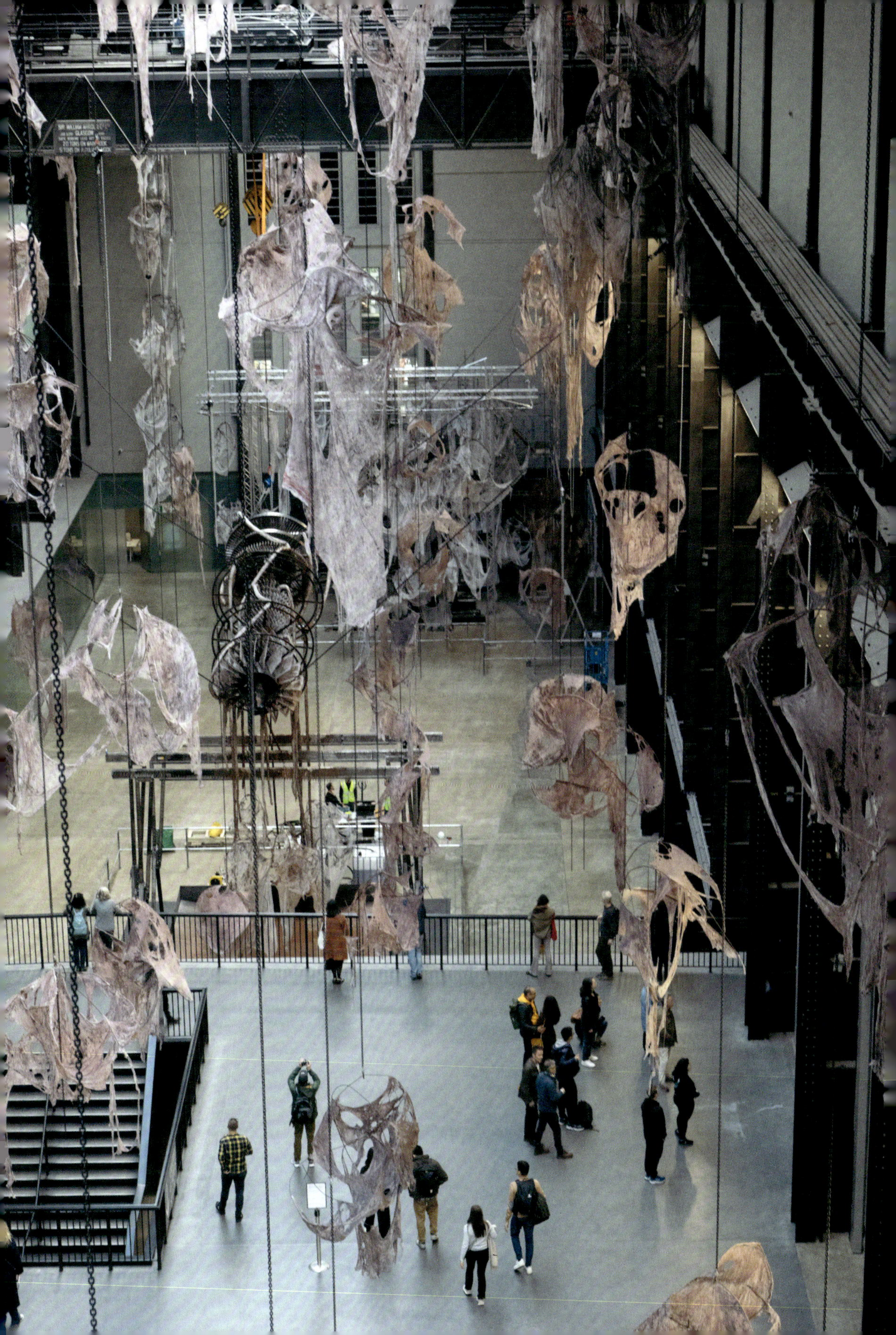

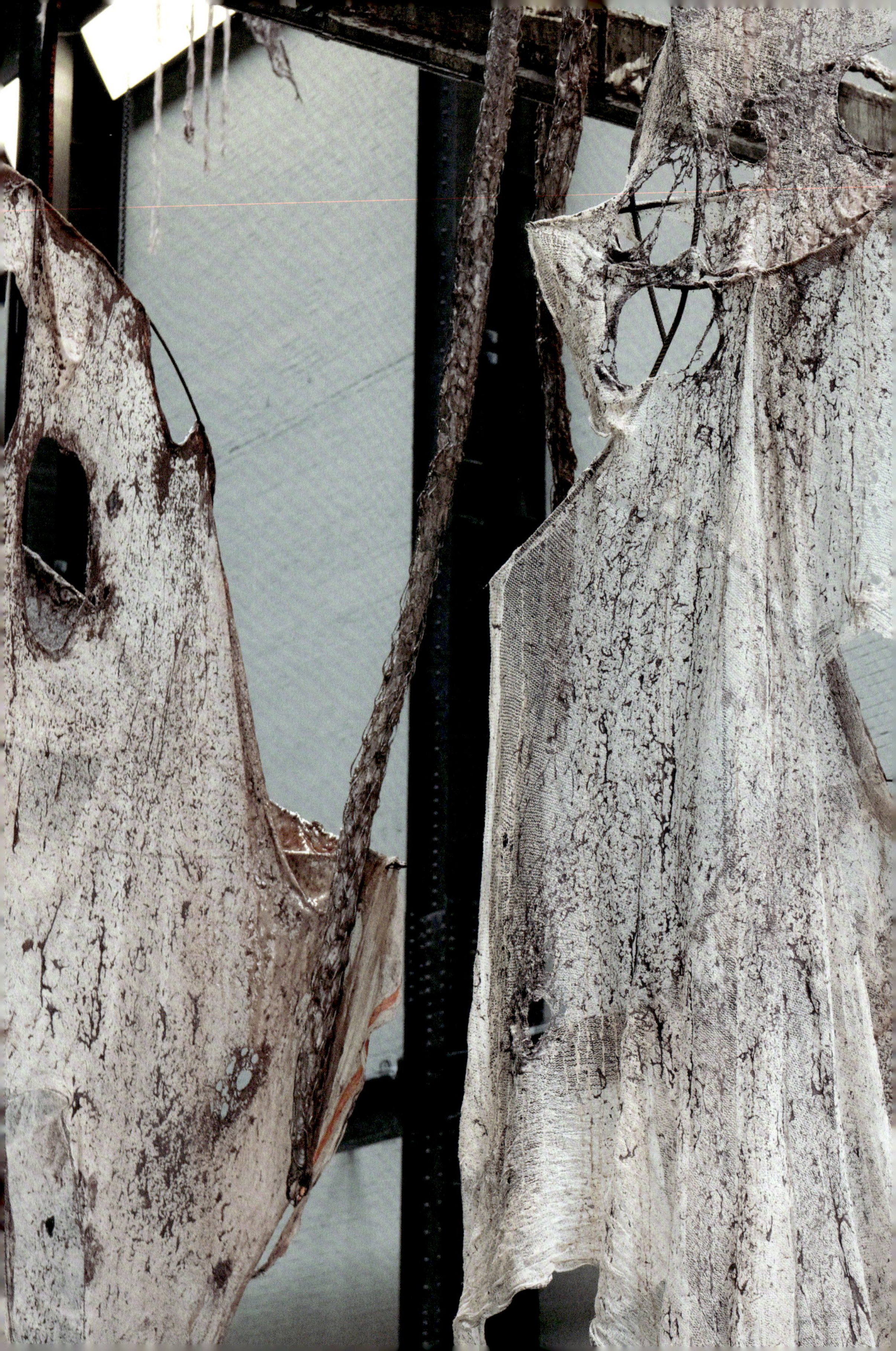

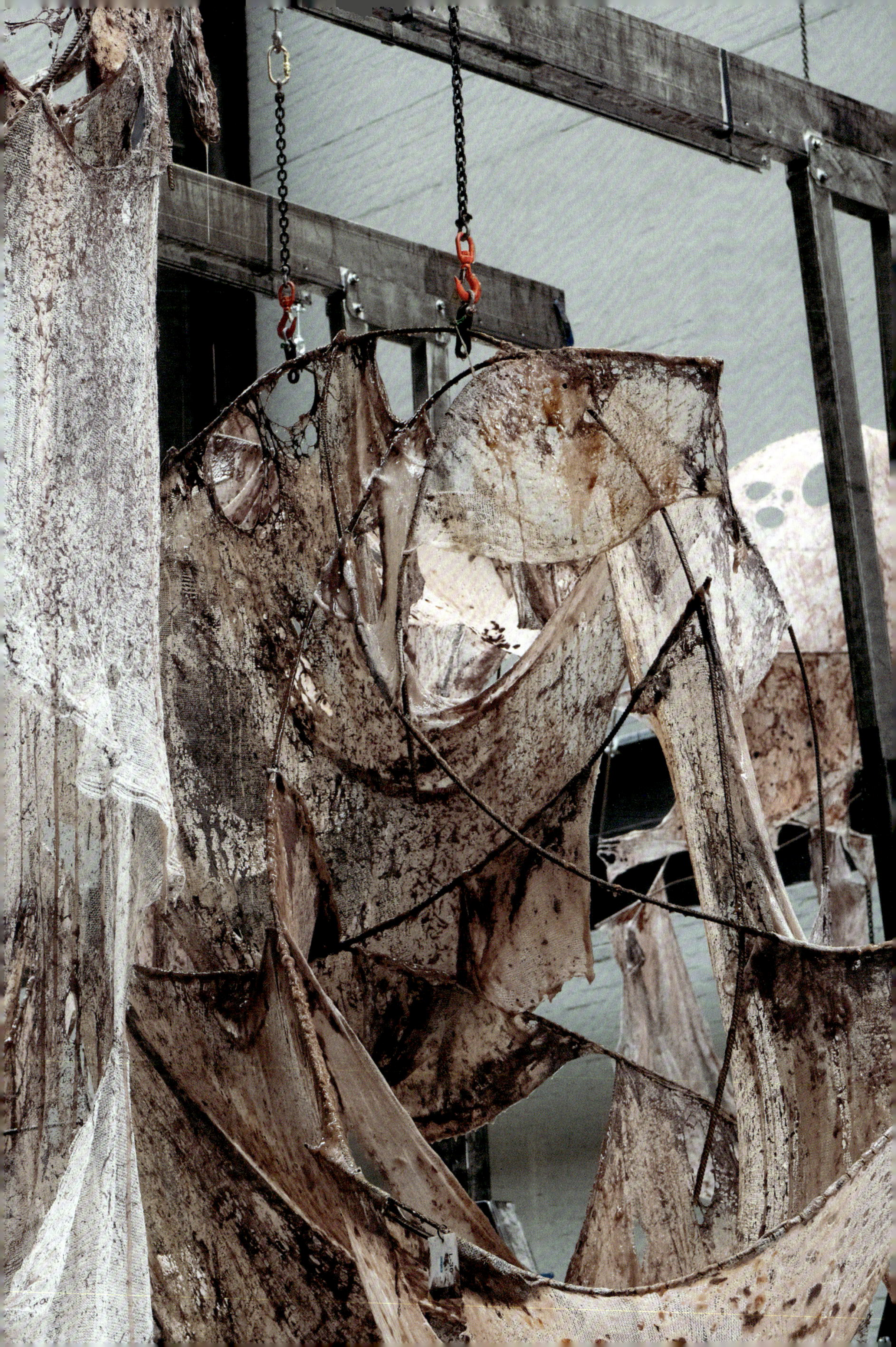

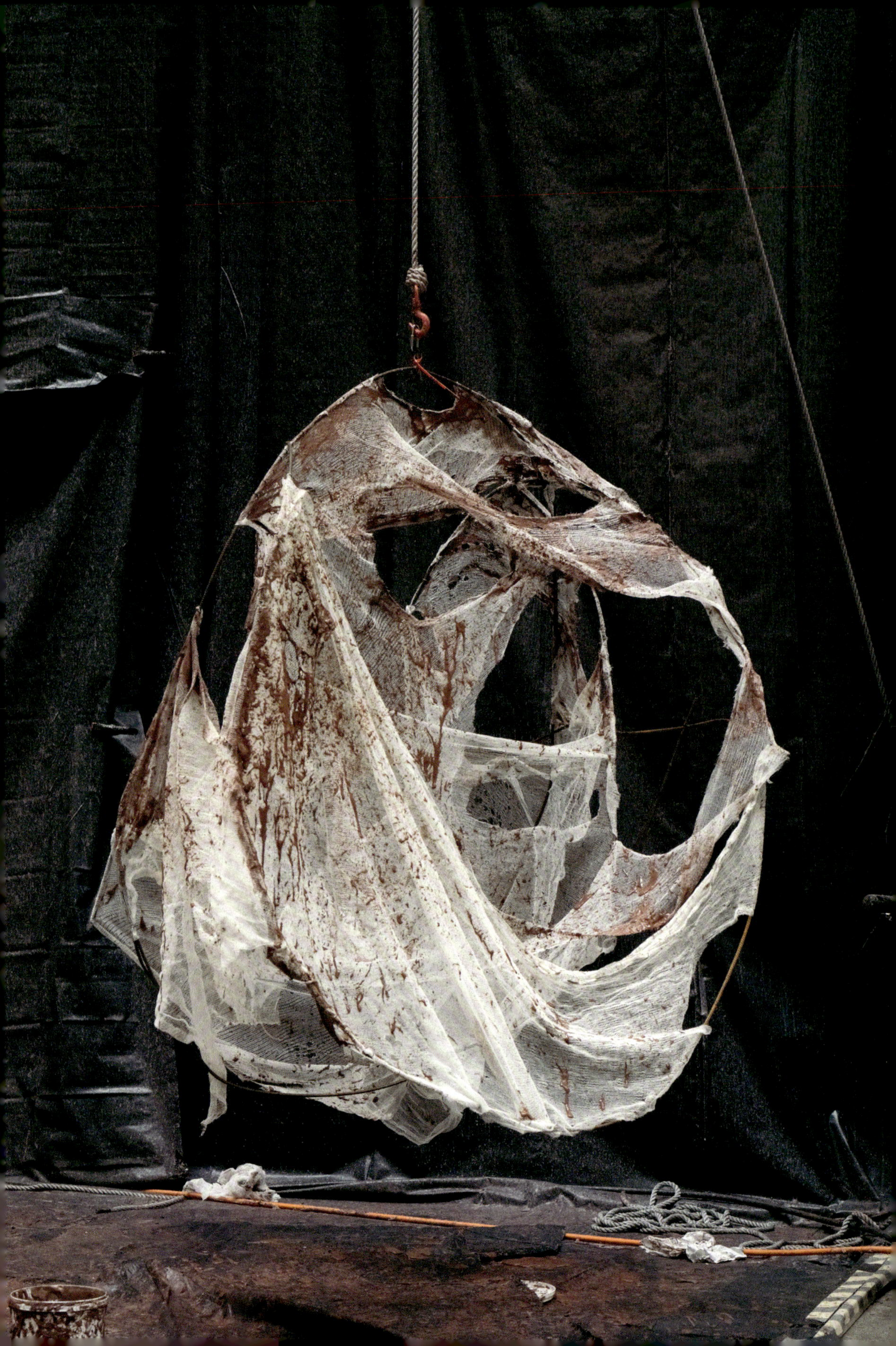

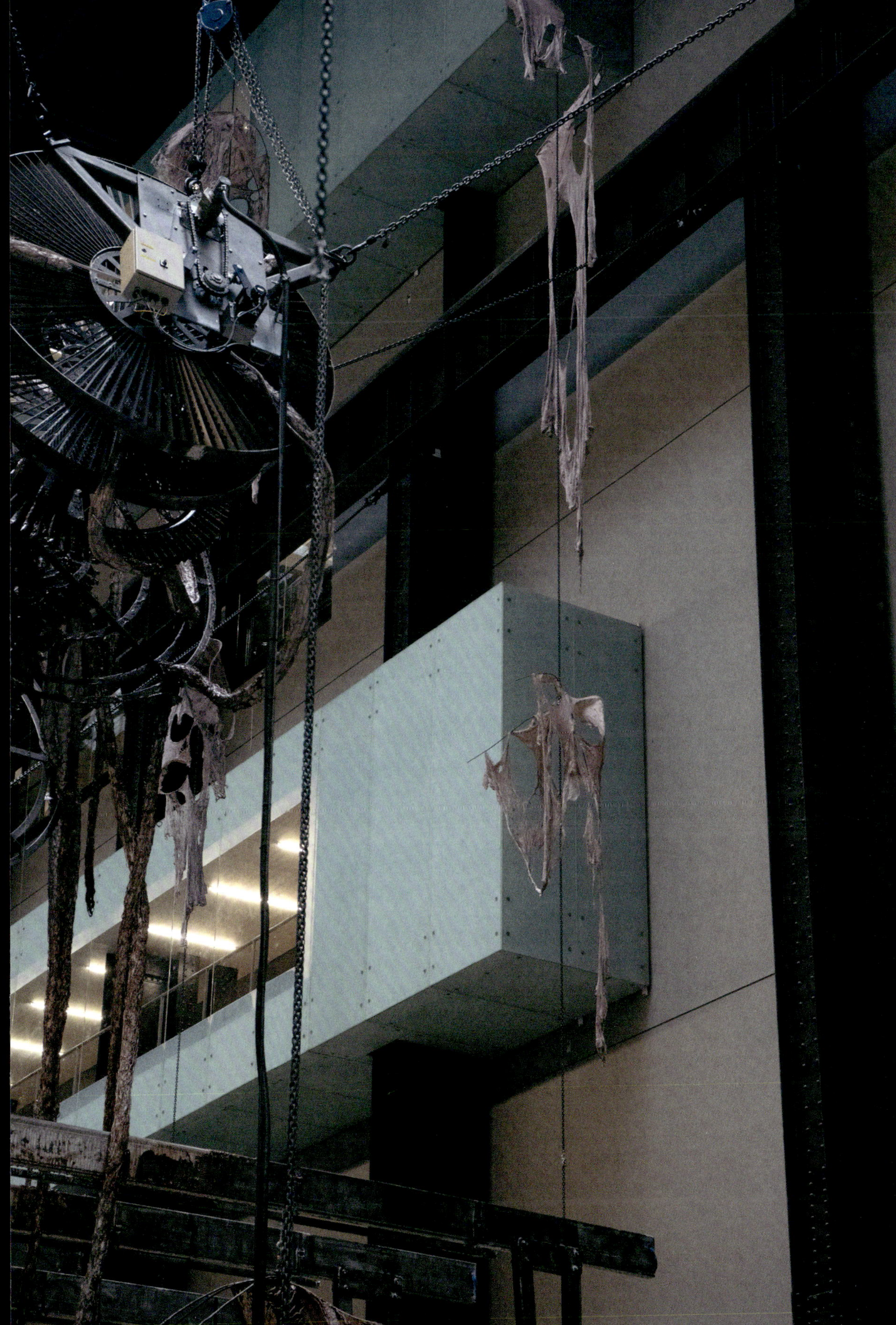

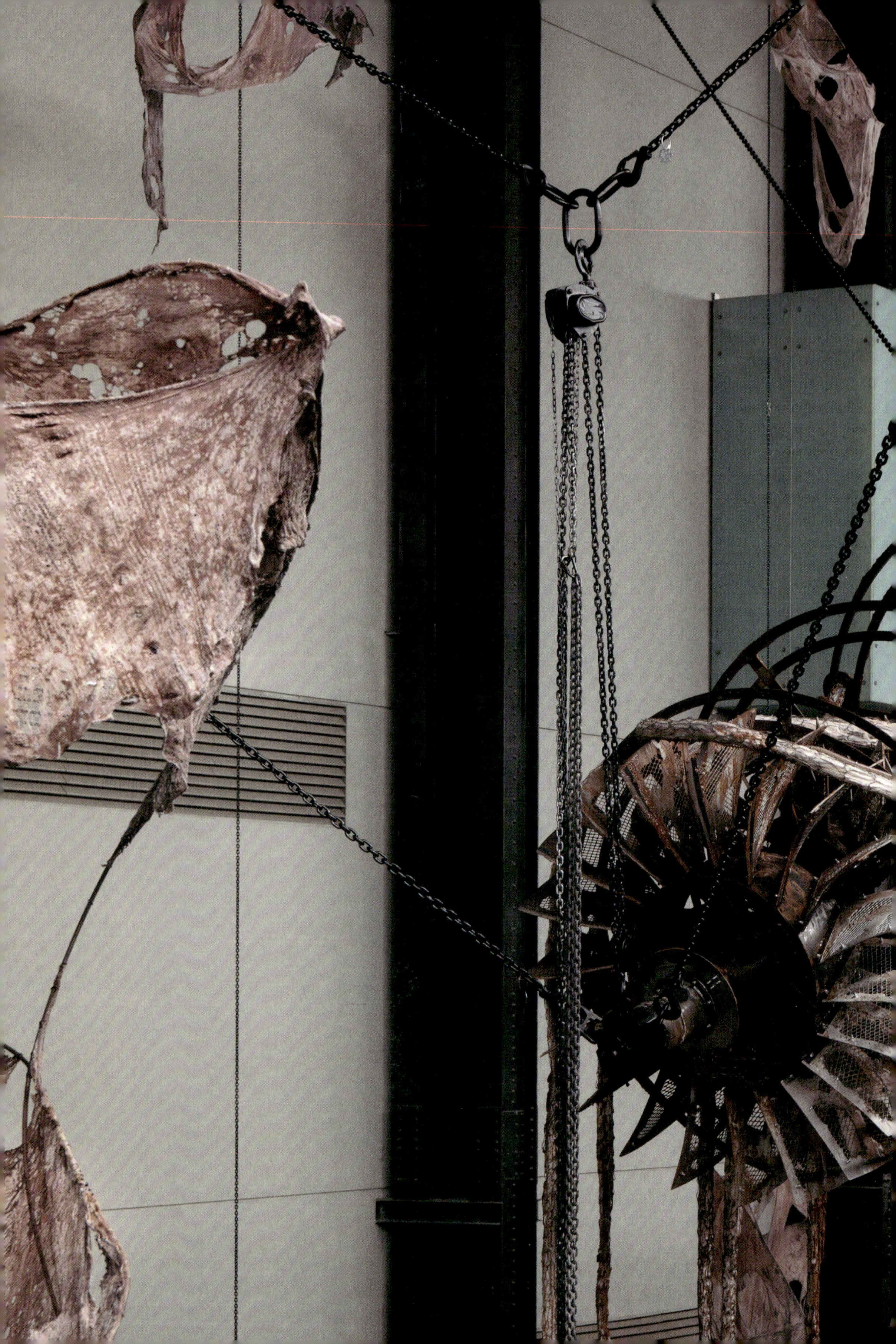

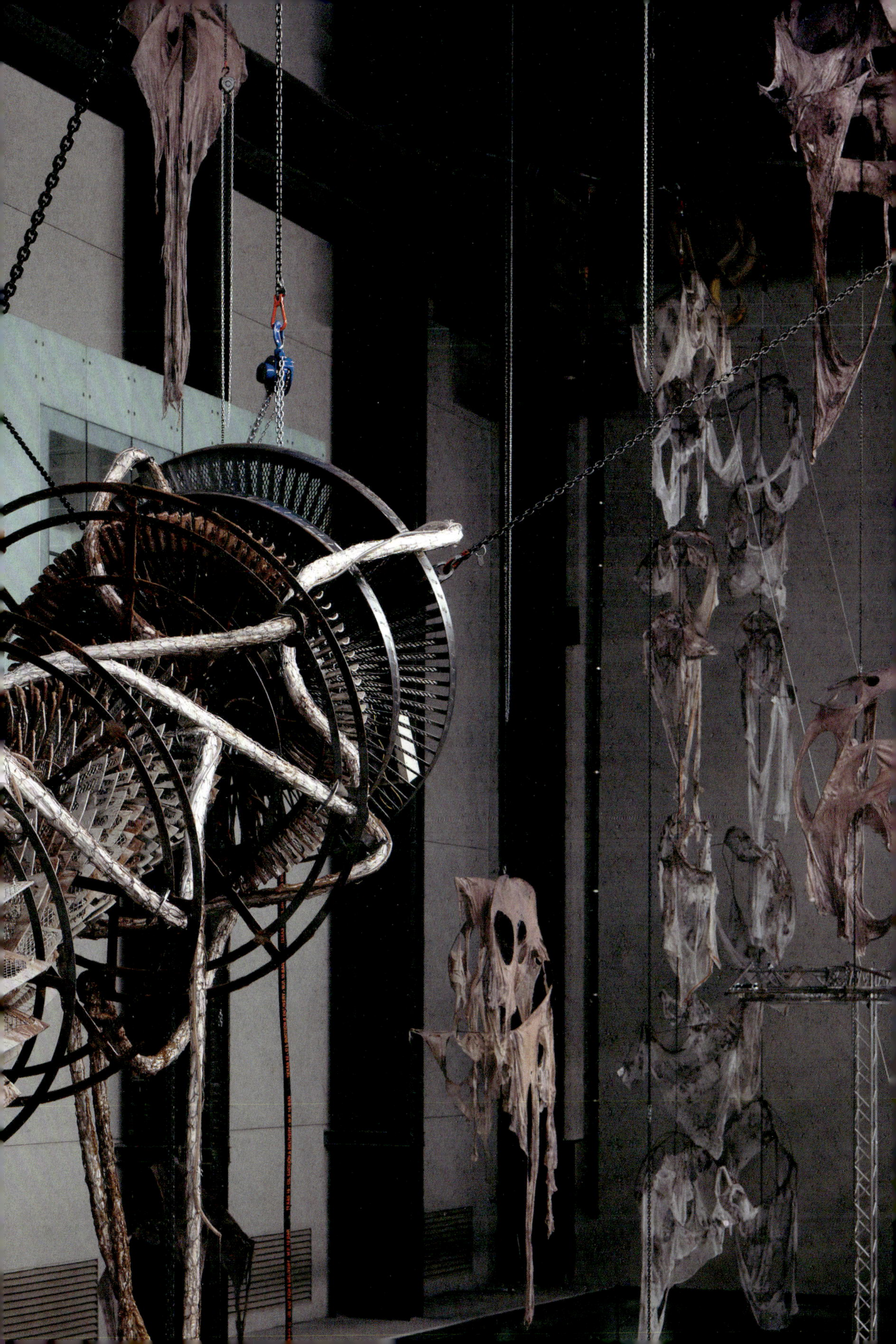

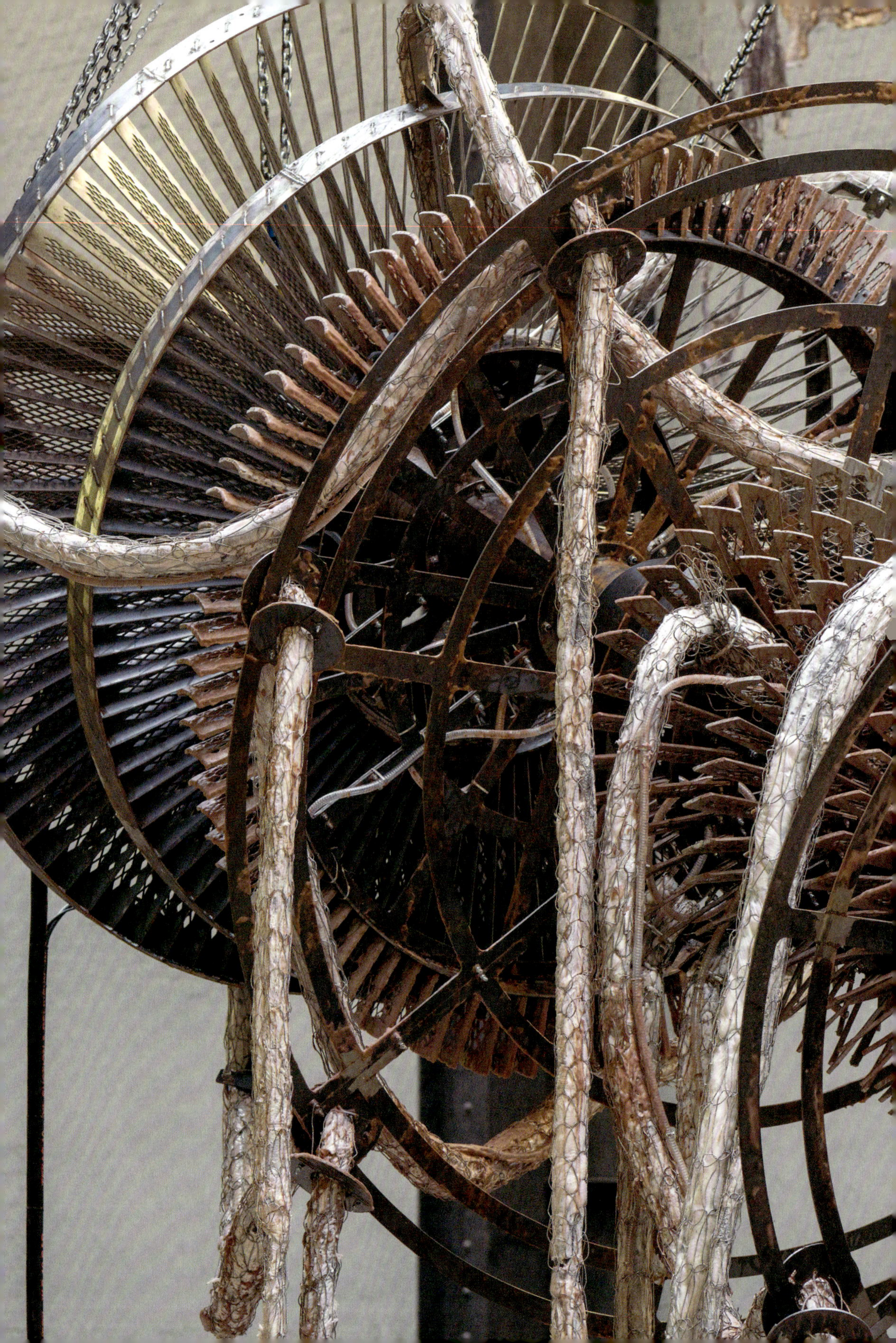

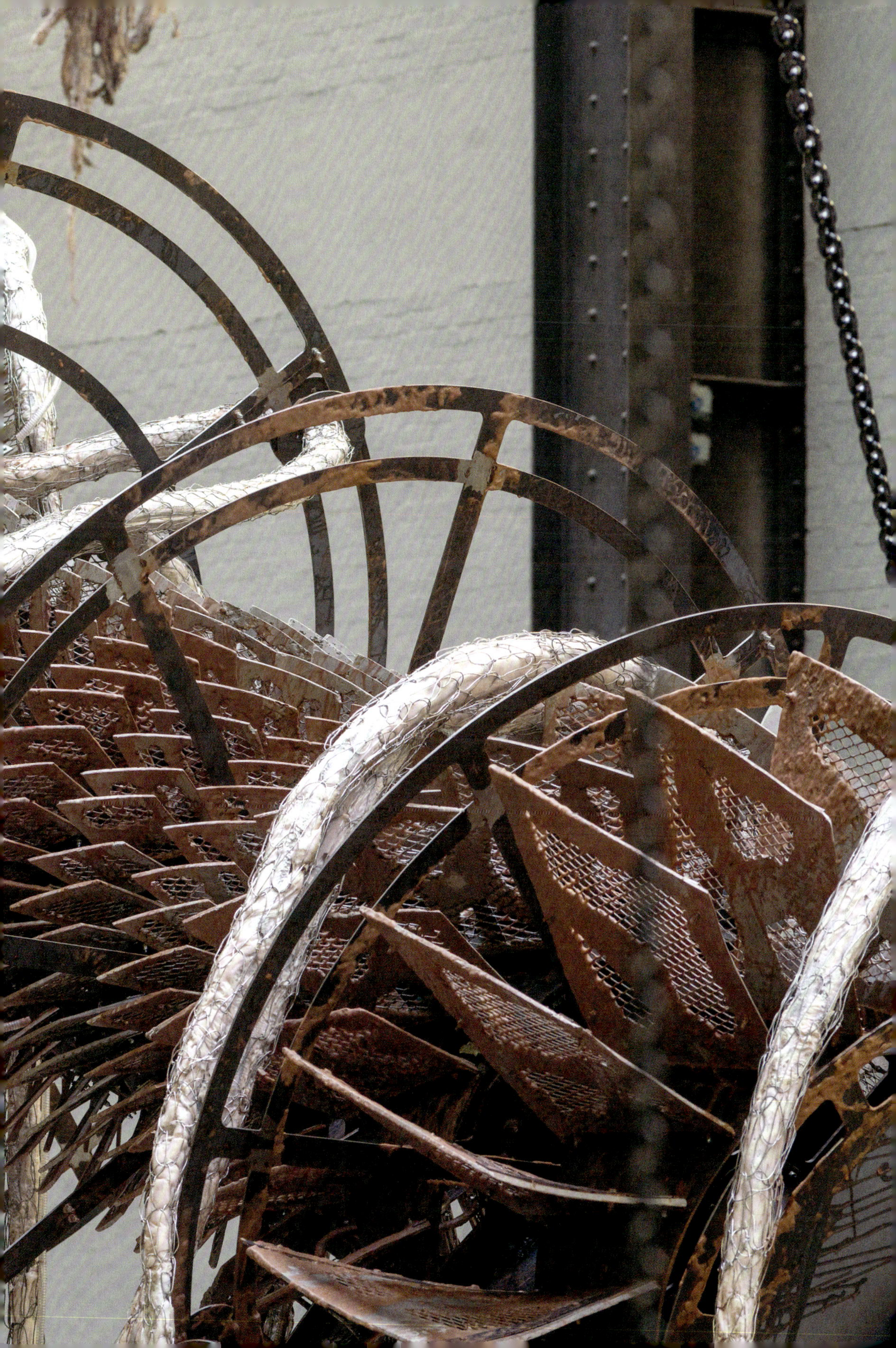

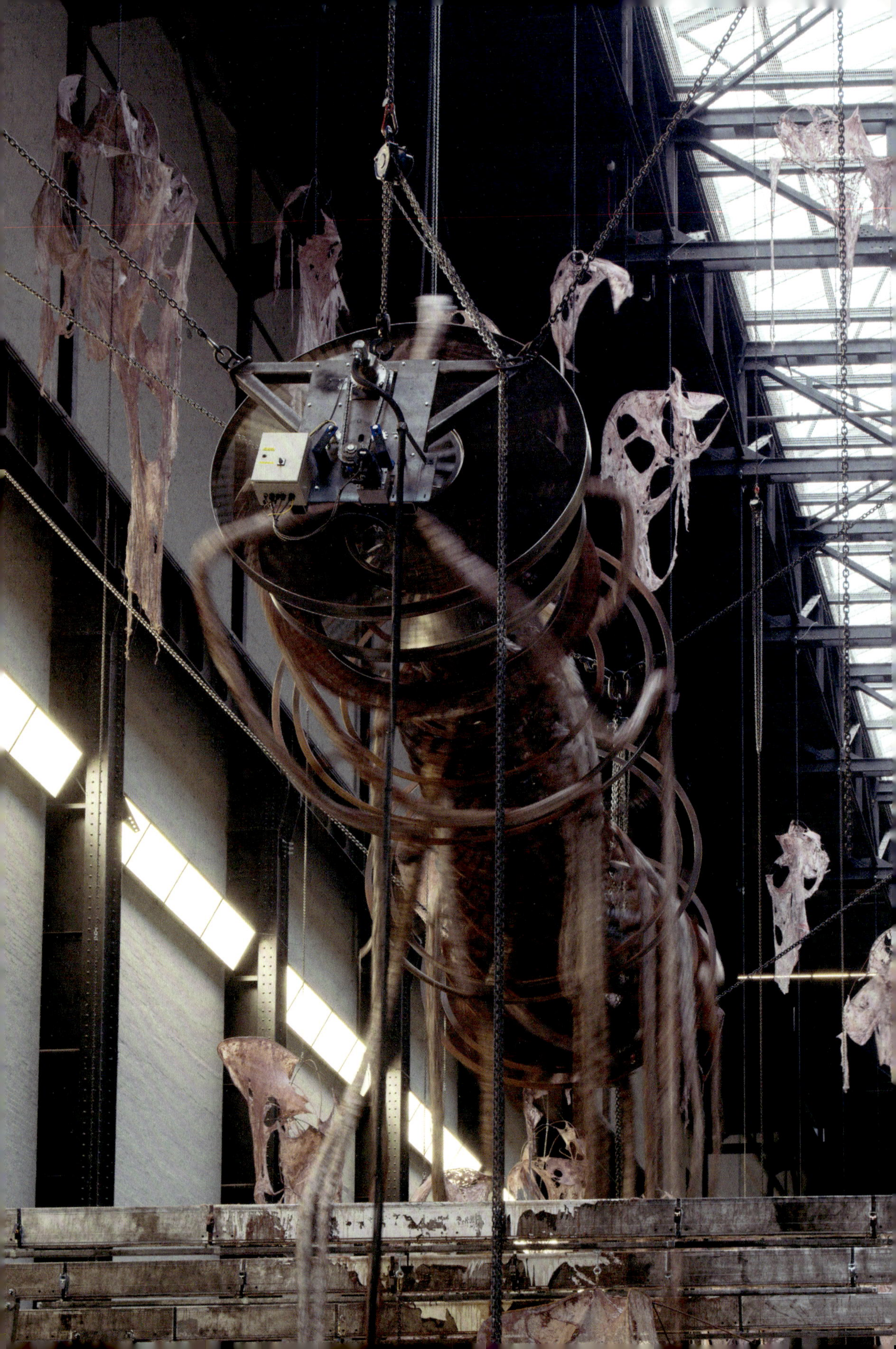

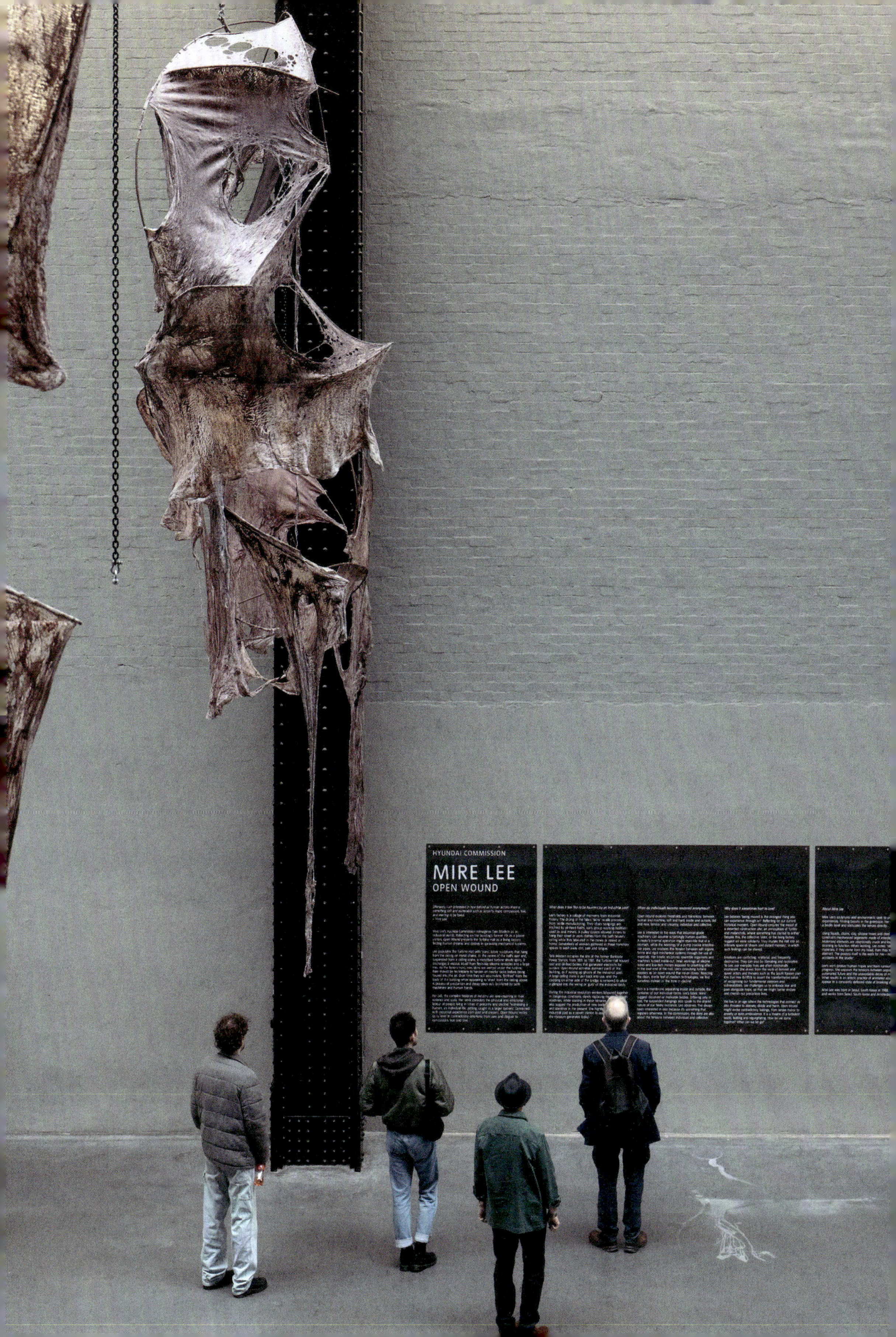
HYUNDAI COMMISSION
MIRE LEE
OPEN WOUND

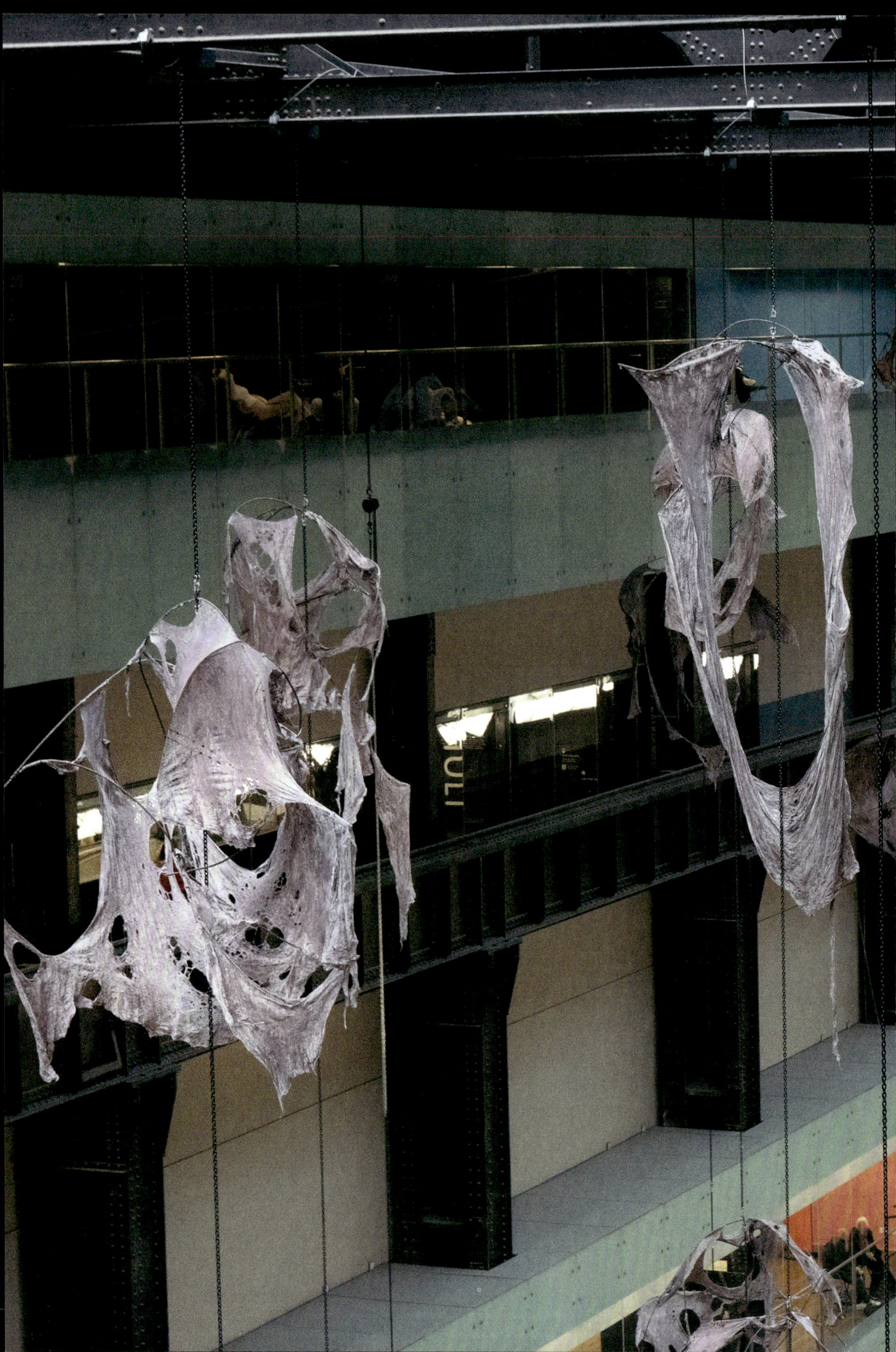

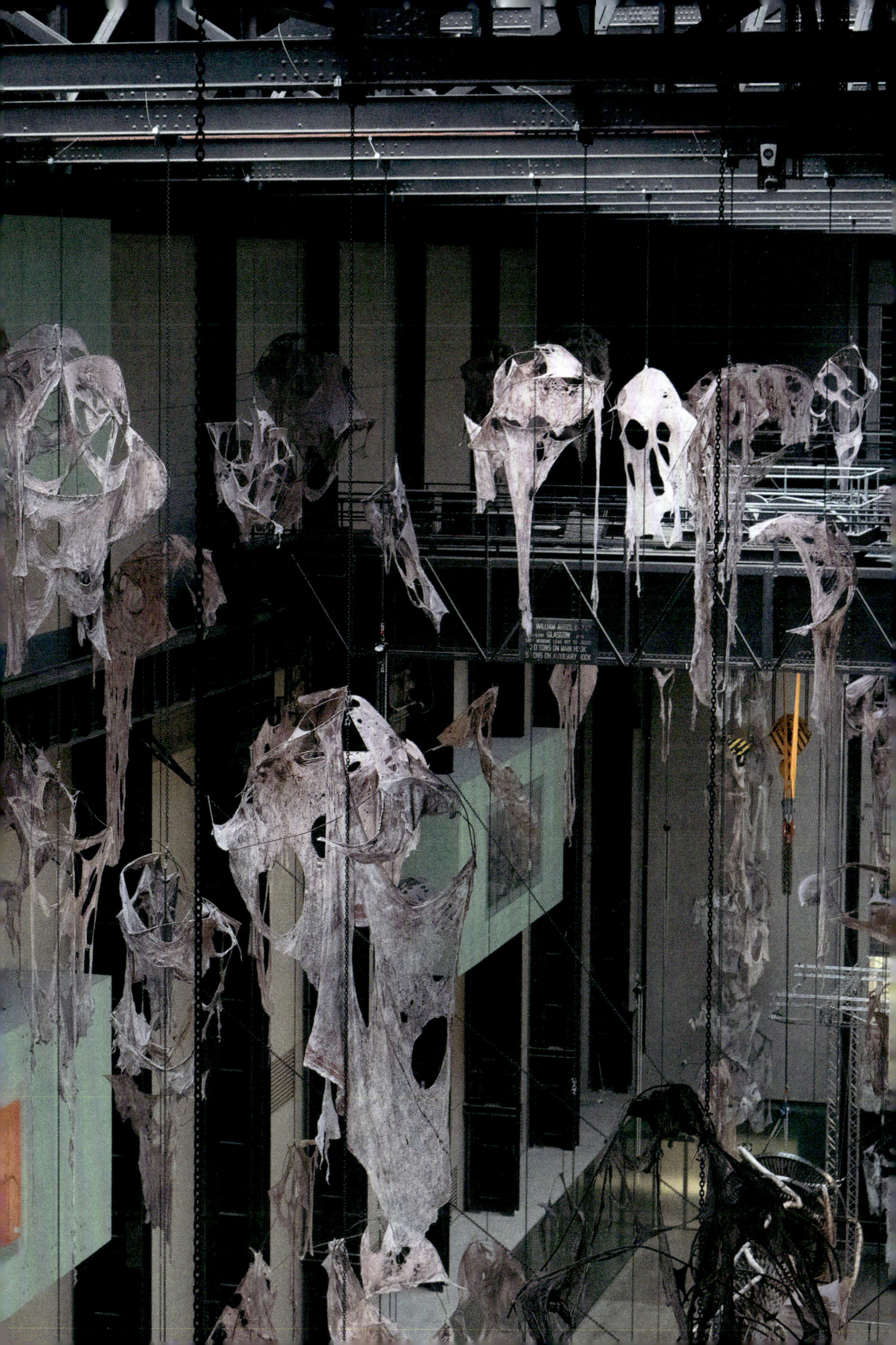

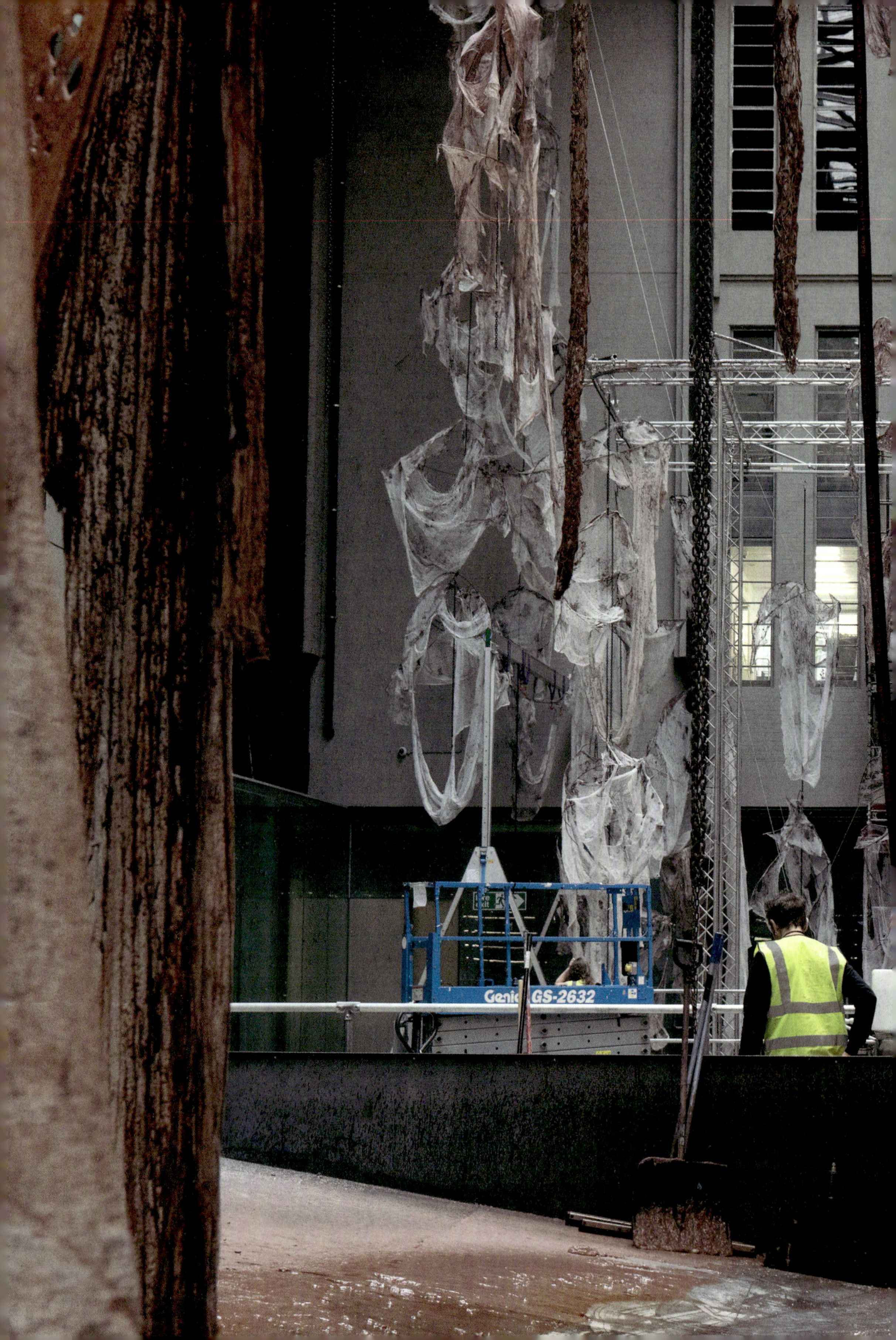

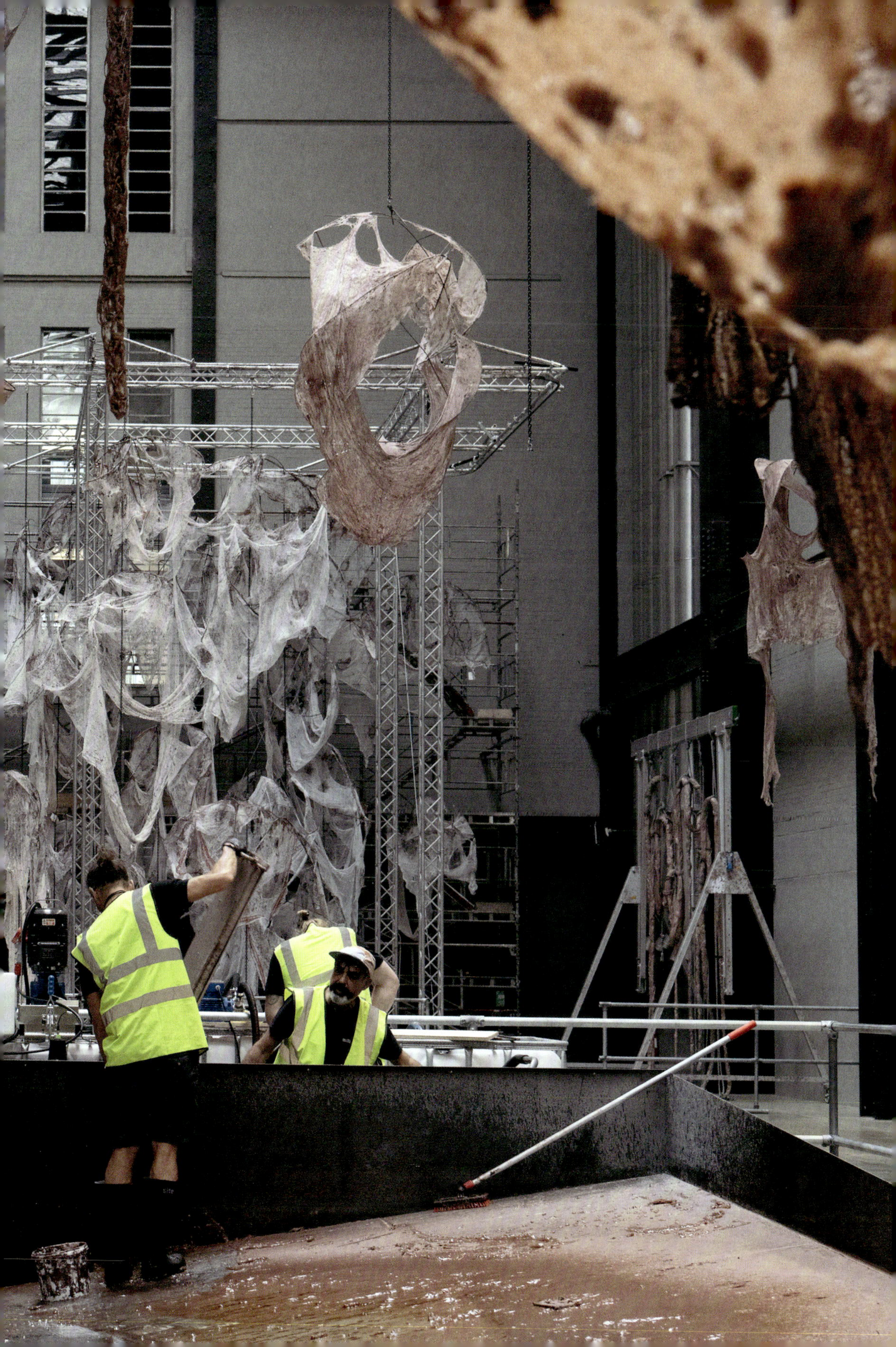

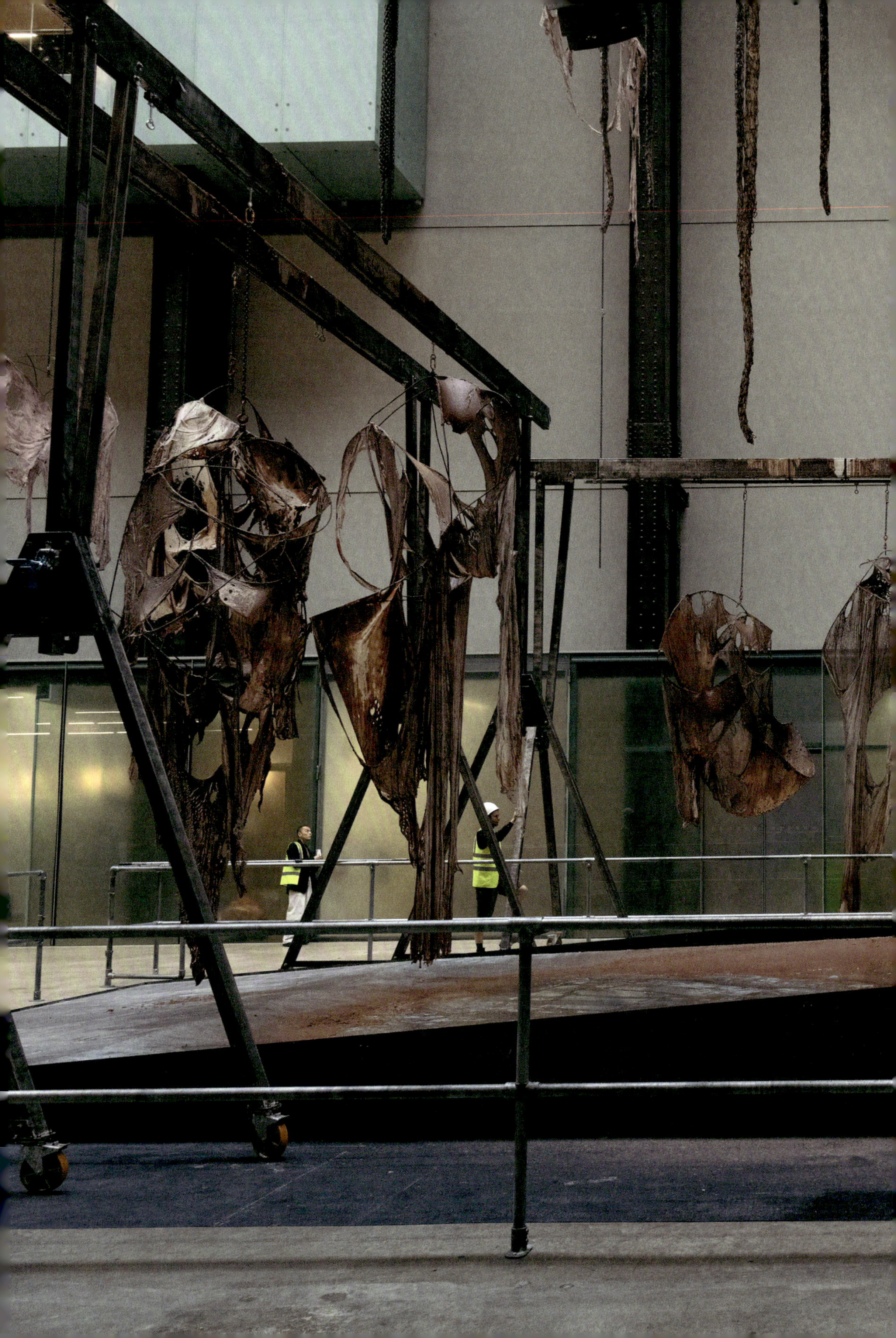

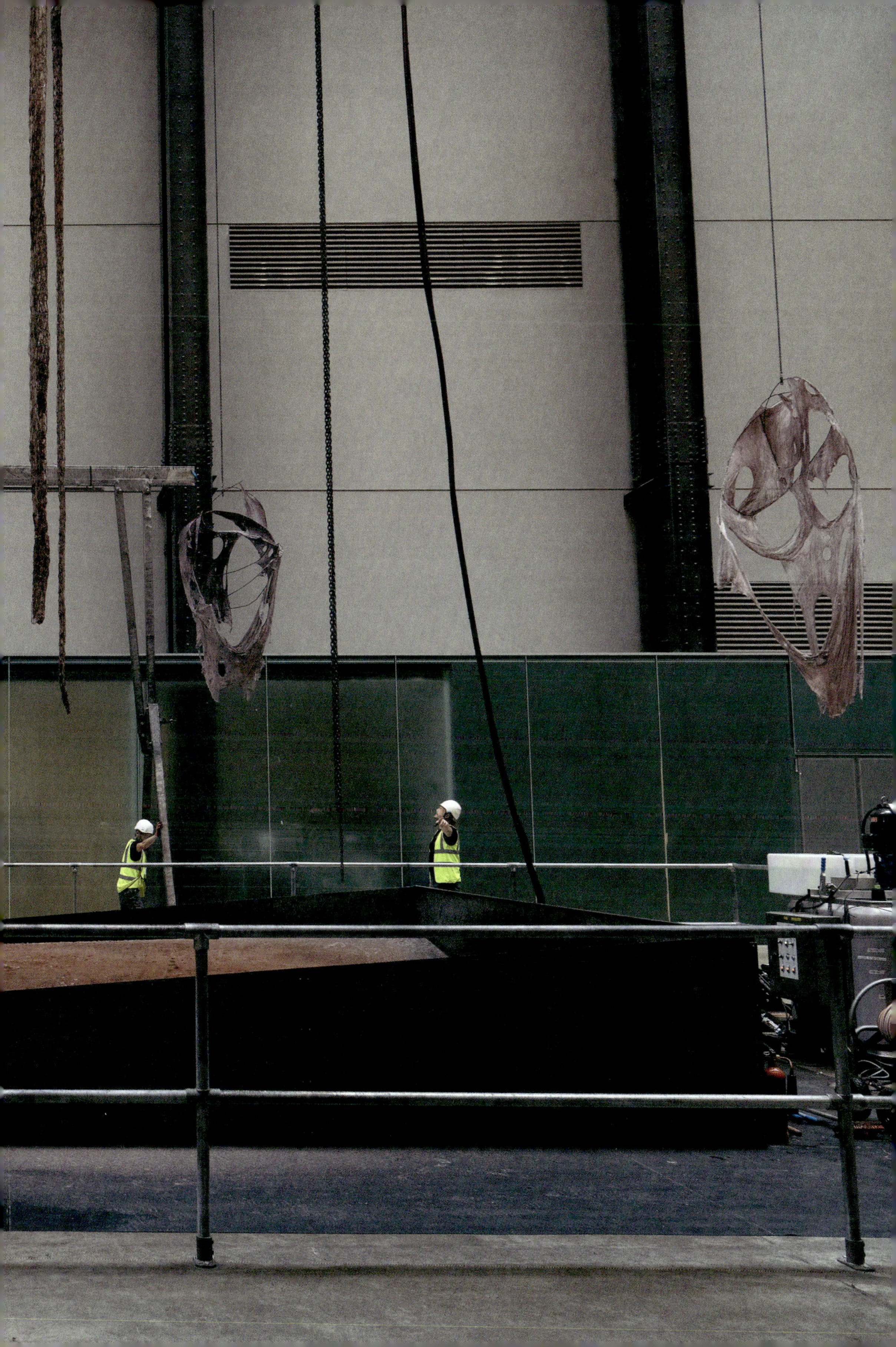

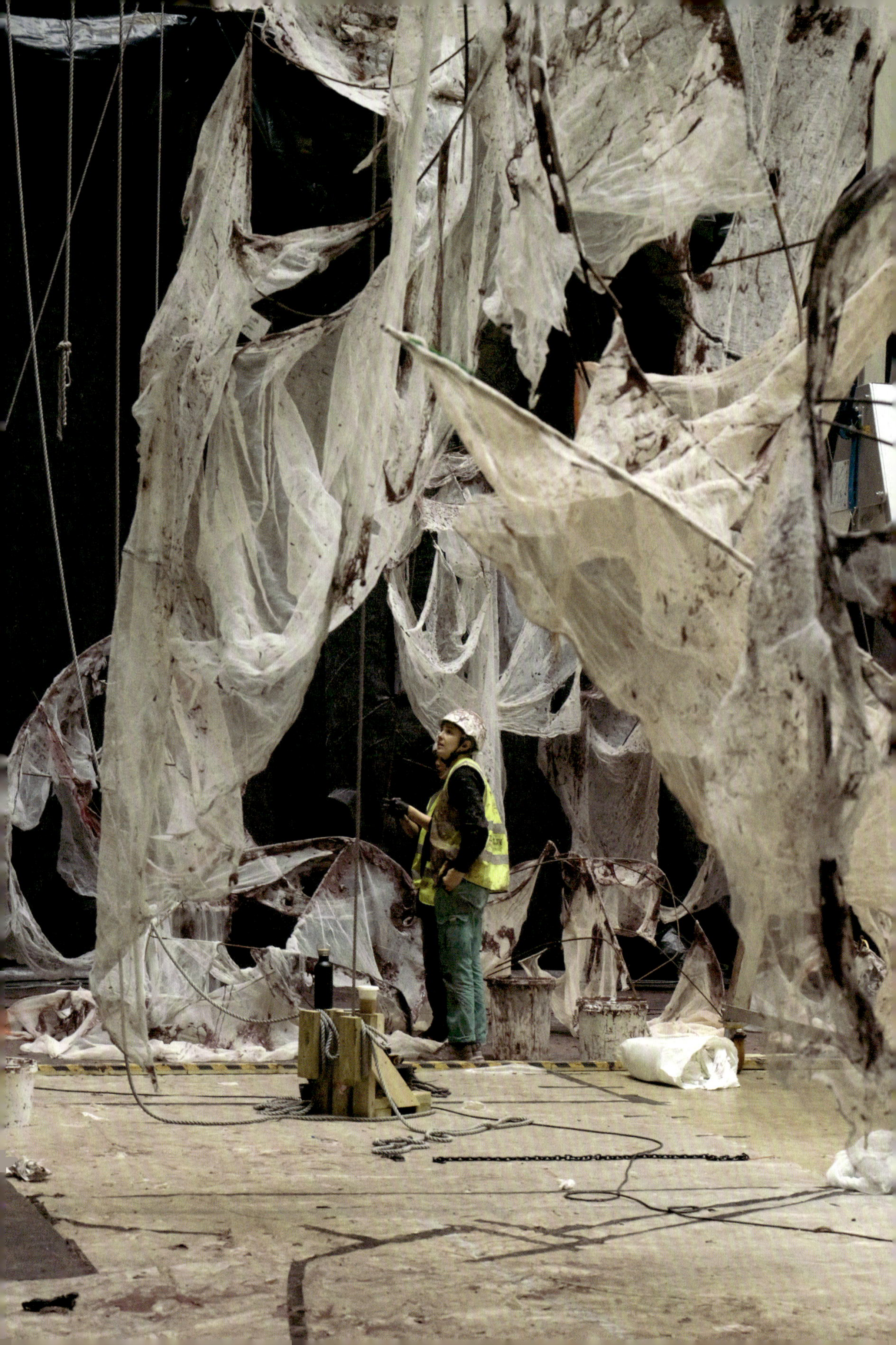

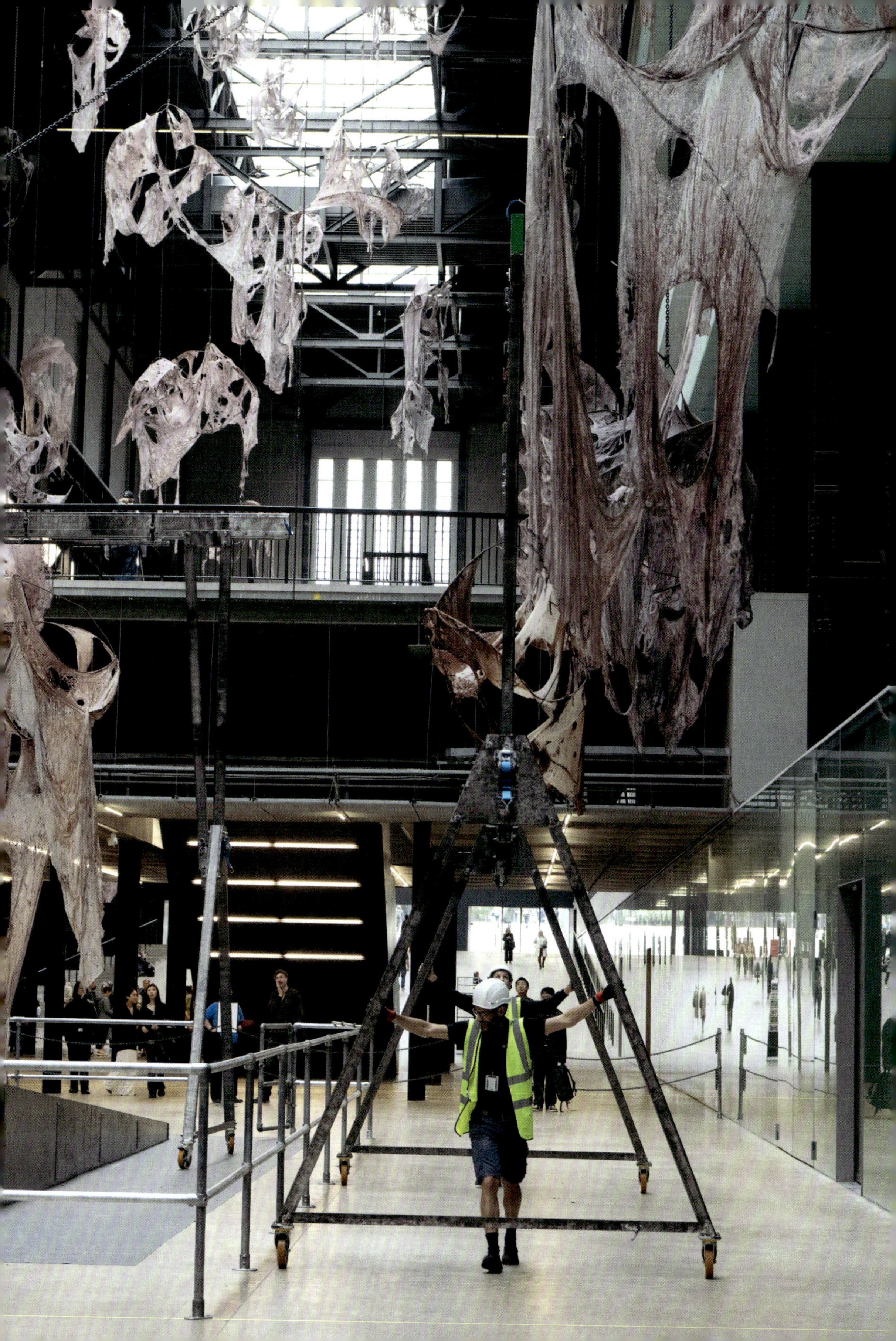

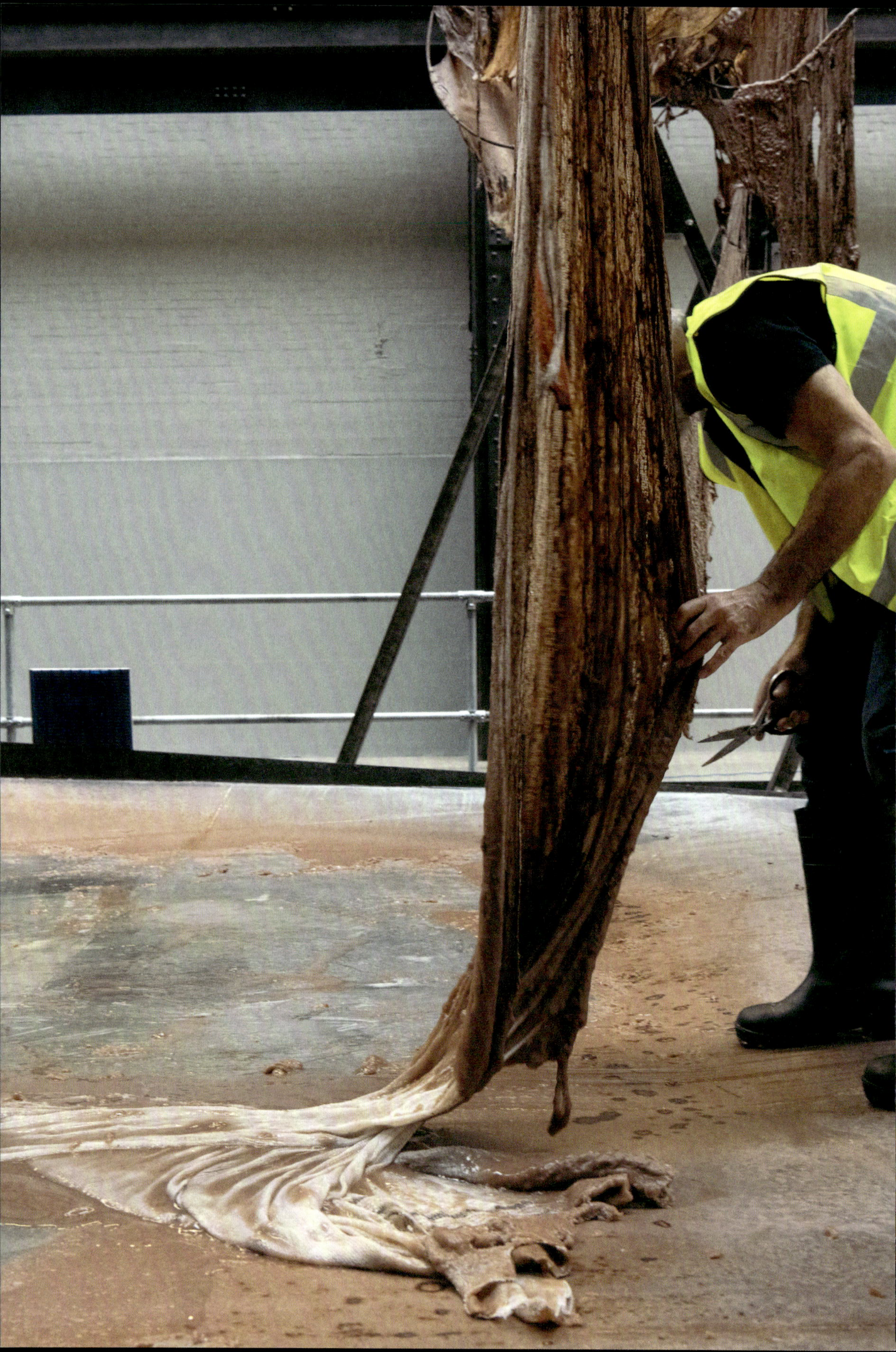

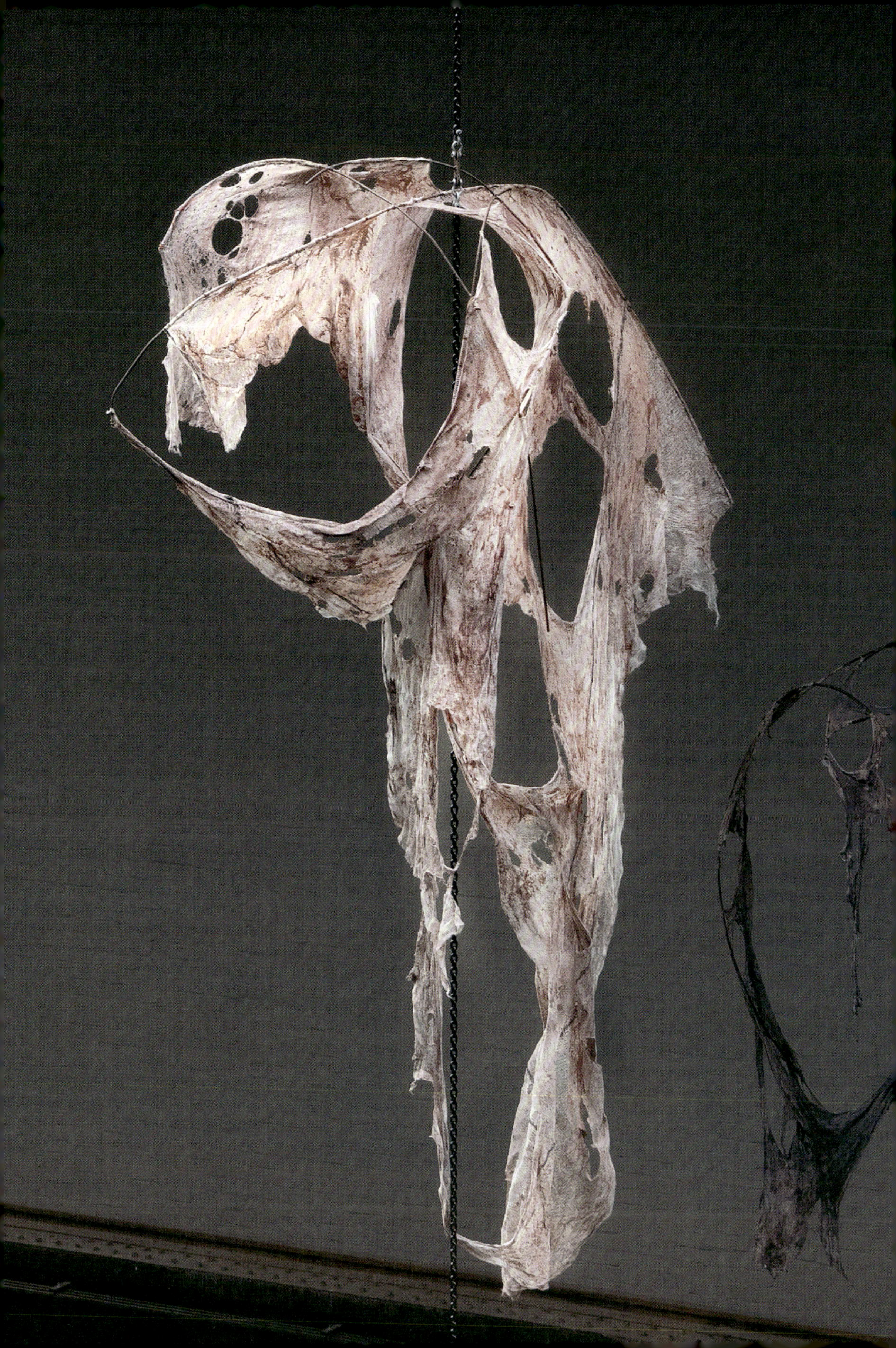

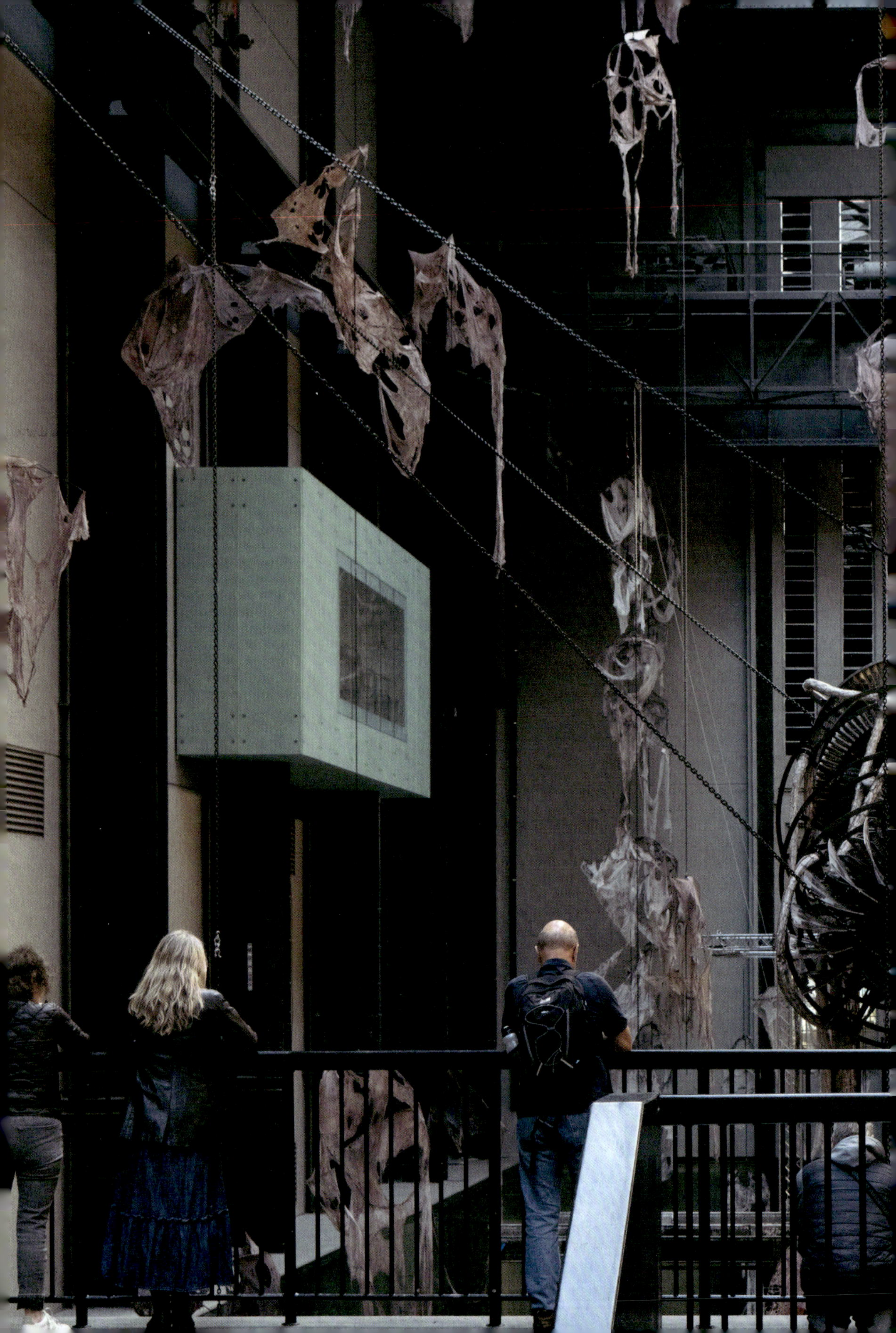

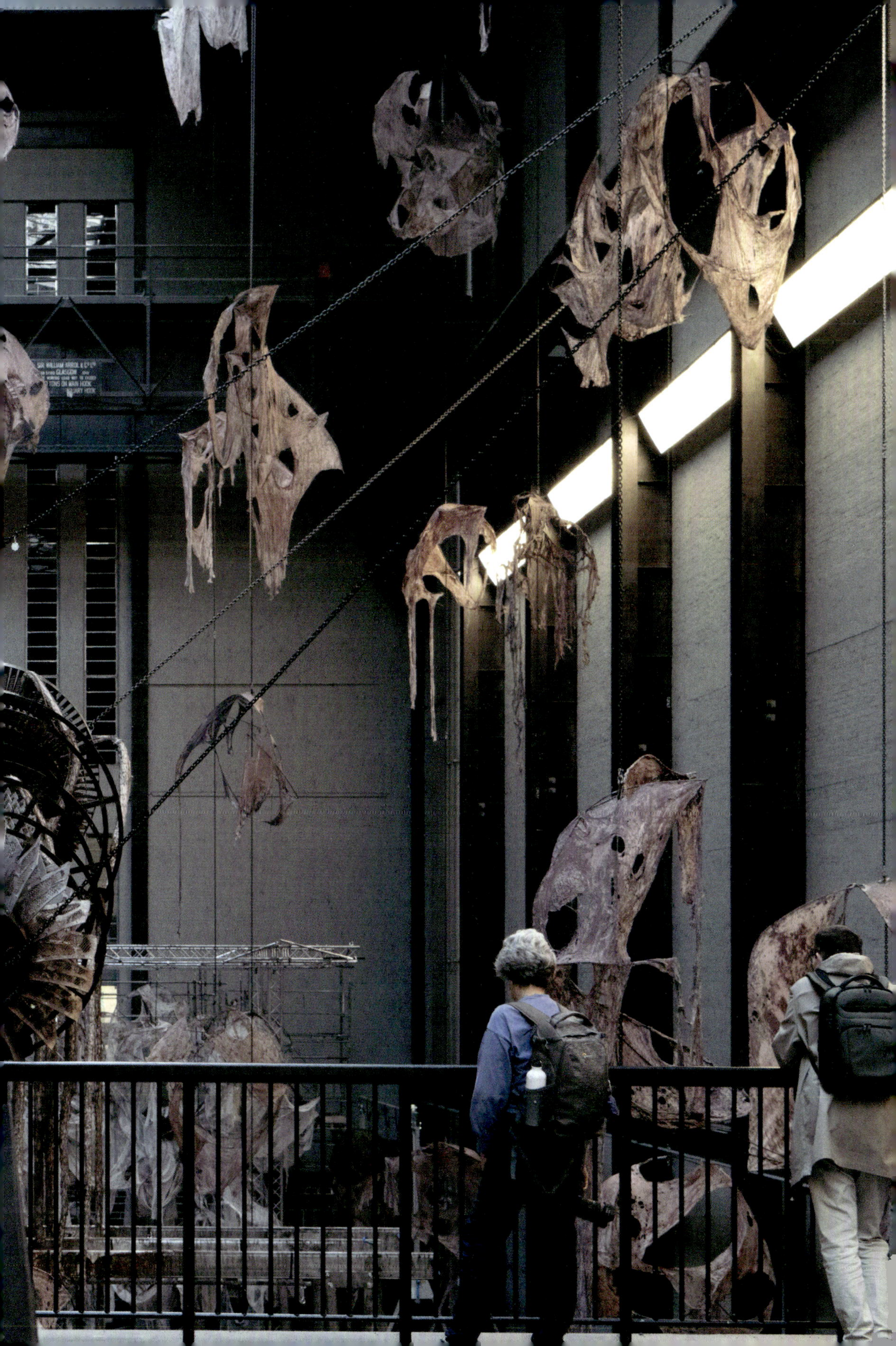

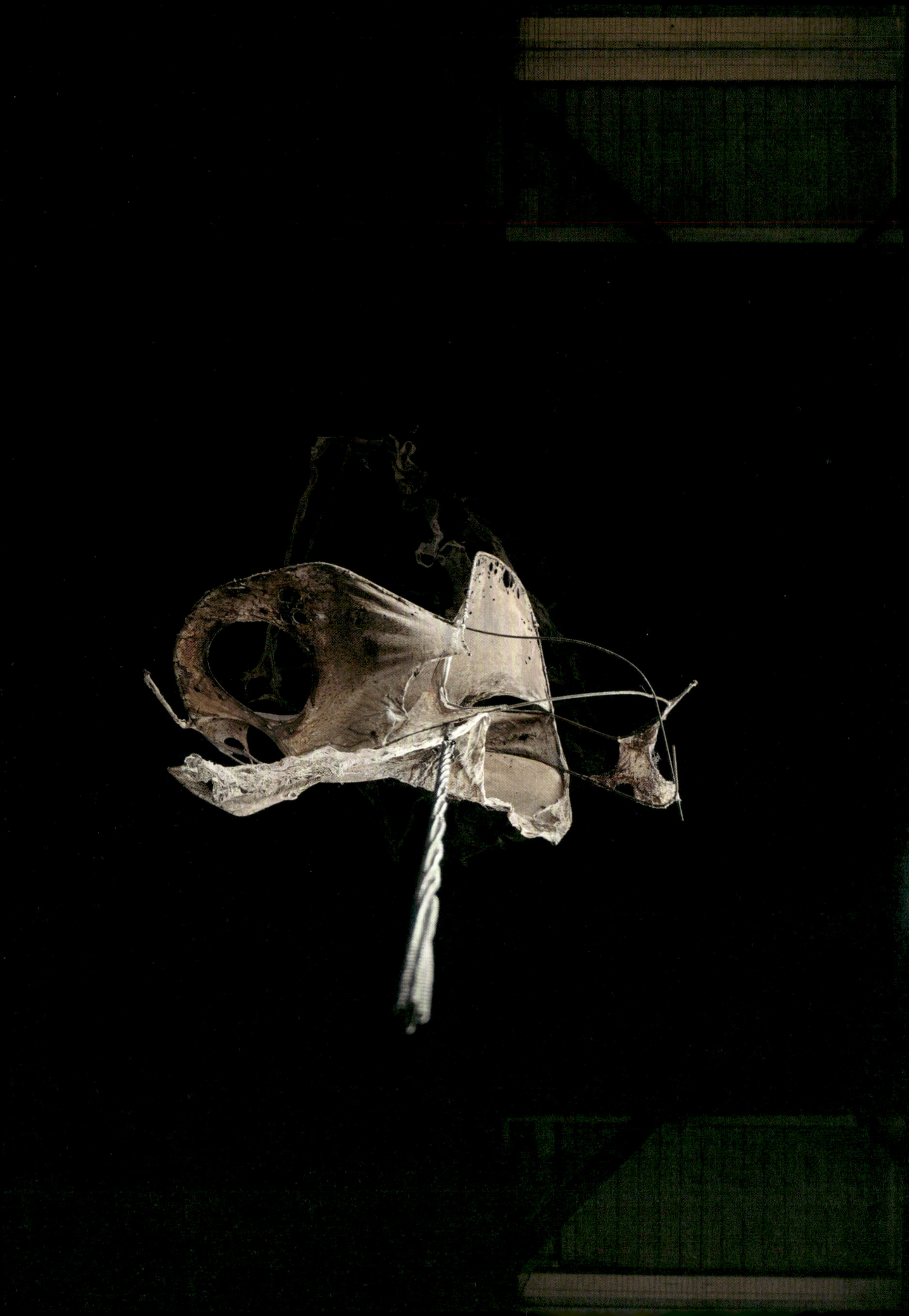

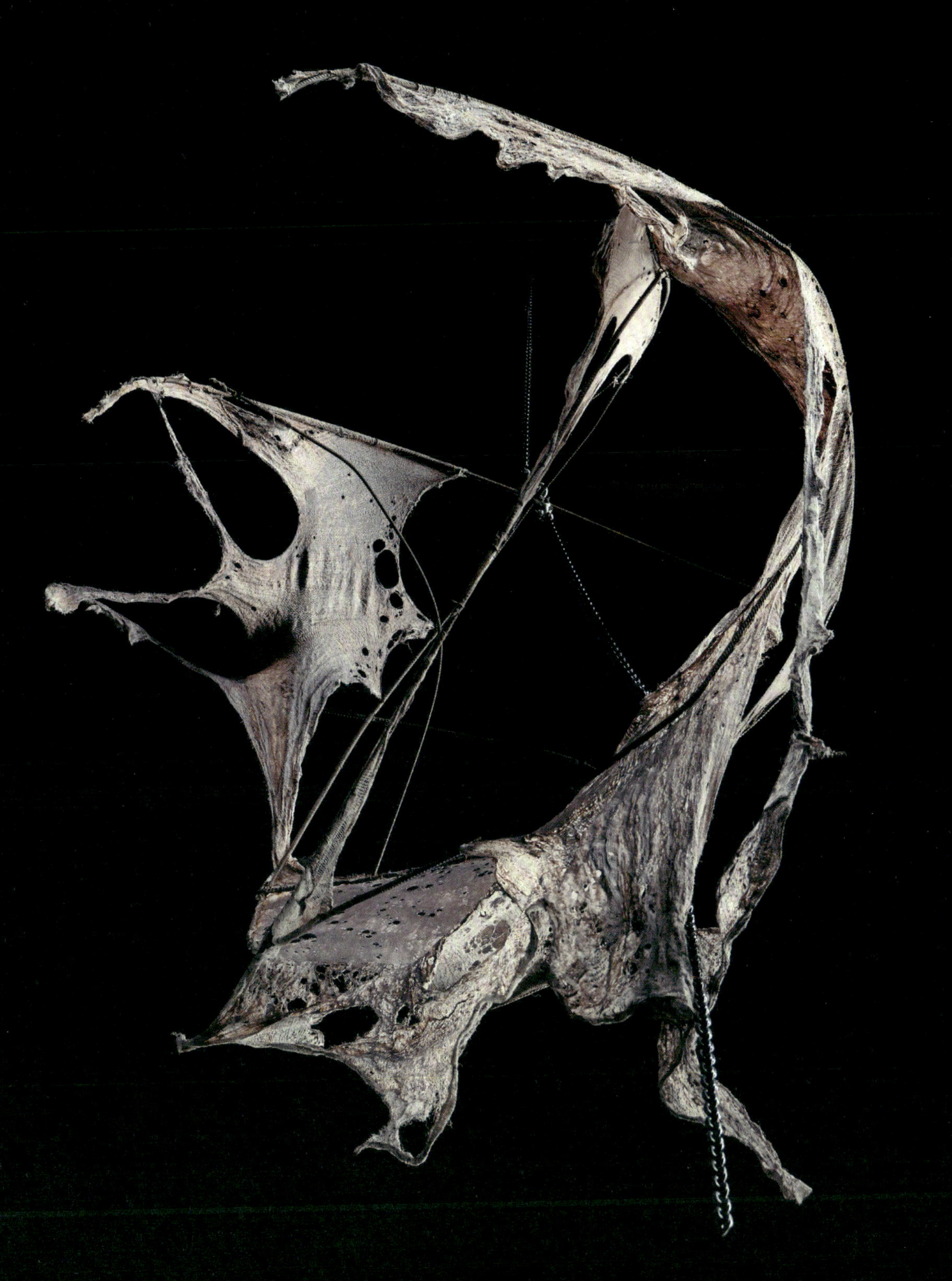

Mire Lee: Biography

Born 1988 in South Korea
Lives and works in Amsterdam and Seoul
2013 BFA in Sculpture, Double Major in Media Art,
College of Fine Arts, Seoul National University, South
Korea

2024
Mire Lee: Open Wound, Hyundai Commission, Turbine
Hall, Tate Modern, London

2023
Mire Lee: Black Sun, New Museum, New York, NY

2022
Carriers, Tina Kim Gallery, New York, NY
Look, I'm a fountain of filth raving mad with love,
ZOLLAMTMMK, MMK Frankfurt, Frankfurt
As we lay dying, Kunstmuseum Den Haag, The Hague

2020
Carriers, Art Sonje Center, Seoul
words were never enough, Lily Robert, Paris

2019
Het is of de stenen spreken (silence is a commons), Casco Art
Institute, Utrecht

2014
War is Won by Sentiment Not by Soldiers, Insa Art Space,
Seoul

SELECTED GROUP EXHIBITIONS

2024
Connecting Bodies: Asian Women Artists, National Museum
of Modern and
Contemporary Art (MMCA), Seoul
cuerpo & ala, alma I cuerpo, Fundacion Medianocheo,
Granada
territory, Sprüth Magers, Berlin
My Last Will, Casino Luxembourg
*Shortlisted Proposals for the Fifth and Sixth Plinth
Commissions*, High Line Art, New York, NY

2023
Dream Machines, DESTE Foundation for Contemporary
Art, Nea Ionia
Berlin Atonal 2023: Universal Metabolism, Kraftwerk
Berlin, Berlin

2022
We, on the Rising Wave, Busan Biennale, Busan
The Milk of Dreams, 59th International Art Exhibition,
Venice Biennale, Venice
Is it morning for you yet? 58th Carnegie International,
Pittsburg

2021
Kunsthal Light Program, Kunsthal Rotterdam, Rotterdam
TECHNO, Museion, Bolzano
Contamination, Kunstverein Freiburg, Freiburg
HR Giger & Mire Lee, Schinkel Pavillon, Berlin
Chapter 4OUR, Het HEM, Zaandam

2020
Breathing through skin, Antenna Space, Shanghai
(Im)Possible Bodies, Niet Normaal Foundation, Den
Bosch
*It is very difficult to be an islands of perfection in a sea
of misery, but please do not doubt our sincerity*, W139,
Amsterdam
As time went on, a rumor started, Gianni Manhattan,
Vienna
Born A' Woman, Suwon Museum of Art, Suwon
Plural Fertilities, Kunstfort bij Vijfhuizen, Vijfhuizen
Other.Worldly, Friesmuseum, Leeuwarden

2019
In Between Uneven Stairs, Tunnel Tunnel, Lausanne
Rijksakademie Open Studios 2019, Rijksakademie,
Amsterdam
Where Water Comes Together With Other Water, 15th
Biennale de Lyon, Lyon
iwillimedievalfutureyou1, Art Sonje, Seoul
Surface Tension, Sharjah Art Foundation, Sharjah
Lubricated Language, AKINCI, Amsterdam

2018
Double Negative, Arko Arts Center, Seoul
SPEICIES, bologna.cc, Amsterdam
RijksOpen2018, Rijksakademie van beeldende kunsten,
Amsterdam
Today Will Happen, Gwangju Biennale Pavilion Project,
Gwangju Civic Center, Gwangju
Fictional Frictions, Gwangju Biennale Pavilion Project,
Mugaksa, Gwangju

The Eye Became Body by Walking into the Hole, Night and Mouth, Art Space Pool, Seoul

2017
It is a lover who speaks and says, Homesession, Barcelona
Moving/Image, Arko Art Center, Seoul
Mobile, Doosan Gallery, Seoul
A Snowflake, Kukje Gallery, Seoul
Read My Lips, Hapjeongjigu, Seoul
Do it 2017 Seoul, Ilmin Museum of Art, Seoul
The Cameraperson, gallery175, Seoul

2016
APAP5, Anyang Public Art Project, Anyang
KIMKIM Art Fair LAVA! Come Back to Me!, KIMKIM gallery, Yangpyeong
The art of not landing, Cake Gallery, Seoul
NERIRI KIRURU HARARA, SeMA Biennial Mediacity Seoul, Seoul Museum of Arts, Seoul

2015
goods, Sejong Center, Seoul
Long Armed Sculpture and Space for Autonomy, Space 413, Seoul
Flat Repository, Take Out Drawings, Seoul
8yoil noons, Barim, Gwangju
Trunk Gallery Window Project, Trunk Gallery, Seoul

2013
Showcase <99°C +1>, Seoul Art Space_ Seogyo, Seoul

RESIDENCIES AND AWARDS

2023
Gold Art Prize

2022
PONTOPREIS MMK 2022

2021
Special Prize, Future Generation Art Prize, Victor Pinchuk Foundation

2018
Rijksakademie van beeldende kunsten

2017
SeMA Nanji Residency, Seoul Museum of Art

PUBLIC COLLECTIONS

Centre Pompidou-Metz, Paris
Fundacion Medianocheo, Granada
LACMA, Los Angeles
Leeum, Samsung Museum of Art, Seoul
M+, Hong Kong
National Museum of Modern and Contemporary Art, Korea
SFMOMA, San Francisco

Bibliography

SELECTED PUBLICATIONS

2024
Kim, Hong-hee, and Kim Hyesoon, *Korean Feminist Artists: Confront and Deconstruct*, London, pp.57–62

2023
Bußmann, Frédéric, Marc Weis, and Martin De Mattia, eds., *My Last Will*, exh. cat., Cologne: Kunstsammlungen Chemnitz, Casino Luxembourg
Carrion-Murayari, Gary, and Madeline Weisburg, eds., *Mire Lee: Black Sun*, exh. cat., New York

2022
Alemani, Cecilia, ed., *Biennale Arte 2022: The Milk of Dreams*, exh. cat., Venice, p.610
Gryczkowska, Agnes, Charlie Fox, McKenzie Wark, and Hans Ulrich Obrist, *HR Giger & Mire Lee*, exh. cat., New York and Berlin
Mohebbi, Sohrab, with Ryan Inouye and Talia Heiman, *Is it morning for you yet?: 58th Carnegie International*, exh. cat., New York
Tang, Billy, 'Post-Industrial Grotesque', in *Extreme Beauty: 12 Korean Artists Today*, ed. Elaine Ng and H.G. Masters, Hong Kong, pp.108–27

2020
Jeon, Hyo Gyoung, Kim Eon-hee, Jiwon Lee, Yeonsook Lee, and Gabi Ngcobo, *Mire Lee, Carriers*, exh. cat., Seoul

SELECTED INTERVIEWS AND PROFILES

2024
Elderton, Louisa, 'Mortal Machines: Mire Lee', *Flash Art*, no.348, Fall, pp.50–65
Foster, Kristina, 'Artist Mire Lee on Her Visceral Tate Modern Turbine Hall Commission', *Financial Times*, 8 October, <https://www.ft.com/content/3e5b2e85-1419-448e-a78e-b6747b3291f2>
Heo, Yun-hee, 'First S. Korean Artist Presents Solo Exhibition at Tate Modern London', *The Chosun Daily*, 10 October, <https://www.chosun.com/english/kpop-culture-en/2024/10/10/CQLTL4AQMZC33NH63LKVNJITUI/>

Hendy, Eloise, 'Mire Lee is Risking It All', *Elephant*, 8 October, <https://elephant.art/mire-lee-is-risking-it-all/>
Hevda, Johanna. 'What Mire Lee Is Bringing to the Tate Turbine Hall (Loving the Alien)', *Frieze Week, Seoul 2024*, September, pp.15–16
McDermott, Emily, 'The Uncontainable Mire Lee', *ArtReview Asia*, vol.12, no.3, Autumn, pp.64–9
Sooke, Alistair, 'Turbine Hall Star Mire Lee: "You Can't Control a Sexual Fetish – It Feels Like Art"', *Telegraph*, 6 October, <https://www.telegraph.co.uk/art/artists/tate-turbine-hall-mire-lee-interview-sexual-fetish-art>

2023
Hessler, Stefanie, 'Mire Lee', *BOMB*, issue 164, Summer, pp.66–78
Packard, Cassie, 'Mire Lee on the Cannibalistic Imagination', *Artforum*, 6 July, <https://www.artforum.com/columns/mire-lee-on-the-cannibalistic-imagination-252809/>
Russeth, Andrew, 'For Mire Lee, Rising Art Star, It All Comes Down to Guts', *New York Times*, 25 June, Arts & Leisure, p.16
Tang, Billy, 'The Sorrow and Desire of Abysmal Life Machines: An Interview with Mire Lee', *ArtAsiaPacific*, issue 135, Sep/Oct, pp.50–7

2022
Li, Alvin, 'Mire Lee's Deep-Rooted Romanticism', *Frieze*, issue 229, September

2021
Greenberger, Alex, 'Mire Lee on Sculpting Body Horror and Vore', *Art in America*, 12 November, <https://www.artnews.com/art-in-america/interviews/mire-lee-schinkel-pavillon-interview-1234609889/>
Lee, Jinshil, Jinjoo Kim, and Yeonsook Lee, 'Interview with Mire Lee: Deforming Sculpture as Emotional Portal', *Seminar*, issue 8, translated by Hakyung Sim

SELECTED REVIEWS

2024
Diehl, Travis, 'Mire Lee: Vorous, Not Unwelcoming', *Spike Art Magazine*, issue 79, Spring
Frankel, Eddy, 'Mire Lee: "Open Wound"', *TimeOut*, 8 October, <https://www.timeout.com/london/art/mire-lee-open-wound>

Freeman, Laura, 'Mire Lee: Open Wound Review – A
Horrible Yet Heavenly Turbine Hall Show', *Times*,
8 October, <https://www.thetimes.com/culture/art/
article/mire-lee-open-wound-review-a-horrible-yet-
heavenly-turbine-hall-show-gs5pzzbfw>
Larios, Pablo, 'Mire Lee', *Artforum*, May, pp.120–3
Lawson-Tancred, Jo, 'Mire Lee's Massive New Work
in Tate's Turbine Hall Provokes Awe and Disgust',
Artnet News, 8 October, <https://news.artnet.com/
art-world/mire-lee-tate-turbine-hall-2549509>
Sooke, Alastair, 'Mire Lee, Tate Modern: The Turbine
Hall Has Been Turned into a Fabulous Gore-Fest',
Telegraph, 8 October, <https://www.telegraph.co.uk/
art/reviews/mire-lee-hyundai-commission-tate-modern-
review/>

2023
Amy, Michaël, 'Mire Lee', *Sculpture Magazine*, 29
August, <https://sculpturemagazine.art/mire-lee/>
Bailey, Stephanie, 'Mire Lee's Visceral Bodies',
Ocula Magazine, 21 September, <https://ocula.com/
magazine/conversations/mire-lee-visceral-bodies/>
Chun, Emily, 'One Work: Mire Lee's "Carriers"',
Art in America, 7 November, <https://artnews.com/
art-in-america/aia-reviews/mire-lee-carriers-one-
work-1234645734/>
Edgington, Colin, 'Mire Lee "Black Sun" New
Museum / New York', *Flash Art*, no.344, Fall
Lawson-Tancred, Jo, 'See South Korean Rising Star
Mire Lee's Gutsy Debut of Squelching Kinetic
Sculptures at the New Museum', *Artnet News*, 4
August, <https://news.artnet.com/art-world/see-south-
korean-rising-star-mire-lees-gutsy-debut-of-squelching-
kinetic-sculptures-at-the-new-museum-2335644>

2022
Dozier, Ayanna, 'Mire Lee's Tantalizing Installations
Are Charged with Death and Desire', *Artsy*, October
14, <https://www.artsy.net/article/artsy-editorial-mire-
lees-tantalizing-installations-charged-death-desire>
Hoare, Natasha, 'Mire Lee', *CURA.*, issue 38, Spring/
Summer, pp.158–63
Yau, John, 'Alone in a Dirty, Sacred Space',
Hyperallergic, 27 September, <https://hyperallergic.
com/764592/mire-lee-carriers-tina-kim-gallery/>

2020
Li, Alvin, 'Vorarephilia: Mire Lee', *Mousse Magazine*,
issue 69, pp.158–61

Copyright Credits

All artwork by Mire Lee © Mire Lee, courtesy
the artist
© Werner Herzog Film / Deutsche Kinemathek
92–3

Photographic Credits

2019 Autumn Exhibitions – Het is of de stenen
spreken (silence is a commons) at Casco
Art Institute: Working for the Commons
featuring Babi Badalov, Ansuya Blom, Ama
Josephine Budge, and Mire Lee 113
Photo by Axel Schneider. Courtesy of the artist
and MUSEUM MMK FÜR MODERNE
KUNST 47
© Busan Biennale Organizing Committee 44–5
Photo: Choi Hyuk kyu 121
Collection Christophel / Alamy Stock Photo 98
Photo: Dario Lasagni 50–1
Edith-Russ-Haus for Media Art 75 (top)
Eoghan Ryan: Circle A. Photo © Edith-Russ-
Haus 2024 75 (top)
Photo by Frank Harrison/Getty Images 66
Photo: George Barrows 98
History and Art Collection / Alamy Stock
Photo 94
Photo: Hong Cheolki 34
Photo: Jiyoung Kim. Commissioned work by
SeMA Biennale Mediacity Seoul 2016 60
Lee Yeon-sook (Rita) 81
Courtesy of Mire Lee and Art Sonje Center 118
Courtesy of Mire Lee; Galerie Isabella
Bortolozzi, Berlin; Rodeo, London / Piraeus
70–1
Courtesy of Mire Lee and Hapjeongjigu 34
Courtesy of Mire Lee, the 2019 Lyon Biennale.
© Blaise Adilon 63
Courtesy of Mire Lee and Tina Kim Gallery
38–9
Courtesy of Mire Lee and Venice Biennale 127
Photo © Mire Lee 75 bottom, 77–81, 87 top,
88–91, 97, 99–104, 106–7, 109–17
Digital image, The Museum of Modern Art,
New York / Scala, Florence 59, 98
Courtesy of The National Archives 64
Courtesy New Museum 50–1
Long Beach Museum 1987 83
nsf / Alamy Stock Photo 122
Photo by Milos Bicanski / Getty Images 86–7
Photo: Sang-tae Kim 44–5
Photo © Sebastiano Pellion di Persano 38–9,
127
The Picture Art Collection / Alamy Stock
Photo 128
Stocktrek Images, Inc. / Alamy Stock Photo 84
© Tate (Marcus Leith) 125
© Tate (Oliver Cowling) 2–16, 20, 22, 26–7,
31–3, 130–55, cover
University of California, Berkeley Art Museum
and Pacific Film Archive; Gift of the Theresa
Hak Kyung Cha Memorial Foundation 82–3
West Virginia & Regional History Centre 84
Photo: Yonje Kim 118
ZOLLAMT MMK, Frankfurt am Main,
2022 47

Text Permissions

Beacon Press 92
Duke University Press 74, 76, 90, 96, 103
Humensis 78

The publishers have made every effort to trace
the copyright holders of the works illustrated
and apologise for any omissions or errors
that may inadvertently have been made.